THE NEWS
AT ANY COST

How Journalists Compromise
Their Ethics to Shape the News

TOM GOLDSTEIN

A TOUCHSTONE BOOK
Published by Simon & Schuster, Inc.
NEW YORK

Copyright © 1985 by Tom Goldstein

All rights reserved
including the right of reproduction
in whole or in part in any form

First Touchstone Edition, 1986

Published by Simon & Schuster, Inc.
Simon & Schuster Building
Rockefeller Center
1230 Avenue of the Americas
New York, New York 10020

TOUCHSTONE and colophon are registered trademarks of
Simon & Schuster, Inc.

Designed by Jennie Nichols/Levavi & Levavi

Manufactured in the United States of America

10 9 8 7 6 5 4 3 2
10 9 8 7 6 5 4 3 2 1 Pbk.

Library of Congress Cataloging in Publication Data
Goldstein, Tom.
 The news at any cost.

 Includes index.
 1. Journalistic ethics—United States.   I. Title.
PN4888.E8G6   1985   174'.9097   85-8171
ISBN: 0-671-49960-2
ISBN: 0-671-62251-X Pbk.

A portion of the chapter "Journalists for the Prosecution"
appeared in the *Columbia Journalism Review*

ACKNOWLEDGMENTS

This book could not have been published were it not for the help of Beryl Abrams, Monica Bayley, Bob Bender, Katherine Bouton, Evan Cornog, Ann Goldstein, Michelle Henderson, Robert Kasanof, Margaret Kennedy, Tom Leonard, Jethro Lieberman, Robert Love, Jon Roosenraad, Joe Spieler, Sean Tierney and Steve Weinberg. Each helped to improve the book; I, of course, take responsibility for its shortcomings.

To Beryl

CONTENTS

1. INTRODUCTION

How shall I speak thee, or thy
   pow'r address,
Thou god of our idolatry, the
   Press?
By thee, religion, liberty, and laws,
Exert their influence, and advance
   their cause;
By thee, worse plagues than
   Pharaoh's land befell,
Diffused, make earth the vestibule
   of hell:
Thou fountain, at which drink the
   good and wise;
Thou ever-bubbling spring of
   endless lies;
Like Eden's dread probationary
   tree,
Knowledge of good and evil is from
   thee.
— William Cowper, "The Progress
   of Error," 1782

If you're too ethical and nice, you're never going to get anywhere in journalism, in my opinion. . . . As a journalist, you do whatever you have to for a story. That's your job.
— Student essay at the University of Florida, 1983

Hastiness and superficiality— these are the psychic diseases of the 20th century and more than anywhere else this is manifested in the press.
— Alexander Solzhenitsyn, Commencement Address, Harvard University, 1978

9

In February 1979, in a story about a major narcotics dealer in Harlem, two reporters from the *New York Daily News* wrote that one alias used by the dealer was Sylvester Peacock (a name, they said later, they included because they found it slightly amusing). In the last paragraph of their story, they gave Peacock's address, including his specific apartment number, although this information was not relevant. There was a Sylvester Peacock living in that apartment at that address, but that particular Sylvester Peacock sold hats. He sued the reporters and the newspaper for libel, and asked $100,000 in damages. At the trial, in Manhattan, in March of 1983, I testified as an expert witness for the *Daily News*.

To recover libel damages in New York State, a wronged person, who, like Peacock, is not a public figure needs to show that the journalists "acted in a grossly irresponsible manner." At the trial I was asked about accepted journalistic practices, including whether certain reporting techniques employed by the reporters from the *Daily News* amounted to a "gross" departure from the norm.

In my testimony, I said that journalistic practices are not written down; rather, they are handed down from one generation of reporters to the next by a combination of osmosis and fiat. Furthermore, I said, the *Daily News* reporters were not grossly irresponsible, because they had checked out as thoroughly as could be expected what proved to be an erroneous assumption. The tip about the alias had come from drug enforcement officials, who had also provided the reporters with Peacock's address. The reporters had made a good-faith effort to verify this information.

On cross-examination, Peacock's lawyer questioned me about another part of the article, in an effort to damage the credibility of the reporter who was mainly responsible for the story.

That reporter, Michael Daly, had been forced to resign from the paper two years after the Peacock story, in the spring of 1981, after he was accused by a British newspaper of having fabricated part of a column about a clash between a British Army patrol and a group of youths in Belfast. Daly admitted that he had made up the name of a British soldier who, he reported, had shot a youth in Belfast. After Daly left the paper, the editor, Michael O'Neill, was quoted as saying that he had developed his own "skepticism" earlier that year about Daly and had raised questions about the accuracy of two of his columns.

Through the skill of the lawyers for the *Daily News,* none of this information, which would have been damaging—if not fatal —to the newspaper's defense, was introduced at the trial. The point of the questions by Peacock's lawyer was to get me to allude inadvertently to the incident and thereby alert the jury to Daly's transgression.

Peacock's lawyer first asked me: "Is it in your view, sir, perfectly acceptable journalism to report as if you are an eyewitness to an event when in fact you are not an eyewitness?" My answer: "Absolutely. It happens all the time."

Peacock's lawyer then read the beginning, or "lead," of the Harlem story:

"A cold wind was ripping up 125th St., and the man in the full-length leather coat dug his hands deep into his pockets as he stepped from the black BMW.

" 'Yo,' one of the teenagers standing in front of the Oasis Sandwich shop just off Park Avenue shouted when he spotted the man crossing the sidewalk. Scattering like pigeons, the teenagers crossed to the other side of the street.

" 'That's Frank James,' one of the teenagers, a stocky sixteen-year-old named Luther Crimshaw, said. 'He's THE man.' "

Appearing incredulous, the lawyer informed me—and the jury—that despite the specificity and richness of detail of this lead, neither reporter had been at the scene. I said that I was not surprised, because this kind of reconstruction was a common practice. Since reporters cannot be everywhere all the time, it is necessary sometimes to reconstruct scenes after the fact. (Having reread the *Daily News* story several times—and with the always helpful benefit of hindsight—I now think that the minute detail in the lead signals that there may have been some inventive reconstruction. Although it is not standard practice, it would have been helpful if the reporters had mentioned they were not eyewitnesses and had composed their account from interviews with others.)

The judge, Martin Evans of State Supreme Court—New York State's basic trial court—was clearly disturbed by this technique. What would happen if a reporter had "just made it up"? I said that would be unacceptable. One of the lawyers for the *Daily News*—the firm also represents *The Wall Street Jour-*

nal, which perhaps allows reporters more freedom than any other newspaper to reconstruct events in their leads—told me, out of earshot of the jury, that even he was surprised that this technique was so widely used.

The *Daily News* won the case. Afterward, it occurred to me that the technique that was so troublesome to the judge and lawyers was one that I had long taken for granted. Their ignorance about this practice brought home to me just how poorly journalists explain how they gather and present the news.

At one level, as an expert witness, I assumed that a reporter for the *Daily News*, one of the country's best newspapers, was honest, ethical, resourceful and wise. On another level, I knew better. As a relatively experienced journalist, I knew that many reporters at the *Daily News*—and, I suspect, at almost all other publications and broadcast stations—were far from honest, ethical, resourceful and wise all the time.

■

When I told journalist friends that I was writing a book about press ethics, the almost universal response was: "Short book." A few added: "Press ethics? That's an oxymoron."

Journalists are more aware of ethical considerations than they were twenty years ago, when I first started reporting. They certainly talk more about ethics. But that is not to say they necessarily behave more ethically.

In my first paid newspaper job, during summers in the middle 1960s when I was at college, I was a reporter for the *Buffalo Evening News*. As I recall, about the only thing forbidden there was smoking in the newsroom (the owner disapproved), so most reporters spent large portions of the day smoking in the bathroom.

I learned, as do nearly all novice journalists, from other reporters. Like my role models, I fabricated stories. I created and wrote about a fictional family—the Etkinowskis—who attended the "community days" I was assigned to cover each week at a local amusement park. I got away with it, and my colleagues considered that admirable. I regularly accepted free passes to local cultural events or other special occasions, like the circus, that I had no intention of writing about. When I was working as a general assignment reporter, one editor asked me to make up some letters to the editor. I did so, and one of those that I made up was published under a fictional name. When I was working at the financial desk, my editor told me that stories about certain companies had to appear in the paper; the advertising department wanted it that way.

When I was a student at the Columbia University Graduate School of Journalism in 1968 and 1969, there was little guidance in ethical matters. Without thinking much about it and without being told not to, I posed several times as someone other than a reporter to get stories. (I even got arrested in a police sweep near Times Square. I protested that I was a journalism student but was not believed. I had purposely, but stupidly, left my wallet, together with my money and my identification, at home, figuring I did not want them stolen as I pursued the seamy side of New York. I then wrote about my night in jail.)

When I worked at the Associated Press, I saw editors and reporters openly solicit and receive lavish gifts, especially at Christmastime, from public relations people. Stories about these people's clients (who were often minor politicians) usually were carried on the wire for several hundred words. When I covered political speeches or civic events, I almost always ate the free hotel dinners provided for reporters.

At the AP, I saw one of the great police reporters—Pat Doyle of the *Daily News*—at work. There was greater interest in police stories then, and the night shift, which Doyle worked, usually yielded interesting ones. The police reporters worked in a grimy converted house that they called "the shack," across from the old police headquarters in Little Italy in Manhattan. Doyle, undoubtedly the most resourceful reporter in the shack, would get exclusive stories night after night. He would call the station house where an arrest had been made, and, circumventing normal procedures, ask for the arresting officer, saying he was "Inspector Doyle calling from headquarters." Then he would write down what the obedient—and gullible—officer told him. Occasionally, he would even talk to the suspect on the phone. Doyle would invite the younger reporters into his office and show off for them.

In 1972, on my first day at *The Wall Street Journal*, I told my boss that I wanted to pay for my own lunches with news sources. My beat was housing and building materials—industries whose public relations people had the reputation of being particularly oily. I had been at my desk for about an hour when I received the first of a dozen or so congratulatory telephone calls from them. I did not take this as a compliment. (The reason I was covering that beat at all was that the paper needed someone quickly and I was around. My predecessor had committed suicide. The editors tried to persuade the person who covered the beat before him to return to it. She quit the paper instead.) My boss said that it would be fine for me to pay for meals, but that I would find it difficult because the public relations people were so persistent and clever. He was right.

At *The New York Times,* where I spent six years as a legal reporter based in New York, I was often in awkward situations. In 1979, for a fee of $1,500 I spoke about the image of lawyers to a group of negligence lawyers meeting in St. Louis. They did not appear to be much interested in what I had to say, but I did socialize with some of them later, and they seemed to think that they were buying my good will, if not that of the newspaper. I had not covered this group before and had no intention of doing so in the future, but they did not seem to understand that. Before making the speech, I had asked for permission. The editor I asked said, "Sure," and remarked as to how jealous he was of the amount of money I was receiving.

At the *Times,* I was forbidden to write about probably the best story I knew—the close relationship between Irving Kaufman, a Federal Appeals Court judge, and the *Times.* Kaufman wrote stirring opinions in support of the press. The *Times* flattered him in its news columns and frequently had him write for the paper. The tightness of the bond was well known to many leading lawyers, and the overwhelming praise and absence of criticism of the judge in the newspaper's pages gave evidence to these lawyers that the coverage by the *Times* was far from objective.

After I left the *Times,* I worked as press secretary to New York City's Mayor Edward I. Koch, from 1980 to 1982. There I saw pack journalism at its worst. Rather than operate independently, the reporters were cliquish. They could be easily manipulated, and they could also be petty and unreasonable. For example, they threatened not to cover the mayor whenever he traveled north of midtown Manhattan or to one of the four outer boroughs unless the city supplied them a car and driver.

When I returned to journalism in 1982, one of my first assignments came from *Rolling Stone.* I was asked to write a profile of Tom Downey, a young congressman from Long Island, a topic I thought unusual and rather localized for that magazine. I was not told until long after I had finished my story how it had originated. Jann Wenner, the magazine's editor and publisher, had asked one of his assistants to tell him who among young politicians had the greatest potential. "Downey," was the reply. Wenner—known in the office as "Citizen Wenner" because of his kingmaking aspirations—proceeded to introduce Downey to important people who could help him raise money and had the magazine do a story on him. Such a situation poses an ethical question of whether a publisher should double as a "kingmaker" and political fund raiser. And while there is nothing wrong in running a story on a promising politician, what *Rolling Stone* did was attempt to convert a standard profile into a piece of propaganda. It would have made no sense for the magazine to carry a negative story about Downey, and what I wrote was indeed complimentary to him, with some significant reservations. In fact, my story was not significantly altered in the editing process, but it certainly was not flattering enough to merit the seven pictures that accompanied it and the headline: "Coming Up Downey: The fastest-rising young star of the Democratic Party is Congressman Tom Downey."

■

Although such things cannot be quantified, the number of ethical transgressions by journalists seems quite high—or at the very least there is a heightened perception of such lapses. The last couple of years have been especially troublesome ones for journalists.

One day in particular stands out as a sobering one for the media. On January 21, 1985, the Monday that Ronald Reagan —who masterfully manipulated television and who largely ignored the print press—was inaugurated to his second term, journalists were on trial in three courtrooms in a single Manhattan courthouse.

That day marked the beginning of the trial in Federal court in Foley Square of R. Foster Winans, a former *Wall Street Journal* columnist who had been accused of illegally leaking information to investors on companies he had planned to write about. (Winans was subsequently convicted and sentenced to eighteen months in prison.)

In a nearby courtroom, a jury continued its deliberations on whether *Time* magazine had libeled Ariel Sharon by publishing a paragraph that linked him to a 1982 massacre of Palestinian refugees in Beirut. In earlier deliberations, the jury had determined that the disputed paragraph was defamatory and false; on that Monday, it was weighing the crucial element of libel— whether *Time* had printed the information while harboring serious doubts about its truth. (The jury eventually decided in *Time*'s favor, but it took the unusual step of singling out the *Time* correspondent who filed the dispatch for having "acted negligently and carelessly in reporting and verifying the information." With all this, Ray Cave, *Time* managing editor, insisted that the mistake was a "small matter" and that the story was "substantially correct.")

In a third courtroom, testimony continued for the fourth month in the libel action brought by General William Westmoreland against CBS and those journalists responsible for a 1982 documentary that accused him of deliberately underestimating enemy troop strength in Vietnam for political reasons. An internal study conducted by CBS had concluded that there were editing mistakes and other violations of the network's news standards in the program. George Crile, the producer of the disputed documentary, had been suspended by CBS for having secretly taped several telephone conversations during the preparation of the documentary. (In February 1985, with the case only days away from going to a jury, Westmoreland settled his suit in return for a bland CBS statement saying that he had fulfilled his patriotic duties as he saw them. Westmoreland's decision to settle followed damaging testimony by his former aides. The settlement was announced just before Mike Wallace, the documentary's correspondent, was to testify.)

Other examples of questionable behavior by journalists that came to light while I was working on this book include:

• In March 1983 a camera crew in Jacksonville, Alabama, kept their camera rolling as a man set himself on fire, and initially did not try to save the man's life.

• In May 1983 outtakes—footage not used ín the final broadcast—were shown at the trial of a libel suit filed by a California doctor against CBS's "60 Minutes" suggested that events had been staged. The film clips showed the CBS reporting team repeating questions for those being interviewed, badgering one interview subject and flattering another.

• In June 1983 it was disclosed that George Will, the columnist, had helped prepare Ronald Reagan for his 1980 presidential campaign debate with Jimmy Carter. After coaching Reagan, Will had gone on television and praised him.

• In October 1983 the Newspaper Guild, a labor union whose 31,000 members include journalists covering presidential campaigns, endorsed Walter F. Mondale for president.

• In December 1983 the *Cleveland Plain Dealer* admitted that one of its reporters, George Jordan, had plagiarized Carl Rowan, a syndicated columnist.

• In January 1984 Alexander Cockburn, the press critic for the *Village Voice,* was suspended for having accepted a $10,000 grant from an Arab studies organization.

• In January 1984 Presidential candidate Jesse Jackson, believing that he would not be quoted because he was having a "background" conversation, told a *Washington Post* reporter: "All hymie wants to talk about is Israel; every time you go to hymietown, that's all they want to talk about." The comment appeared in the *Post,* and the reporter later said he felt it was his duty to disclose this private conversation.

• In March 1984 the National News Council, which had been established in 1973 to assess complaints about the major news organizations, went out of business, in large part because it lacked the support of most of these organizations.

• In June 1984 Alastair Reid, a longtime writer at *The New Yorker,* admitted to having invented characters and rearranging conversations.

■

As long as this list is, it covers only a fraction of the situations in which journalists' ethics are tested. Day in and day out, journalists confront a formidable array of ethical quandaries. In their devotion to objectivity, are they allowed to show compassion or patriotism? Can they maintain their objectivity while exercising ordinary civic responsibilities, such as sitting on a local school board? While witnessing events, to what extent may journalists shape these events? Should they cooperate with investigators and prosecutors? Should the same rules that restrict the conduct of reporters apply to media executives, who do take political stands and who occupy positions of influence in their communities?

Journalists employ a wide variety of techniques to lend an aura of verisimilitude to their stories. Many of these techniques are of dubious propriety: ambushing the subjects of interviews, using stolen documents, masking one's identity. The standard justification of journalists—that their ends justify the means— ordinarily fails to withstand close scrutiny. Some journalists are even willing to take such unacceptable short-cuts as fabricating stories or copying the work of others.

While not "professionals" by any standard definition, journalists still belong to a special occupation. They have been granted privileges by the Constitution. But too often journalists degrade these privileges by invoking them to defend ethical transgressions and improprieties. Such overabundant references to the First Amendment protections of the press threaten to erode these very safeguards.

The media are unloved and distrusted by the general public. Fifty-three percent of those responding to a poll conducted for *Newsweek* in 1984 by the Gallup Organization said they believed "only some" of what they read or heard in the news media, and only 46 percent said the media get the "facts straight" in things they were involved with or knew about personally. Later in 1984, a poll conducted by Louis Harris & Associates found that only 17 percent of the public had "a great deal of confidence in the press"—down from 19 percent the year before.

Journalists have brought much of this on themselves. They are almost inarticulate on the subject of what they do and why they do it. They often are careless or incompetent, and they acknowledge mistakes reluctantly.

Mistakes can lead to litigation, and the low esteem in which the media are held is reflected in the sizable monetary damages juries have awarded plaintiffs in libel actions. Sharon's loss was an exception, as was Sylvester Peacock's. Statistics compiled by the Libel Defense Resource Center in New York City indicate that between 1980 and 1983, in 85 percent of the libel actions involving media defendants in which juries reached verdicts, they did so against these defendants. (That statistic is, however, a bit misleading inasmuch as 90 percent of such cases are dismissed in advance of trial for lack of merit, and 70 percent of the verdicts against the press are reversed or modified on appeal.)

One important libel case where the plaintiff prevailed initially involved William Tavoulareas, then president of the Mobil Corporation. He had been accused by *The Washington Post* of setting up his son in a London-based shipping firm that then obtained many of its contracts from Mobil. A jury awarded Tavoulareas $2 million, but in May 1983 federal judge Oliver Gasch set aside the award. He wrote that there was no evidence —which would have been necessary to sustain the award—to show that the article "contained knowing lies or statements made in reckless disregard of the truth." However, the judge also wrote that the article "falls far short of being a model of fair, unbiased, investigative journalism."

This key distinction was overlooked by Benjamin Bradlee, executive editor of *The Washington Post*, in his response to the judge's decision. "We're delighted that our reporting was vindicated, and it's a great day for newspapers everywhere," he said, inadvertently endorsing the low standards the judge complained of. (The case has been appealed and was not resolved by early 1986.)

As individuals, journalists are probably no more or less ethical than doctors, lawyers, politicians or business executives. (In a 1983 public opinion poll, the press commanded roughly the same level of respect as business, organized religion and Congress.) In other fields—in politics, business and the law—problems have emerged that are similar to issues facing journalists. Examining how others have dealt with these problems is useful in judging whether journalists have behaved properly.

For instance, journalists, especially prominent ones, would do well to follow the example set by judges and cut down on their outside activities that conflict with their primary duty. The change in the way judges have conducted themselves was outlined by Frank Coffin, the Chief Judge of the United States Court of Appeals based in Boston. In a 1980 book, *The Ways of a Judge*, Coffin wrote:

"I can remember the time when judges commonly served on the boards of businesses and industries; arbitrated all kinds of disputes outside court; headed up fund drives, and publicly maintained their partisan political ties. The feeling was that because a judge was eminent, he should be exploited. Today the ethic is that just because the judiciary is so precious, it should be jealously conserved for its own work."

Substitute the word "journalist" for "judge" in this passage, and it becomes analogous to many codes governing the behavior of reporters. Now substitute "publisher" for "judge"; just about everything that judges and reporters are forbidden to do publishers feel free to engage in.

The techniques employed by journalists are also used in other fields. For example, the tape-recording of conversations by one participant in a conversation without the knowledge of the other was once common among lawyers. This practice and the secret taping of face-to-face conversations were declared unethical in 1974 in a formal opinion of the American Bar Association Committee on Ethics and Professional Responsibility. Secret taping of calls placed from federal government phones may also violate federal regulations which prohibit such taping. And it is a crime in at least thirteen states to tape-record a telephone conversation without first informing the other party to the conversation.

For many years secret taping has been condoned, and even encouraged, in the business and political worlds. What was probably the most dramatic disclosure of secret government taping since Watergate was reported on December 28, 1983, by *The New York Times*. Charles Z. Wick, a lawyer, and the director of the United States Information Agency, had secretly tape-recorded his office telephone conversations with government officials, his own staff and friends. At first, Wick denied that he had done this, but he quickly retreated from that position. Wick was investigated by district attorneys in two states, Florida and California, although neither investigation resulted in criminal charges. Ultimately, Wick wrote more than 120 personal letters of apology. Although it is unclear whether he violated the law, Wick's conduct may well have been in violation of the spirit of the code that governs his behavior as a lawyer. Wick was nevertheless quickly exonerated by his long-time friend President Reagan.

There was more than a hint of hypocrisy in all this coverage. Newspapers and television stations played up this story during the slow news days between Christmas and New Year's. But few pointed out that secret taping was standard practice in many newsrooms. *The New York Times*, at least, used the Wick incident as a learning tool. On the very day the story broke in the *Times*, A. M. Rosenthal, its executive editor, wrote a memorandum to the staff "reminding" them that secret taping was forbidden.

An underlying rationale for the ban on secret taping—whether expressed as a policy of the *Times*, in the lawyers' code of ethics or in the statutes of thirteen states that prohibit it—is that people do not ordinarily expect that their conversations will be recorded.

"We are not entitled to assume that strangers will turn out to match our idealized expectations," notes Sanford Levinson, a professor at the University of Texas Law School. "But we are entitled to the belief that persons who present themselves to us will not actively be wishing us ill and using the encounter as a means of furthering their malevolence toward us."

This assumption of good faith is undermined by secret taping —and it is undermined by those who mask their identity. It does not make much difference, says Levinson, whether the infiltrators are undercover policemen or newspaper reporters who "in an effort to ferret out important information, have masqueraded as assembly-line workers, naive consumers and bartenders." Only a "narrow" lawyer, said Levinson in a 1982 essay, "Under Cover: The Hidden Costs of Infiltration," can be "happy with the argument that this kind of activity is protected by the First Amendment whereas police undercover work should be controlled by the Fourth Amendment." (Among its provisions, the First Amendment prohibits Congress from "abridging the freedom of speech, or of the press." The Fourth Amendment guarantees "the right of the people to be secure in their persons, houses, papers, and effects, against unreasonable searches and seizures.")

In the late 1970s the government, in its Abscam operation, set out bait by having undercover agents tell targeted congressmen that they were willing to pay for political influence. Although every Abscam defendant who stood trial was convicted (two juries did return verdicts of not guilty on one or two counts), these "sting" techniques remain controversial. John Z. DeLorean, the former auto maker who was videotaped making what appeared to be a large narcotics purchase from undercover agents, was acquitted in 1984 in a highly publicized trial in Los Angeles, in part, according to the jurors, because they wished to punish misbehavior by government agents.

By and large, more restrictions are placed on law enforcement officials than on journalists. Agents of the state are prevented by the Fourth Amendment from entering a private place without a warrant. Yet television crews on occasion go into private places with their cameras rolling. A police officer cannot stop someone on the street without establishing "probable cause"—a standard that must later stand up in court. But a journalist, notes the commentator Jeff Greenfield, "can chase a citizen down the street, cameras rolling, and paint a picture of guilt that no explanation can eradicate." Police officers are required, under the *Miranda* ruling, to inform criminal suspects, before they are questioned, of their right to remain silent. Journalists, of course, have no such obligation; with the justification of getting a better story, they sometimes do not identify themselves as journalists.

Because few legal restraints are placed upon them, journalists need to show greater self-restraint. In a well-received speech in 1984 to a group of publishers, Louis D. Boccardi, then executive vice president of the Associated Press and now its top executive, asked a pertinent question: "Have we reached a point where we must recognize an obligation *not* to do some of the things the First Amendment gives us every right to do?"

Merely because a right exists does not mean that it needs to be exercised indiscriminately. Bearing in mind the observations of Judge Coffin, journalists must be cautious of their extracurricular involvements. Journalists are free to do many things— endorse candidates, serve on community boards, crusade for causes—that should not be encouraged. Similarly, journalists employ many techniques—entrapping the unwary, ambushing the unsuspecting and assuming false identities—that should be shunned. Journalists need to abandon the mentality that impels them to pursue a story at any cost.

Part I

THE QUANDARIES OF JOURNALISTS

2. ON THE JOB TWENTY-FOUR HOURS A DAY

I think one of the most incredible dilemmas is to be in a position where you really have a good story, but it's going to hurt somebody you like. And then you're really torn. And usually what wins, if you're a journalist—and you know, by definition if you're a journalist you're somewhat unbalanced—you go off with a good story.
— Richard Cohen, columnist for *The Washington Post*, during a panel discussion, 1981

A cameraman has to keep rolling, no matter what happens. . . . It was something I agonized over, but all my training and my whole life had been "keep filming anyway." But he was a man—I knew him well.
— Neil Davis, explaining why he kept filming when an American soldier was killed in combat in Vietnam directly in front of him
—as quoted in a documentary, *Front Line*, 1981 (Davis was killed in September 1985 while covering an attempted coup in Bangkok.)

There is a need in this world for teachers and social workers and Boy Scout leaders and politicians—men and women whose primary reason for existence lies in their effective relationship with others. Orange juice. But there is also room for and need for the kind of people who make journalists, who view the orange as a totality to be turned over and examined as a whole and then slowly unpeeled, taken apart lovingly, and described and tasted slice by slice. They are part of the world but they also stand by themselves and never become squeezed into the juice.
— A. M. Rosenthal of *The New York Times* in his introduction to *A Prince of Journalists: The Life and Times of Henri Stefan Opper de Blowitz*, 1974

In 1925, the following story appeared in the *Louisville Courier-Journal:*

"Cave City, Ky., Feb. 2—Floyd Collins is suffering torture almost beyond description, but he still is hopeful he will be taken out alive, he told me at 6:20 tonight on my last visit to him.

"Until I went inside myself I could not understand exactly what the situation was. I wondered why someone couldn't do something quick, but I found out why.

"I was lowered by my heels into the entrance of Sand Cave. The passage way is about five feet in diameter. After reaching the end of an eighty-foot drop I reached fairly level ground for a moment.

"From here on I had to squirm like a snake. Water covers almost every inch of the ground, and after the first few feet I was wet through and through. Every moment it got colder. It seemed that I would crawl forever, but after going about ninety feet I reached a very small compartment, slightly larger than the remainder of the channel.

"This afforded a breathing spell before I started again on toward the prisoner. The dirty water splashed in my face and numbed my body, but I couldn't stop.

"Finally I slid down an eight-foot drop and, a moment later, saw Collins and called to him. He mumbled an answer.

"My flashlight revealed a face on which is written suffering of many long hours, because Collins has been in agony every conscious moment since he was trapped at 10 o'clock Friday morning. . . ."

Floyd Collins, a mountain youth, had been exploring an underground passage, trying to find something that might attract tourists, when a fifty-pound boulder fell on top of his left foot. He remained trapped until he died, two weeks after this article appeared. His agony, his fears and his declining hope were recorded by William Burke Miller, a twenty-year-old cub reporter for the *Courier-Journal.* "Skeets" Miller was five feet five inches tall and weighed less than 120 pounds, and because of his small size was able to squeeze through the cold and slimy passageways of the cave. He risked his life to wriggle through the tunnel, and he carried milk and whiskey and chicken-salad sandwiches to the trapped youth. He led many rescue parties to save Collins, who was unable to move.

Collins's torment became front-page news across the country. His death, after eighteen days in the cave, was the lead story in *The New York Times* under a three-column headline. Once Collins's body had been dug out, it was placed for a time in a glass-covered coffin inside a nearby cave. In *Only Yesterday*, Frederick Lewis Allen, the historian, related how the plight of Floyd Collins "gave the clearest indication up to that time of the unanimity with which the American people could become excited over a quite unimportant event if only it were dramatic enough."

In his daring and enterprise, Skeets Miller went beyond what is commonly understood as the reporter's role of observing events. This was an exceptional circumstance: a journalist placed in a situation in which he might save a life. In 1926 his courage was acknowledged when he was awarded the Pulitzer Prize, the youngest person to be so honored.

With regularity journalists face fundamental questions involving their role. Which comes first—the job or commitment to country, to community, to personal values or to friends? These questions come up in a variety of ways, and some are clearly more difficult to resolve than others. Should a reporter work for the Central Intelligence Agency? What about serving on a local school board? Should a reporter cover a press conference held at a private club that discriminates against women, or blacks, or Jews? Can a reporter make known strongly held views? What happens when a reporter has a close personal friendship with a source? Is a reporter on the job twenty-four hours a day?

Ordinarily, no journalist embodies virtue the way the young Skeets Miller did. The clash between the human instincts of a journalist and the desire to get a good story is usually more complex and subtle.

The conflict was raised by the book *In Cold Blood*, in which Truman Capote tells the story of a brutal multiple murder in Kansas by two young men, Perry Smith and Dick Hickock, and of their capture, trial and execution. The book was generally received enthusiastically by critics. An exception was Kenneth Tynan, who charged Capote with winning the friendship of the two men and then failing to help them. Tynan felt that Capote could have helped arrange better psychiatric evaluation for the men, and that might have saved them from death.

In his review, in March 1966, in the London *Sunday Ob-*

server, Tynan wrote: "For the first time an influential writer of the front rank has been placed in a position of privileged intimacy with criminals about to die, and—in my view—done less than he might have to save them. The focus narrows sharply down on priorities: does the work come first, or does life? . . . Where lives are threatened, observers and recorders who shrink from participation may be said to betray their species; no piece of prose, however deathless, is worth a human life."

Capote called the attack "McCarthy-like" and said that one of the most distinguished forensic psychiatrists in the United States had been in continual contact with the killers for five years and had concluded that there was no hope of proving them insane within the law of Kansas.

The question of a journalist's compassion was raised again after *The Washington Post* carried a moving story by Janet Cooke in 1980 about Jimmy, an eight-year-old heroin addict. Several months later, after Cooke won a Pulitzer Prize for the story, it was discovered that she had invented Jimmy. After that, "Jimmy's World" generated more discussion of journalistic ethics than any other recent story. The discussion focused on the use of confidential sources (Cooke was able to get away with writing fiction because she was not forced to disclose her sources to her editors), on the pressure on young reporters to perform and on the pursuit of prizes.

What was never adequately explained, though, was why the *Post* editors—even before the article was published—chose to ignore the plight of a young child. At one of the many postmortems of the incident, Charles Seib, a former ombudsman—or readers' representative—of the *Post,* recalled how, two weeks after the story appeared, he talked to an editor who had been directly involved in handling the report.

Seib asked this editor, whom he did not name: "If you had it to do over again, would you do it the same way?"

The editor replied to Seib: "No, I don't think I would. Before I printed the story I would go to the mother. I would make some effort to get her to get the kid out of there, to get him into treatment, to get him to a doctor. The *Post* could pay the bills. We wouldn't get her involved with the authorities. I think I would have done it that way."

Seib commented on this editor's reaction to a group of news executives shortly after the hoax was disclosed. "And of course the irony is," he said, "if he had followed that human instinct and realized he was dealing with a life and not just a good front page story, he would have found the story wasn't true. There would have been no Pulitzer Prize—and no scandal or the rest of it. . . . If compassion, if humanity, if a value for life had entered into the discussion earlier in this game, we wouldn't be playing out this dismal last inning now."

In March 1983 another young journalist, Gary Harris, a part-time assistant at WHMA-TV in Anniston, Alabama, became a reluctant national figure in a potential life-and-death situation. Harris, who was eighteen years old, stood by the side of Ron Simmons, a television cameraman, who kept his camera rolling as an unemployed roofer set himself on fire late one chilly night. For thirty-seven seconds, the television crew videotaped Cecil Andrews, who was protesting his joblessness in the town square in Jacksonville, a small college town near Anniston. Andrews doused his chest with lighter fluid. He fumbled for a match, struck it, and moved it toward his chest. The match went out. He lit another and moved it toward his leg. That too went out. He doused himself in more lighter fluid. He crouched on one knee, and lit a match to his blue jeans. This time it took. The fire crept up his body, then spread quickly, and he became a ball of flames. The two onlookers made no move. Finally, Harris, who unlike Simmons, was not encumbered by bulky equipment, moved forward, and tried to extinguish the flames with his reporter's notebook. From the videotape, it is not clear whether Harris was frozen in disbelief or terror, or whether he was a mesmerized voyeur watching a story unfold.

By the time a volunteer firefighter had put out the flames, Andrews had second- and third-degree burns over more than half his body. Excerpts from the tape were shown on Anniston television, and within a week the story became national news. *The New York Times* ran it on page one. The same day, the footage, heavily edited, appeared on the three television networks. In the days that followed, there were conferences on journalistic ethics, inspired by this incident, and one question was asked again and again: Does a journalist have a responsibility to do more than observe and then report events? In almost every instance, the crew members from Anniston were castigated for their insensitivity. They came to symbolize the worst part of journalism, the mentality that demands a story at any cost. "Like it or not, what Simmons and Harris did was squarely in today's mainstream tradition of news gathering," commented Hodding Carter III, host of "Inside Story," a television program that examined the performance of the press. That critical observation is flawed.

In the past several years, there have been several recorded instances of heroic actions by photographers and television crews. In almost every case that has been documented, when other bystanders were not present to intervene, photographers chose to save lives instead of snapping a picture. "Quite simply, you do not photograph a drowning man when you are the only one that can swim," says Tim Walton of KICU-TV, in San Jose, California.

The camera crew in Jacksonville reacted slowly, but that was not necessarily because they were in search of a good story. Of the two men in the crew, Harris was in the better position to help put out the flames. But he was a teenager, hardly a scarred veteran reporter with nerves and sensibilities toughened by experience. Several weeks after unwelcome celebrity was thrust upon him, Harris raised the same issues of heroics and lost honor that haunt the young Englishman who in a moment of panic deserts his apparently sinking ship in Joseph Conrad's *Lord Jim.* "If you've never been through it," said Harris, "people say, 'I woulda did this' and 'I woulda done that'—but unless you've really been there, those seconds, you just—if I was to do it again I couldn't say exactly what I would do. It's just—it's what's pumpin'. It's just—it was a scary situation."

■

Skeets Miller, Truman Capote, *The Washington Post* editors and the camera crew in Jacksonville were placed in situations in which they had to decide whether merely to watch or to participate as well. That choice, not unique to journalists, has a special resonance. Indeed, the journalist's quandary—to watch the world or to help change it—has been a popular theme in fiction and in film precisely because it applies to others besides journalists. In *Under Fire*, a 1983 movie, Nick Nolte plays a courageous news photographer in Nicaragua during the final days of the Somoza regime. At first, he is full of glib one-liners: "I don't take sides, I take pictures." But he loses his neutrality, becomes progressively caught up in the Nicaraguan civil war and eventually fakes a photograph in order to help the rebels. His commitment stands in sharp contrast to the detached professionalism of the mercenary played by Ed Harris, who is so cold-blooded in seeking out adventure that at one point he forgets which side he is fighting on.

It is rare in real life for war correspondents to affect the course of revolutions, but many inevitably take sides. Until Vietnam, when correspondents discovered and wrote about a credibility gap, they mostly kept to themselves any doubts about American misconduct and were generally patriotic.

In 1865, after covering the American Civil War, Junius Henri Browne, a renowned correspondent for *The New York Tribune*, wrote how he kept his misgivings to himself: "What is war, after all, but scientific assassination, throat-cutting by rule, causing misery and vice, and pain and death by prescribed forms? It seems high time War had ceased to be. It is a palpable anachronism . . . but my duty was to write of, not against, War; and, stretched on the earth beside my tent, in the shade, on a warm, bright, beautiful day, full of the loveliness of October, I proceeded to discharge my journalistic obligations as best I could, reserving my sentimental opinions about war for private ears."

As late as World War II, journalists accepted censorship voluntarily. On the job, most reporters wore uniforms and dutifully saluted those who outranked them. In the 1950s and early 1960s, there was a broad consensus among American journalists that the United States played a salutary role in world affairs. In 1961, toward the end of the Cold War, James Reston, then Washington bureau chief of *The New York Times,* intervened with the paper's publisher to tone down a story about the planned CIA-backed invasion of Cuba at the Bay of Pigs. The story, which had been scheduled to lead the paper, was edited and moved to a less prominent position on the page. Any reference to the imminence of the invasion was removed. The reasoning was that it was in the national interest to withhold certain facts, including the involvement of the CIA. After the invasion failed, President Kennedy acknowledged that perhaps the *Times* in its self-censorship had been overly cautious; and had it printed what it knew, he told Turner Catledge, the managing editor, "you would have saved us from a colossal mistake."

But with Vietnam as the catalyst, judgments by journalists of what patriotism required of them changed quickly. Helping the CIA—a common practice among journalists in the 1950s and early 1960s—was no longer acceptable behavior. Before his retirement in 1974, Joseph Alsop, the columnist, occasionally undertook clandestine work for the CIA. "I'm proud they asked me and proud to have done it," Alsop told Carl Bernstein, who wrote a long article in 1977 for *Rolling Stone* on dozens of journalists who had served as intelligence agents. "The notion that a newspaperman doesn't have a duty to his country is perfect balls. . . . I've done things for them when I thought they were the right thing to do. I call it doing my duty as a citizen." In the article Alsop was alone among journalists in discussing on the record work he had done for the CIA, and his view of patriotism was clearly not the prevailing one.

By the time the United States invaded Grenada in October 1983, the seeming indifference of journalists to patriotic values was cited by the Reagan administration as a reason for denying them access to frontline combat—the first time this had ever happened. Initially, the Reagan administration said that secrecy was necessary to ensure the invasion's success and that military leaders were too busy to be concerned with the safety of journalists. Then, several weeks later, Secretary of State George Shultz, in an interview, bluntly defended the exclusion of reporters. In contrast to World War II, when "reporters were involved all along" and "were on our side," it now seemed to him "as though reporters are always against us," and because of this "they're always seeking to report something that's going to screw things up." And, he added, "When you're trying to conduct a military operation you don't need that."

This extreme view of journalists—that they should be distrusted and denied access unless they are cheerleaders for the government—was not embraced for long. After the news blackout at Grenada, a commission of military officers and former journalists drafted rules for news coverage of future surprise combat actions. There was agreement that military operations should be covered "to the maximum degree possible consistent with mission security and the safety of U.S. forces."

■

Whether lives are at stake or patriotism is at issue, journalists must decide to what degree they should be involved in the events they cover. There is a large difference between being a witness and being a participant. The journalist's role lies somewhere in between, and it shifts with the situation and with the type of journalism being practiced. When someone is drowning and no one else is around, a journalist obviously ought to act. But in wartime, with lives constantly at risk, a journalist cannot do his job if he must be responsible for each life around him. And among journalists themselves there are important distinctions—a magazine writer or a columnist ordinarily interprets events as well as reporting on them and so he will have greater latitude than a news reporter in distinguishing between watching and participating.

Journalists cannot suspend their critical faculties, but traditionally they are told not to let their personal views, no matter how deeply held, intrude on their reporting. In the summer of 1983, Helen Rattray, editor of *The East Hampton Star,* a small weekly with a highly literate readership on the eastern tip of Long Island, broke this rule. She refused to cover a party given on behalf of a local politician running for reelection at a club at which few Jews are members.

"A journalist should be ready to go anywhere 'on assignment,' " Mrs. Rattray, who is Jewish, explained in her column in the paper, "and I certainly could have interpreted attendance at the party as a working rather than a social occasion, but the issue was too complicated. I have long had an unshakable personal rule against being a guest at places that would not admit me, and every one of my relatives and friends, to membership. I believe that those who represent the public have a similar obligation."

As appealing as Rattray's principle may seem, if it were to be applied on a grander scale the structure of journalism would collapse. The notion of a marketplace of ideas would vanish if foreign correspondents did not cover regimes they disagreed with, if political reporters paid attention only to candidates they themselves would vote for, if sports reporters refused to report on teams whose managers they disliked.

At *The Philadelphia Inquirer,* reporters are specifically instructed to refrain from showing their views in their writing as well as in their activities outside the office. In the paper's written code, one of the most thoughtful in journalism, staff members are told to "be careful not to offend or give wrong impressions to members of the public by blatantly espousing or expressing viewpoints on public and philosophic issues; for instance, wearing an antiwar button at a rally or festooning an Inquirer workspace with one candidate's placards could create a belief, intended or not, of partiality."

But this principle is not universally practiced. *The New York Times*, for instance, is a tradition-bound paper, and reporters are generally discouraged from letting their personal point of view seep into the news columns. But one of the most emotional, sensitive writers on the paper is A. M. Rosenthal. In 1959, Rosenthal, then a foreign correspondent with the *Times*, was expelled from Poland. He was told by a spokesman for the Ministry of Foreign Affairs that he had written "very deeply and in detail about the internal situation" and that the Polish government "cannot tolerate such reporting."

Nearly a quarter of a century later, as executive editor of the *Times*, Rosenthal returned for the first time to Poland and wrote candidly of his feelings in the *Times Magazine:* "When I was a reporter, I had felt sympathy toward the country and its people. And I had felt sorrow for the Polish national history of suffering. Politically, there was warmth in me—for the anti-Communism of the people, which I shared. . . ." His journalism is very personal, not at all detached. He describes in the 1983 magazine article how "staggered" he was to discover the desperate living conditions of the Poles.

Of course, this was a magazine article, in which a writer is granted more freedom. Rarely, though, are writers permitted the degree of journalistic license that appeared in that article. Rosenthal, who as executive editor sets the tone for the *Times*, expresses an undisguised sympathy for one side in the Polish conflict. Rosenthal is, of course, entitled to his views, but the problem with his article is that his extreme public partisanship is inevitably imputed to a newspaper staff that is supposed to be impartial.

At the same time, journalists need not be eunuchs. In *How True*, Thomas Griffith, a former editor at *Time* and *Life* magazines, wisely writes: "The true relationship between a journalist's beliefs and his reporting is something like that of a juror's desire to reach an impartial verdict. Jurors are not required to be empty minds, free of past experience or views; what is properly demanded of them is a readiness to put prejudices and uncorroborated impressions aside in considering the evidence before them. As much is asked of the journalist."

The difficulty comes for alert and sensitive reporters when they wish to translate their "past experiences and views" into action. After a while, many reporters come to feel that they can run things better than those they are covering. If they wish to remain journalists, that is a temptation they must resist, even if they have something to contribute.

Anthony Lewis, before becoming a columnist for *The New York Times*, was an excellent reporter who wished to do more than merely report. He was so adept at covering his beat that his old job of covering the Supreme Court and the Department of Justice now is divided among at least two and sometimes three reporters. He knew his beat, he formed views, and he went beyond the role of observer. Lewis took strong positions about many issues, including the reapportionment cases that were to be decided by the Supreme Court in 1964. In an interview several years later that appeared in Victor Navasky's *Kennedy Justice*, Lewis recalled that "at an early point in the briefing period" he spoke to Robert F. Kennedy, then the attorney general, and told him that he thought Archibald Cox, the solicitor general, "was personally unconvinced of the one-man, one-vote standard," and he thought that "it would be a tragedy to have the Department of Justice take an antagonistic position." Lewis went to see Cox at his farm, and he apparently was listened to; after Lewis's intervention, changes were made in some of the passages in the government's written brief. Alterations were made in places where the solicitor general seemed to be wavering in his support for the notion that at least one house of every state legislature be apportioned on this basis of population.

Arthur Schlesinger, Jr., in his biography of Robert Kennedy, said Lewis played "a lively role behind the scenes." Navasky called him an "active kibitzer." In manipulating behind the scenes a story that he was covering, in giving advice privately to a public figure, Lewis—an exceptional journalist with an exceptional intellect—went beyond the bounds of appropriate journalism. The proper way for Lewis to change policy would have been to write a story or a series of stories about faults in the government's position. Instead, unbeknownst to his readers, he became a lobbyist and a part of the very story he was covering.

Anthony Lewis could not have influenced policy had he not known those whom he covered. Reporters at all levels of sophistication are encouraged to get to know sources informally —an occasional drink, a casual dinner. After six years of covering legal affairs in New York City at *The New York Times*, I had become friendly with many of the people I covered. I liked some and disliked others. (Some I disliked because they were unpleasant to be with, others because I thought they were doing a poor job.) I had social friends and professional friends. It was hard to separate the two, and it was hard for me to figure out whether people were friendly only because I might be helpful to them. Occasionally, my advice was sought on professional matters, and I gave it. I was asked who might make a good judge or what might be the best day to release a report. In return, I was sometimes given tips that led to good stories.

After so long on a single beat, I began to lose my distance and adopt the viewpoint of the people whom I was writing about more often than I should have. And I began to think that they valued my advice, when in fact, the better explanation was that they were merely trying to curry favor with a representative of the *Times*.

Moreover, I was getting bored and stale. I was aware of this and told my editors and asked for another assignment. But I was told I could not be transferred because I was too valuable where I was. "I certainly can understand your desire to cover other things," Rosenthal wrote me. But at that time, he said, "we have a very strong need for more legal coverage rather than less." Shortly after, I left the paper.

At the *Times*, I found it difficult to separate work life from personal life. Some of the best reporters are on the job twenty-four hours a day. Inevitably, for these journalists, business life spills into social life, and the hazards can be insurmountable.

Only recently have the possible conflicts between a reporter's romantic and professional lives been discussed seriously. In Philadelphia, in the 1970s, a reporter had a love affair with a source—hardly an uncommon occurrence. This particular affair became public because the source, Henry J. "Buddy" Cianfrani was charged with committing several crimes. Laura Foreman, the reporter, while covering Philadelphia Mayor Frank Rizzo's reelection campaign in 1975 for *The Philadelphia Inquirer*, met and began to date Cianfrani, a state senator and a Rizzo ally. He gave her gifts—tires for her sports car, jewelry, furniture and a fur coat. She wrote stories about him and other stories for which he served as a source. In 1977, Foreman moved to the Washington bureau of *The New York Times*. She continued to go out with Cianfrani, but no longer wrote either stories about him or stories that affected him. Later that year, shortly before Cianfrani was indicted with mail fraud, racketeering and income tax evasion charges, the relationship, which had been common knowledge in the *Inquirer* newsroom, became known publicly. On August 27, the *Inquirer* published an article on page one disclosing that Foreman had told FBI agents that she was romantically involved with Cianfrani and had accepted gifts valued at more than $10,000.

On September 11, at the request of A. M. Rosenthal, Foreman submitted her resignation to the *Times*. "She committed a major journalistic offense," said Rosenthal after her resignation. At that time, the press, along with government lawyers, was investigating possible conflict of interest charges involving the banking affairs of Bert Lance, President Carter's close friend, who finally resigned as director of the Office of Management and Budget on September 21. "We investigated Bert Lance not for what he did as budget director, but for what he did in Georgia," said Rosenthal. "How could we apply different standards to Laura Foreman?"

After Cianfrani was convicted and sent to prison for mail fraud and racketeering, Foreman wrote in *The Washington Monthly:* "If it was a bad situation, it was bad because we were in love, not because of the gifts Buddy bought me, which were the immediate cause of my downfall. Otherwise, I think my critics were wrong. I don't think I got too close to the people I covered. I got closer than most, it's true, and the situation was tricky at times, but I think it paid off in terms of what I was able to write." Foreman concluded that "reporters should try to walk the narrow line of friendship with politicians they cover if it will help them write better stories. I don't think they should fall in love with them—that makes honest reporting well-nigh impossible." In 1980, after Cianfrani was released from prison, they were married.

Since the fall of 1978, the *Inquirer's* guidelines have specifically addressed this issue: "If a relative—spouse, parent, child, brother or sister, for example—or a close friend is involved in a political campaign or organization, a staff member should refrain from covering or making news judgments about such a campaign or organization."

When Laura Foreman moved from New Orleans to Philadelphia in 1973, she was determined to learn as much about her new community as she could in as short a time as possible—a sound instinct that she carried too far. One of the shortcomings of journalism is that too often it is an occupation filled with itinerants. Many journalists do not stay long in one place, and they do not become familiar with the communities they cover.

Appropriately, in many news organizations journalists are told they must forfeit community involvement in return for the privilege of reporting and editing news. While the networks and most large publications take a position limiting the outside activities of their employees, there is no consensus among them about just what is permissible. Individual publications often lack an internally coherent policy. Some are too rigid. Other codes prohibit "conflicts of interest" without specifying what they are. For example, at *The Atlanta Journal & Constitution,* "Service in community and civic organizations is to be encouraged so long as there is no conflict of interest"—a pleasant sentiment, but since it does not specify what such conflicts are, it is not a helpful guide to conduct.

The *Chicago Tribune* is a bit more specific. Those wishing "to become active in public service organizations or community groups should discuss the matter with division level editors." According to the policy statement, "common sense" is the guideline. "Membership in a political party, a church auxiliary group or a neighborhood association is obviously not a problem. Activism in a zoning fight, acting as the publicity chairman, or taking the leadership role in any group likely to generate news or controversy is a violation of this policy." At the *New York Daily News,* which is owned by the Tribune Company, "employes are encouraged to be active in religious, civic, cultural, or social organizations. But they should not use their position with the newspaper to give these organizations any special attention or favor. Nor should they become public advocates for causes, whether to raise the pay of teachers or to oppose abortion."

At *The Denver Post,* reporters are not allowed to serve on community-related boards or school boards. At *The Indianapolis Star,* it is permissible for reporters to serve on nonprofit community boards. At the Kansas City papers—the *Star* and the *Times*—"membership in professional journalistic organizations, and voluntary work (excluding general fund-raising or public relations) for religious, cultural or social groups, are acceptable." At *The New York Times,* "public service commitments should be far removed from any conceivable professional duty; a foreign desk copy editor might properly serve on the Great Neck school board, but a Long Island correspondent should not." At *Newsday*, says Anthony Marro, the managing editor, "the general rule is that reporters and editors should not hold public office or serve on school boards. Personally, the extent of my civic involvement is to give blood at the local school's annual drive."

ABC discourages its employees from taking positions on matters of public controversy. Employees who do so may be reassigned or asked to resign. This, however, is not absolute: "The limitation on political activity is not intended to preclude participation in a local school board election or appointment to a town council committee."

At *Newsweek* magazine, which is owned by the Washington Post Company, there are rules limiting outside conduct, but many editors and writers openly serve on outside boards. When he was editor in the 1970s, Osborn Elliot served on the Board of Overseers of Harvard. Jerrold Footlick, a specialist on law and education at *Newsweek*, has served on the board of trustees of a small college and has advised groups whose spokesmen occasionally get quoted in the magazine.

"My outside activities have never been commercial," Footlick told me. "They have always had to do with eleemosynary institutions"—those supported by gifts, charity or charitable donations. When he covered legal affairs, he served on the board of the National Council of Crime and Delinquency, a national nonprofit organization that studies crimes and its causes. "I knew they did terrific research," said Footlick. "They did not have an axe to grind. I quoted them, but I never did a profile." On the organization's letterhead, he was identified as a *Newsweek* employee. "Sure, that was valuable to them," Footlick says, but he did not think this was harmful. Yet that identification on its masthead gave the appearance he was taking a stance since the National Council on Crime and Delinquency is not a neutral research group—it takes strong positions, including the controversial one that new prisons not be built.

"A rule prohibiting what I have done would not be a good rule," says Footlick. "I have a very clear conscience on these things. If you take it to the extreme, a journalist could not do anything. I don't believe we are automatons. We exercise independent judgment."

A better rule, I think, would forbid journalists from serving in positions they were named or elected to in order to capitalize on the prestige of their employer or otherwise to make use of their journalistic connections. For instance, in New York City, the Legal Aid Society has long named journalists, mostly from *The New York Times*, to its board—less for what they could contribute at board meetings than for their ties to the *Times*. That should be stopped. On the other hand, unless they cover education or perhaps local politics, reporters should not be banned from serving on a school board.

It was on this last issue that Jacquelyn Brown McClary of the *Knoxville News-Sentinel* came into conflict with her editor, Ralph L. Millett, Jr. McClary was born in Montgomery, Alabama, grew up and was educated in Birmingham in the 1960s and received a degree from Talladega College in Alabama in 1973. She studied journalism at Fordham University in New York City and then went to work at *Business Week*, first as a copy editor and then as an environmental writer. In the early 1980s she and her family moved back to the South, and she went to work for the *News-Sentinel*. She covered the zoo, a local college, local churches and the courts.

In the spring of 1983 she was a general assignment reporter, and her job did not involve covering events in Alcoa, a town of seven thousand about twenty-five miles from Knoxville, where she and her family had moved. McClary was concerned about the quality of education there, and she ran for the school board. In June 1983 she was the first black woman elected as an official in the town. She was then dismissed from the newspaper for having violated the paper's guideline prohibiting "participation of an employee in any political activity that could raise questions as to the newspaper's objectivity."

After she was fired by Millett, McClary wrote: "When I decided to seek the nonpartisan school board seat after being asked to run by a community group, I saw no conflict between my job and my civic responsibility. . . . Reporters have something extra and special to offer the communities we live in."

At the time, Millett served as chairman of the Knoxville Parking Authority, an advisory body appointed by the mayor, and sufficiently significant that its meetings were covered as news events. "I see no valid comparison between this and an elected, legislative office," Millett said after McClary was fired. The case was submitted to binding arbitration. The arbitrator found for McClary, and she returned to the paper. Millet resigned from the parking authority.

In this instance at least, a double standard was eliminated. It was proper for McClary to take an active part in her community as long as she did not (as Anthony Lewis had done) cover the story she was involved in. Millett, like A. M. Rosenthal when he wrote on Poland, became too involved in a situation that reporters under his supervision were expected to cover in an impartial way.

3. JOURNALISTS FOR THE PROSECUTION

... I am not a scientist. I am a journalist. I did not gather with indifference all the facts and arrange them patiently for permanent preservation and laboratory analysis. I did not want to preserve, I wanted to destroy the facts. My purpose was no more scientific than the spirit of my investigation and reports; it was . . . to see if the shameful facts, spread out in all their shame, would not burn through our civic shamelessness and set fire to American pride. That was the journalism of it. I wanted to move and to convince.
— Lincoln Steffens, *The Shame of the Cities*, 1904

There should be relentless exposure of and attack upon every evil man, whether politician or businessman, every evil practice, whether in politics, in business, or in social life. I hail as a benefactor every writer or speaker, every man who, on the platform, or in book, magazine, or newspaper, with merciless severity makes such attack, provided always that he in his turn remembers that the attack is of use only if it is absolutely truthful.
— Theodore Roosevelt, at the laying of the cornerstone for the new office building of the House of Representatives, 1906

Probably best known for the tranquil resorts of Captiva and Sanibel islands, Lee County on Florida's Gulf Coast became in the summer of 1983, in the words of a local paper, the scene of "Southwest Florida's longest-running soap opera." It was a story of sex, politics, corruption—and it raised the question of how far a journalist should go in trying to change conditions. In this instance, a relatively inexperienced reporter cooperated with law enforcement agents.

The story began when an indiscreet county commissioner bragged to a local television reporter about liaisons with prostitutes supplied him by a local contractor seeking county business. The curtain dropped on the soap opera in November 1983 when Lee County Commissioner Ernie Averill was sentenced to five years in prison for accepting illegal compensation.

During pre-trial maneuvering the previous summer, the state attorney's office gave credit for breaking the case to two confidential informants. One was the director of the county airport; the other was Chere Avery, a thirty-eight-year-old reporter for WBBH-TV in Fort Myers, the country's 118th largest television market.

Avery first met Averill when she was covering county government. Over time, they developed a closeness that few journalists and sources enjoy, and they even shared personal secrets. At a pre-trial hearing, Avery testified that they had once discussed one of her childhood fantasies: she being kidnapped by a pirate and rescued by a buccaneer. Despite their closeness, she did not feel obligated to keep the secrets that Averill confided to her. She testified: "If you say, 'Keep this off the record,' that means I don't put it on the news. That doesn't mean I don't tell someone."

When Averill bragged to her, she told her husband, an assistant state attorney, and others in the prosecutor's office. Later, when asked why, she replied under oath: "I felt it was my duty, OK?"

When the county commissioner and the contractor planned a pleasure cruise along the scenic Intracoastal Waterway near Fort Lauderdale on Florida's other coast, Avery alerted the prosecutors. In return, they agreed to permit a cameraman from her station to join them when they staked out the commissioner. Avery could not be there, she said later, because she was sick. The story was held for three months, until the investigation had been nearly completed.

Avery continued in her job, covering county government and also serving as evening anchorperson. Several months after the trial, in a room in a hotel on the ocean in Miami Beach, she explained to a group of young journalists and journalism students why she had acted as she had. First, she said, she got a tip from Averill about possible fraud in the construction contracts. "One of my first thoughts was—how do I break this story? How do I go about proving it? I need a paper trail. I need another source." At her station she was responsible for reporting on three to five stories a day in addition to her anchor duties. "I'm not an investigative reporter. I'm not labeled investigative reporter. My station doesn't give me a week or months or years to develop a story. The only time I could investigate was in my spare time."

She did not know whether a crime was being committed. "If it was a crime, I felt it was my duty to inform the law," she told the journalists. "I had suspicions, no facts. I had a suspicion a crime was being committed. I didn't think I could sit on it. I was suspicious enough to fear for the health, safety and welfare of thousands of taxpayers. So I contacted the state attorney's office. It is hard for a media person to isolate him- or herself from the rest of civilization. I'm not sorry for what I did. I'm only sorry for some of the way the media reported it."

She played down her role. "I didn't give them any information that indicted, arrested or convicted these people. It was just a suspicion. I didn't think that by being a journalist I should give up my right to citizenship. I had a feeling I wasn't going to be able to break the story."

The extent of Avery's cooperation is unusual but not unique. A report by the Department of Justice on leaks that occurred during Abscam and two other undercover operations mentions an unnamed reporter who was treated officially as an informant. The report, issued in 1981, goes on to say, however: "The value to the government of tips or leads from informant newspeople is likely to be marginal at most. Truly trustworthy information probably will find its way into the public domain on the air or the printed page, since reporters are not likely to sit for long on a good story."

Chere Avery's willingness to cooperate with the authorities, while understandable, given her relative inexperience and the small size of her station, is at sharp odds with the widely accepted notion that the press, by what it reports, should serve as a check on government.

In a "Letter to the Reader," an occasional feature of the *News-Press* in Fort Myers, Ron Thornburg, the executive editor, commented on what Chere Avery had done: "Reporters can't be watchdogs of government if they draw a paycheck from the state or if they are in any way dependent on government. That's not to say that reporters are above the law, but they aren't policemen or prosecutors, either. It's easy to see why. The public must feel free to tell reporters lots of things they wouldn't tell a policeman or prosecutor."

This is the traditional view of the press. "The press and the government are natural adversaries," says Burt Neuborne, legal director of the American Civil Liberties Union. "When elements of the press talk about being partners, that's like *me* talking about being partners with the government. Sure, I live in the same universe and I respect some [officials]. But I fight them. That's my institutional role."

Many prosecutors do not want the help of the press, or at least they say they do not actively seek it out. "We can do things you can't do, and you can do things we can't," Stanley Marcus, the United States Attorney for Southern Florida, told a group of investigative reporters meeting in Miami in the spring of 1984. "The press is an independent, investigative body, not an arm of the state. . . . The presence of a nosy, snoopy press heightens the desire for the prosecutor to get the story first. The public is the beneficiary of this competition between press and prosecution."

Between these extremes—of Chere Avery, acting as an informant to the prosecutor, and of Stanley Marcus, a prosecutor, seeking a worthy competitor in the press—lies a vast middle ground.

There are many different relationships between journalists and prosecutors:

• Some journalists wish to lower the intensity of investigations by journalists. (In a sense, all reporting is investigative, but the phrase "investigative reporting" usually describes sustained attempts to uncover illegal activities or conflicts of interest.) In the spring of 1983, Michael O'Neill, the former editor of the *New York Daily News*, remarked that the "great investigative wave that surged through American journalism after Watergate seems to be ebbing." That was a trend he welcomed. In an earlier speech, O'Neill counseled editors: "We should make peace with the government; we should not be its enemy." In his graduation address in the spring of 1983 at the University of Texas, Joe Dealey, chairman of the company that owns *The Dallas Morning News*, urged journalists not to be "obsessed with a mission to overly investigate, to muckrake, to serve misguided ideals, or to arouse passions and animosities."

• Some journalists preach accommodation with law enforcement officials. In the fall of 1983, at a meeting in Palm Springs of Investigative Reporters and Editors (IRE, which now has 2,000 members, started as an educational clearinghouse organization and first gained attention as its members collectively tried to investigate the death in 1976 of Don Bolles, an Arizona reporter), Tom Renner of *Newsday*, then the group's president, complained about the arrogance of the press and its antagonism toward law enforcement agencies. "Good reporters have exchanged information without compromising their dignity or integrity for decades," said Renner, who criticized reporters who preferred to walk a "one-way street where it's all right for us to take and yes, demand, information" from law enforcement "but refuse to provide reciprocal help when called on by those we seek information from." In the audience, there was some applause, some "right on's," and some groans. (Renner is a longtime investigative reporter and coauthor of several books on the Mafia in which he has relied heavily on the FBI and the police for information.)

• Some journalists cooperate with law enforcement officials in order to move forward with what they see as their larger mission. "Every time I go into these investigations, I want to get an indictment," says Clark Mollenhoff, a veteran Pulitzer Prize winner who teaches journalism while writing for the *Washington Times*.

• Some reporters are crusaders, like the muckrakers at the turn of the century. Jack Newfield of the *Village Voice* feels "we are in special need of writers" who are "committed in their bones, to not just describing the world, but changing it for the better." At the Miami conference of investigative reporters, Geraldo Rivera, then of ABC's "20/20," told the audience: "We are part of the process of positive social change. We are embarrassed to admit we are crusaders. There is nothing wrong with the goal of trying to change the world."

Under certain circumstances, journalists are expected to co-operate with the law, just as they would be expected to save a drowning man. In the written code of ethics that governs the behavior of lawyers, a lawyer may not tell authorities about past crimes a client has committed. But the lawyer has an obligation to inform on his client if there is reason to believe a crime is about to be committed. Similarly, there is a consensus among journalists that a journalist has a responsibility to inform the police of an imminent crime. To illustrate this point, Gilbert Cranberg, former editor of the editorial pages of the Des Moines newspapers and now a professor at the University of Iowa, uses a hypothetical instance of a reporter who picks up the telephone and is told by the caller that he is headed for the statehouse to shoot the governor. That reporter, notes Cranberg, would "instinctively" notify the police.

Beyond situations like the one described by Cranberg—situations that come up infrequently—there is little agreement on how reporters and law enforcement officials ought to treat each other. Some television stations, with their infinite appetite for dramatic footage, have been especially accommodating to police and prosecutors. Other stations have sought and received the blessing of law enforcement officials for their undercover work.

In 1981 reporters at KSL-TV in Salt Lake City conducted an undercover "test" to find out how easy it was for unqualified applicants to receive food stamps and unemployment compensation. In order to avoid being prosecuted, the reporters obtained the advance approval of the Utah attorney general. "They promised to deposit anything gained in a safe deposit box, and we determined there would be no intent to defraud," says Paul Tinker, the chief deputy attorney general. The tape made by the reporters has been used as a training film for new employees in some Utah state offices. This was a trade—a *quid pro quo.*

That same year a "20/20" camera crew went to Iowa at the request of a local prosecutor to join him in catching insurance salesmen suspected of making fraudulent sales pitches. A sting operation was set up, and "20/20" secretly taped the salesmen at work. Some of this footage was used on the television show, and the tape, without being subpoenaed, was turned over to the prosecutor. Charles Thompson, a "20/20" producer, appeared before the Iowa County Attorneys Association and told them: "I don't look at you people as the enemy. And if we can give you the technical assistance or if we could give the information and we don't compromise your prosecution and you don't compromise my ethics, I see nothing wrong with it. And I think we ought to be on the same side."

There are dangers in Thompson's position. When reporters become part of law enforcement, they cannot be impartial. It is standard procedure for most print and television journalists to resist efforts by prosecutors to compel testimony about confidential sources. When the sources are not confidential, there are those who wish to cooperate but, unlike Thompson, they feel more at ease doing so under the compulsion of a subpoena.

"Reporters feel more comfortable in turning over information when ordered to," says Richard Arcara, district attorney of Erie County in Upstate New York. In Buffalo, the largest city in the county, the relations between law enforcement officers and reporters have generally been cordial. In the summer of 1983 a ten-year-old Buffalo girl was abducted and raped, and that night her father—a truck driver and street-corner preacher—was arrested and charged with stabbing the man who was later accused of the rape. What lifted this particular incident from obscurity was the fact that the stabbing was captured on tape by a television crew that was doing a story on the abduction and was on the scene when the stabbing occurred. It was later broadcast on WKBW-TV, the local ABC affiliate, and nationally on ABC's "Nightline." The story received wide national attention as an example of vigilante justice.

Arcara wanted the tape; Phil Beuth, the general manager of the station, was willing to oblige as long as a subpoena was issued. "In essence, the tape was the same as if someone had recorded it at home," said Beuth in explaining why he saw no damage in turning it over. In fact, in Buffalo there was a company that recorded television news clips each night and tried to sell them to people who were mentioned. Under these circumstances, Beuth thought it would have been pointless not to turn over the tape. But in order not to appear too accommodating, he quite appropriately insisted that he be "compelled" to do so by a subpoena.

It is most sensible for journalists to take the stubborn position that prosecutors are entitled to no material gathered in reporting stories and then to carve out exceptions on a case-by-case basis, as Beuth did.

That is how Jerry Uhrhammer, who now works for the *Press-Enterprise* in Riverside, California, has been operating for more than twenty-five years as an investigative reporter at several newspapers. In the fall of 1982 he testified as a character witness, at the request of a prosecutor, on behalf of a key prosecution witness at a trial in Eugene, Oregon. Two years earlier, while he was working at the *Eugene Register-Guard*, Uhrhammer had developed as a source a former college football linebacker who was helpful in his investigation of bogus grade transcripts of football players at the University of Oregon. Later, at a trial unrelated to those accusations, Uhrhammer's source was called as a witness for the prosecution, which was attempting to convict another football player of burglary. The defense lawyer tried to impugn the ex-linebacker's integrity. The prosecutor thereupon asked Uhrhammer for help. He agreed to testify.

"The linebacker had gone out on a limb to help us," said Uhrhammer. "He put himself on the line. Everything he gave us checked out to a gnat's eyelash. We felt a personal obligation. There was a certain amount of citizenship involved. It was in society's best interest to see justice done."

Like many of his colleagues, Uhrhammer feels that collaborating with law enforcement agents is inevitable. "Sometimes you give up very little," he says in outlining what is probably the most sensible approach to collaboration. "Sometimes you give up a bit more than you like. That's trading. It's been done for a long time and will continue to be done for a long time."

Day in and day out, there is trading of information between reporters and law enforcement agents. Relationships between reporters and police and prosecutors are not unlike those that are developed by any good reporter who covers a beat.

The Indianapolis Star has even put in writing the etiquette of trading information in "A Guide for Editorial Employees": "One of the toughest questions reporters often face is trading information with law enforcement. We feel it should be limited. Some of the best reporters in the country trade information with law enforcement, but with two disclaimers: (1) Never give information which would identify, or tend to identify, a source. (2) Never trade information with any law enforcement person unless that person is of PROVEN reliability. The main thing to remember is that you are a reporter, operating under the principles of independence and impartiality, not, in any way, an unofficial arm or helpmate of law enforcement."

Despite the rhetoric of an adversary relationship, there is one built-in feature in the transmission of information that puts journalists and their publications in the position of being more than willing collaborators in making law enforcement look good. That happens when prosecutors leak confidential information to the press.

It is a truism that prosecutors who leak can expect more flattering coverage than those who do not. Collateral benefits flow to reporters, who often receive credit for scoops. But those exclusives are often trivial. In the scheme of events, it is hardly significant to learn that "Mr. X is going to be indicted tomorrow, according to informed sources." There usually is nothing lost in waiting until tomorrow to find this out. It would be much better if reporters spent their time uncovering information that would lead to the indictment of Mr. Y or Ms. Z.

When prosecutors leak to journalists, journalists invariably get manipulated, and the target of the leak usually gets unfair treatment by being stigmatized in the press. Most of the time, reporters do not understand or try to discover the motive of a prosecutor, and it is rare that officials confer benefits on reporters without some selfish motive. Occasionally a prosecutor who is unable to secure an indictment under the rules of evidence seeks to harm his target by means of unfavorable publicity. He will leak derogatory information about such a target to reporters grateful to get exclusives and who then proceed to injure someone who, at least in the eyes of the law, is not culpable. In most jurisdictions it is a crime for a prosecutor to leak grand jury information, but no one has ever been prosecuted for it since that would require prosecutors to investigate themselves. Receiving such information is not a crime, so reporters are not subject to prosecution for printing such material. But just because it is not against the law is insufficient reason why such material should routinely be published.

When Edwin Meese was nominated for attorney general in early 1984, Bill Boyarsky of *The Los Angeles Times* recollected how Meese started as a prosecutor in the dilapidated municipal courtrooms of Oakland in the 1950s: "The press was part of the system and I, as a beginning reporter, was an enthusiastic member of the club. The police or deputy district attorneys would alert us to coming arrests and the resulting stories convicted the suspects in the papers and made heroes of the police and the district attorneys."

One of the rare instances in which law enforcement agents were chastised for leaking occurred in 1981 when the federal government took disciplinary action against two government lawyers and five FBI agents for prematurely releasing information about three undercover investigations of public corruption, including the Abscam sting operation. A report detailing the disciplinary actions dispassionately and shrewdly analyzed the motives of the leakers, noting that some of them may have been moved by a desire to promote the "institutional image" of either the Department of Justice or the FBI. At the same time the FBI was in particular need of restoring a reputation that had been badly tarnished during the 1960s and 1970s when the focus of the agency was on capturing bank robbers and political dissidents rather than on pursuing organized crime, official corruption and drug trafficking.

Orchestrated leaks have long been used by the FBI and Department of Justice. In the early 1960s *Life* magazine was a favored beneficiary; publicity was an important weapon used by Attorney General Robert F. Kennedy in his effort to send Jimmy Hoffa, the teamster leader, to jail. Memoranda that were later made public show that Kennedy had urged a disaffected teamster official to use the pages of *Life* as a vehicle for announcing his break with the union. One note, from a staff member at *Life* to the managing editor, said that Kennedy "makes the suggestion that the piece go into" the background and philosophy of Sam Baron, the disaffected Teamster, "to help explain his disgust with Hoffa and his motivation for breaking with the Teamsters." Later, the note said that Kennedy "agrees that a ghost writer makes good sense. . . ." The article, called "I Was Near the Top of Jimmy's Drop-Dead List," ran in *Life* in 1962. It did not matter how committed Kennedy was to his cause. What he did was improper, and *Life* was wrong to collaborate.

An elaborate arrangement with *Life* was worked out in the early 1970s by Whitney North Seymour, Jr., the federal prosecutor for the Southern District of New York, the jurisdiction that includes Manhattan. Robert Leuci, whose life was later chronicled in the book and movie *Prince of the City*, was a rogue policeman who had agreed to work undercover to help develop drug and corruption cases. Leuci, who was under great pressure in the investigation, became demoralized and afraid for his family, Seymour recalls in his memoir, *United States Attorney*. The prosecutors concluded that they "should try to get a responsible journalist to write up Leuci's experiences and show the world that he had done courageous things in the interest of justice." A formal agreement with *Life* was signed, in which the magazine agreed to publish the article when the investigation was over. But the deal collapsed after *The New York Times* learned of the investigation and the unusual arrangement with *Life*. Much to Seymour's annoyance, the *Times* carried the story about Leuci and the investigation before it had been completed.

Some leaks are relatively benign. From time to time a reporter finds out about a continuing investigation. In return for the reporter's not writing about it, a prosecutor, as a matter of courtesy, may give the reporter an exclusive or some advantage in preparing a story. "If a reporter comes to me and helps by holding off on something he knows, I might give him a slight head start before I announce an indictment," says Mario Merola, who has been the Bronx district attorney since 1973.

Robert Fiske, a former federal prosecutor of the Southern District of New York, recalls how shocked he was when a reporter presented him with details of a major investigation that his office was conducting. "God knows how he knew," says Fiske, whose office still had an active wiretap in the target's office. "Every day we were still getting good information. Publication at that time would have wrecked the investigation." At Fiske's urging, the reporter did not run the story. In return, Fiske promised that if he had a "whiff" that any other reporter was on to the story, he would notify the obliging reporter. He kept his word.

When prosecutors are responsible, it is incumbent on reporters to be responsible as well and temporarily withhold information until an investigation is concluded. The trouble is that the world of law enforcement is often not this neat.

The most dangerous leaks are ones that come from the office of an ambitious and zealous prosecutor. In recent years the prosecutor's office with the reputation for leaking information the most frequently was that of Maurice Nadjari, who served in the middle 1970s as a special prosecutor in New York City to investigate corruption in the criminal-justice system. Four decades earlier, Thomas Dewey had served in a similar capacity, and on the basis of his success there he went on to the governorship of New York.

Nadjari, too, talked of running for statewide office as his tenure came to a close. For most of the four years Nadjari served, years in which I sometimes covered him, his office received extensive and generous coverage far out of proportion to what it accomplished. Nadjari's first press secretary, William Federici, who had been an investigative reporter at the *New York Daily News*, was one of the highest-paid people in the office, creating the impression that Nadjari was as interested in generating publicity as in pursuing wrongdoers. Many of the city's better reporters fell into step with Nadjari because they thought the judges and prosecutors whom Nadjari was investigating were corrupt. Often they would print the name of a judge or official said to be "under investigation." Only a few indictments were ever secured in such cases. It was rarer that trials were held. There were still fewer convictions, and most that were obtained did not stand up under appeal.

But the favorable way that Nadjari was treated by the press was more than just an instance of a prosecutor eager for publicity and of journalists happy for ready-made exclusives. Nadjari's position was created in 1972 in response, in large part, to articles published in *The New York Times* which described widespread corruption in the police department. Nadjari would say, at least in the presence of some editors at the *Times*, that he owed his job to the *Times* and that he would resign should the newspaper ever be displeased with his performance. Few criticisms of Nadjari ever appeared in that newspaper.

Newsrooms were drenched with leaks from Nadjari. When Governor Hugh Carey, then being discussed as a possible vice presidential nominee, tried to fire Nadjari late in 1975, Nadjari went on the offensive with leaks to reporters whom he favored. He suggested that Carey may have been corrupt. These damaging leaks came during a slow news period—between Christmas and New Year's Day; and in edition after edition, the disclosures appeared on the front page, giving the erroneous impression that Carey would soon be indicted. Because of the atmosphere created by these leaks, Carey was forced to rescind the dismissal of Nadjari. Because of the negative publicity, Carey was no longer mentioned as a possible vice president. Not until months later was it apparent that there was nothing to the suggestion that he was corrupt.

In Nadjari's last months in office, leaks became a dominating issue, overshadowing what Nadjari was supposed to be doing —rooting out corrupt officials. Unprecedented hearings were held by a state investigative commission on the subject of these leaks. In the commission's report, Nadjari was accused of improperly leaking information, of lacking controls in his office to prevent leaks, and of allowing investigations to be "influenced by a concern for media favor." In the closing months of his four-year tenure, Nadjari's reputation was such that even when defense lawyers would leak information in their possession, people would assume it came from Nadjari.

What was particularly unfortunate about the Nadjari years were the lost opportunities. There undoubtedly was corruption in the criminal justice system, but he was unable to uncover evidence that would stand up in court. What was particularly dangerous about Nadjari was the intensity of his unchecked zeal.

His critics frequently cited a speech that he made in 1971 to the National College of District Attorneys, in which he said: "Man's greatest experience is the act of lovemaking. I sometimes wonder if the moment when the jury foreman rises to utter those sweet words of verdict—'We the jury find the defendant guilty as charged'—is not as satisfying an experience." At a lecture at Fordham Law School in 1975 about a prosecutor's trial tactics, he told students, "You're going to lead that jury down the road to conviction because that defendant has been judged guilty—and properly so—by you."

Not until a few months before he left office did the complaisant press do what it should have been doing all along—monitor him and offer intelligent criticism.

■

If Nadjari, with his sense of indignation and his single-mindedness, had been a journalist rather than a prosecutor, he would have been a muckraker, a crusader. After he was in office a couple of years, one of Nadjari's severest critics in the press was Jack Newfield of the *Village Voice*, who accused him of using unconstitutional shortcuts. After Nadjari left office, Newfield wrote that, in the beginning, Nadjari's "mission was noble and necessary" and that the prosecutor was perceived of "as a hero, as a lone warrior against a corrupt system."

Had Newfield not been a crusading journalist, he may well

have been a prosecutor, and his description of Nadjari goes a long way in summing up how crusading journalists view themselves. They are unhappy with the world and they want to make it better. Unlike many investigative journalists who choose to cooperate only sparingly with law enforcement and on a case-by-case basis, they have no hesitation about exchanging information with friendly prosecutors.

Advocacy journalists like Newfield are committed to a point of view. If they are forthright and reveal their viewpoint to readers, different rules apply to them than to daily reporters. Readers expect different stories in the *Village Voice*, a journal of opinion, than they do in *The New York Times*. Although the *Voice* is a weekly and has a circulation of 150,000, which is modest in comparison to the three major dailies in New York, Newfield is probably the best-known print journalist reporting on local matters in New York City, and probably the most influential. He is read by those in power and those who wish to be in power, and many other reporters and columnists are influenced by his writing.

I first met Newfield in April 1974, at lunch to discuss a story I had written that dealt with him. My lead was one of the most backward ever to see print: It said that a committee of the city bar association had exonerated three state supreme court judges of charges leveled against them in an article two years earlier by Newfield. This was the first time the *Times* had carried any reference whatsoever to the accusations, contained in an article called "The Ten Worst Judges in New York." The committee of the bar association—an establishment institution —was unable to determine whether Newfield was right or wrong in the case of three other judges, and it did not deal with charges relating to two of the ten he attacked.

That left two judges. The report agreed with Newfield on these judges. That is to say, a panel of the bar association concluded that two sitting judges were incompetent or worse. That was news indeed, much more interesting to the average reader than a dry discussion of Jack Newfield's ability as a journalist. But this real news was buried in my story, in part because journalists denigrate a story they did not get first, and in part because some *Times* editors bore a special antipathy toward Newfield and his brand of advocacy journalism. So the fact that the bar association report at several points accused Newfield of being inaccurate and irresponsible was played up in my story, while the credit he received for performing "a service to the community" was played down.

In the end, the bar association report was ambivalent in its treatment of Newfield. Even though it contained stiff criticism, Newfield boldly said that he had been exonerated. "I have been vindicated on the major substantive points, and the bar association has found only nitpicking points to disagree with." Shortly after this, Newfield picked another list of "Ten Worst Judges" and observed that "the press may be the only institution that can possibly hold judges accountable."

After that lunch, which was pleasant enough, we stayed in sporadic touch, although we were never friendly. Soon after I started working at City Hall for Mayor Koch—whom Newfield once had supported but had come to dislike—I ran into him, and he said something vaguely congratulatory about my new job and how it would be a good experience for me to be working on the inside. (It is one of those ironies of journalism and capitalism that until 1985 Rupert Murdoch, Koch's good friend, owned the *Village Voice*, the newspaper that has been the mayor's most consistent and unpleasant critic. But it has been an enormously profitable property, and that usually ended the discussion of why Murdoch, who has been so keen on expressing his political views through another of his papers, the *New York Post*, left the editorial policy of the *Voice* alone.)

For more than two decades, Newfield has attacked politicians he disagrees with and has befriended those he likes. In the introduction to his latest book, *The Education of Jack Newfield*, a collection drawn from his twenty years as a reporter, Newfield tells how greatly influenced he was by the autobiography of Lincoln Steffens, the muckraking journalist at the turn of the century, and by Steffens's description of his great mentor, Jacob Riis, who "not only got the news; he cared about the news. He hated passionately all tyrannies, abuses, miseries, and he fought them. He was a 'terror' to the officials and landlords responsible, as he saw it, for the desperate condition of the tenements, where the poor lived. He had 'exposed' them in articles, books, and public speeches, and with results."

That, notes Newfield, is his "professional credo." And, he says, "I have cared about the news. I have hated passionately the overdogs who hurt tenants, or old people, or innocent citizens. And I have tried to get results, by going on radio and TV shows, and by confronting politicians and decision makers, and by sharing my files and information with other journalists."

There is a need and a place for crusaders or advocacy journalists, and part of the reason Newfield enjoys such prominence is that there are not enough of them in New York City. But in a world full of ambiguity, Newfield's universe often seems inhabited only by "good" people and "bad" people. Those who disagree with him are the villains. When he finds himself in a dispute, the debate is often not decided on any evidence but merely on his word against someone else's.

For example, Newfield is a close friend of New York's Governor Mario Cuomo. In *The New Yorker* and in the *New York Daily News*, Ken Auletta, a reporter who spent much of 1983 following Cuomo around, chronicled several conversations in which Newfield urged the governor to make certain appointments to his administration and to veto others. ("He has more access to Cuomo than most county leaders," says Auletta.)

Newfield denied this and attacked Auletta's integrity. In a long letter published in the *Village Voice*, Newfield said that Auletta was tainted because he had once worked in politics: "Auletta accuses me of being too cozy with politicians, especially Governor Mario Cuomo. But I have worked for the *Village Voice* as a writer and editor for 20 years. I have never received a dime in compensation from a politician; Auletta has. He worked for Brooklyn Democratic Party boss Meade Esposito. And he worked for Howard Samuels," who three times ran for governor and who was the first president of New York's Off-Track Betting Corporation. Newfield also attacked Auletta because his father received contracts from the city's Department of Parks and Recreation. In self-righteous pique, Newfield asks: "By what standard of purity and probity does Auletta judge my integrity? I have no family members being enriched by city contracts; Auletta does. . . . If a parent of mine profited from city contracts I wouldn't know how to write about government without violating the minimum standards about conflicts of interest."

A few years ago, a series in the *Village Voice* by Wayne Barrett, a protégé of Newfield's, helped to prompt an investigation of possible campaign irregularities by Congressman Charles Schumer, a Brooklyn Democrat. In an affidavit sworn to in May 1983, John Scanlon, a New York public relations executive and an admirer of Schumer's, said that Newfield told him that he was going to "get" Schumer " 'any way I can,' or words to that effect." Newfield denied that such a conversation ever took place.

In a preliminary version of this chapter that appeared in the *Columbia Journalism Review*, I wrote that Barrett and Newfield had coauthored the series in the *Voice* about Schumer. That was incorrect. In a letter to the editor about my mistake, Newfield said that he had told me "twice" that he had not written the articles, which suggests that I purposely introduced this error into the story. In fact, neither my notes nor my memory bear him out on this.

In his letter Newfield amply demonstrated his single-mindedness. Several of his articles, he boasted, "led to the indictment and conviction of some bad characters." These included, he has said, "nursing-home owner Bernard Bergman, city councilman Sam Wright, teamster union leader John Cody, and landlord-arsonist Joe Bald." It is as if Newfield were the prosecutor, the judge and the jury. It is dangerous for a journalist, even a crusading journalist committed to changing social conditions, to usurp all those roles.

4. JOURNALISTS AS UNACKNOWLEDGED LEGISLATORS

"**H**ere's this morning's New York Sewer!" cried one. "Here's this morning's New York Stabber! Here's the New York Family Spy! Here's the New York Private Listener! Here's the New York Peeper! Here's the New York Plunderer! Here's the New York Keyhole Reporter! Here's the New York Rowdy Journal! Here's all the New York papers! Here's full particulars of the patriotic locofoco movement yesterday, in which the whigs was so chawed up; and the last Alabama gouging case; and the interesting Arkansas dooel with Bowie knives; and all the Political, Commercial, and Fashionable News. Here they are! Here's the papers, here's the papers!"
— Charles Dickens, *Martin Chuzzlewit*, 1844

Arriving in Washington for the first time in 1965, an English journalist could not help being surprised that it was a common practice for American political journalists to break bread with American politicians in each other's homes. They seemed to be too unseparate, and it was puzzling to know how the political journalist could, in these circumstances, maintain his posture as a critic. After all, the breaking of bread in another's, or in one's own, home is a ceremony; and, having accepted the hospitality of a politician, or extended his own, the political journalist is not in a strong position to go to his typewriter the next morning and write that the man is a liar.
— Henry Fairlie, *The Kennedy Promise*, 1973

59

In the past several elections that New York Mayor Edward I. Koch has run in, Jack Newfield has been a visible member of the organizations seeking his defeat. With Newfield, the adversary relationship slipped into personal antagonism. But the reporters who regularly covered City Hall during the winter of 1982 could not have been more unlike Newfield. Most were unaggressive, as if they were hibernating, and the traditional role of the press—that it should act as critic of government—was largely absent from City Hall.

Working conditions for the thirty or so reporters who regularly cover City Hall are far from ideal. The building, in lower Manhattan, is a beautifuly proportioned Federal-style structure completed in 1812, but reporters from the wire services and major New York newspapers work in a messy, cramped twenty-by-thirty-foot room that once served as a courtroom where cases involving lunatics and drunkards were heard. The room is an open space, like most newsrooms. But unlike newsrooms, there was supposed to be competition among the various reporters, and competition ordinarily does not flourish in the absence of privacy.

By 1982 most of the veteran City Hall reporters had disappeared, along with many New York newspapers. (Twenty-three small plaques commemorating New York newspapers that have folded hang as a sad reminder on the doorway of the reporters' room.) Until the early 1970s many full-time reporters moonlighted, working for politicians or running political public relations businesses on the side. In 1982 most of the occupants of the room were young and generally well paid. But few were interested in how city government operates; they wished to serve a year or so at City Hall and then move on.

In my two years as press secretary to Koch, I discovered that the politicians' world of "contracts," or favors, was often indistinguishable from the reporters' world of contracts. I had been at City Hall for a few months when a reporter who had been a friend before I arrived there let me know that the other reporters were waiting for me to show some clout. My friend suggested that I arrange for the mayor to have a party for the reporters—this, he said, would be sufficient to demonstrate that I mattered. And so, on a Saturday afternoon at the end of May, the mayor gave a picnic at Gracie Mansion, his official residence, for the reporters and their families. The mayor was happy, the reporters were happy, and I was relieved.

Small favors were always being done for reporters. The mayor's schedule would be rearranged so that he could attend a social event involving a reporters' organization, such as the New York Press Club's annual boat ride. The mayor also was eager to endorse any good cause that a spouse of an editor or publisher had taken an interest in, from helping the blind to promoting understanding of Japanese culture. If invited, he would attend a reporter's wedding or party. His presence was always appreciated.

It was relatively easy for the mayor and his staff to set the agenda for the reporters, who are collectively called Room 9, after the number on the door of their office. As in most government office buildings across the country, the parent news organizations paid no rent for their space. The reporters were physical—and spiritual—captives of the bureaucracy they were supposed to cover.

They were physically too close to one another, and professionally they were too close to the people they covered. They were like firemen, passively waiting for an alarm. When notified by the mayor or a member of his press office of a news conference, they had to cover it. Koch had at least one such conference each day, and these, along with orchestrated leaks and the many handouts distributed by the mayor's office, were the principal sources of news.

Business at City Hall begins at 8 A.M. or earlier. It is a small building with only three entrances. A single gate controls access to the mayor's end of the building. Just watching who goes in and out, especially early in the day when many private meetings take place, gives a clue to what issues are on the mayor's mind. But reporters usually did not drift in until ten or later, and they showed little initiative. I can recall only one occasion in two years when a reporter asked me and my staff to assemble materials as part of an investigative effort. He never picked them up.

The mayor and many of his advisers were pleased that Room 9 was usually so pliant. That is not to say that there was disrespect for the press. Great consideration was given to how issues were played in the papers and on television, and when important decisions were made they were followed by attempts to line up the support of the editorial boards at *The New York Times*, the *New York Daily News* and the *New York Post*.

By this time the *Times* had "redlined" the city, as the banks had done a decade earlier. (Indeed, the *Times*, in its emphasis on Manhattan and the affluent suburbs, had assigned only one reporter—at the Brooklyn courthouses—to the other four boroughs with their 5½ million residents.) At one time the *Daily News* had excellent political coverage, but by 1981 its local coverage had become the least aggressive and least interesting of the three papers. Its City Hall bureau had shrunk from seven or eight reporters to three, and its members often were phantoms, rarely at City Hall.

The radio reporters covering City Hall were generally competent, but they viewed the wire services—not the newspapers—as their competition, so their coverage was workmanlike but unimaginative. The wire services—Associated Press and United Press International—had their hands full just rewriting press releases. New York's seven VHF television stations did not regularly cover City Hall. In fact, not a single television reporter in New York, the nation's largest market, was assigned full-time to cover city government. This was particularly striking since the New York stations are rich and have a great deal of programming to fill, especially after several of them introduced two-hour early-evening news shows in the early 1980s. Television reporters would come downtown only for an occasional feature or for major press conferences—but even in such cases, they usually needed a follow-up call from the press office to remind them it was an important event.

Into this vacuum swept the *New York Post*, owned by Rupert Murdoch, the Australian publisher and businessman. To a degree unimagined by most New Yorkers, the *Post* set the agenda for the other papers. It carried more exclusive stories about city government than the others, and it played them more prominently, particularly in the very late editions of one day or the very early editions of the next morning. This meant that in the morning, radio reporters, eager for a fresh story for their noon newscasts, would frequently question the mayor about the latest disclosure in the *Post*. The other reporters would listen. Often the mayor embellished upon his original remarks. And a day later the *Times* and the *News* would carry stories on what the *Post* had run earlier. Although City Hall reporters were responsible for covering all aspects of municipal government, their coverage was what I called "Kochcentric"—the reporters relied disproportionately on the mayor for news, much to the displeasure of the other officials.

Each March reporters from Room 9 take part in a political

spoof, which is put on by the Inner Circle, an organization of one hundred political reporters and public relations people who were once reporters. They donate the proceeds of their extravagant show to charity—what little is left of the money once the expenses are deducted. Over the years the black-tie dinner has evolved into one of the most important social events of the year in New York politics. Powerbrokers maneuver for desirable tables. The show is usually sold out. And, in a reversal of roles, it is the reporters, behaving like the politicians whom they cover, who decide who among the powerful are to be blessed with tickets and prime tables.

It is like dozens of other spoofs across the country, in capital cities like Albany, New York; Montgomery, Alabama, and Tallahassee, Florida. Reporters seem to feel an irresistible urge to dress up in costumes of the opposite sex, to sing off key and to make fun of those whom they cover. (Until 1980, the proceedings in New York had been "off the record"—meaning nothing could be reported—although hundreds of politicians and reporters were present.) In New York, after the reporters put on their long skits, the mayor comes on and teases and insults them. It is a sign of status for a reporter to be singled out by name for ridicule in the mayor's carefully prepared monologue. "My thanks to Inner Circle President Doug Edelson," Koch said in 1982. "Doug has discovered a great way to avoid a hangover. He doesn't stop drinking."

The mayor then brings on the cast from a Broadway show. The casts from *Annie, Ain't Misbehavin'* and *42nd Street* have performed in recent years; in 1982 Koch was joined by Ann Miller, Mickey Rooney and others from the cast of *Sugar Babies*. The mayor and the Broadway stars he invites are the prime attraction at this $250-a-head dinner, and Mayor Koch knows it. Without his imprimatur, the event might founder. One year, after being criticized publicly for insensitivity for appearing on stage wearing an Afro wig with the cast of *Ain't Misbehavin'*, Koch decided to torture the reporters. He said he was not sure he would participate in the show again. Delegations from Room 9 came to call on him, imploring him to perform. After causing great worry, Koch told them, as he knew he would all along, that he would oblige. He did so because he loved to perform and because he knew it was useful to have the reporters who covered him every day in his debt, rather than angry with him.

In January 1982 the biggest news event at City Hall was

expected to be the unveiling of the city's preliminary budget. This was less of a story in 1982, when the city was rebounding economically, than it had been a few years earlier when New York City was near bankruptcy. After the budget announcement, Koch planned to take a vacation with some friends in Spain. It would be a slow period for the reporters, a time to prepare for the Inner Circle show. On the Friday the preliminary budget was unveiled—the last working day before Koch went abroad—Governor Hugh Carey unexpectedly announced that he would not seek election to a third term the next fall.

Even though Koch had discussed privately with some of his friends and advisers as early as the previous November whether he should run for Governor, these discussions were not taken seriously. Carey was expected to run, and the mayor had often repeated a pledge that he would run for no job other than that of mayor—a pledge that separated him from most other politicians, who routinely seek higher office.

While the mayor was on vacation, the *Post* began a campaign to draft him for governor. Upon his return it printed coupons asking readers to indicate if they thought the mayor should run. About fourteen thousand did. And Koch did decide to run, four weeks after he returned. (Soon after the *Post* began its coupon drive, the *Syracuse Herald-American* began one of its own, declaring, "We Don't Want Koch for Governor." Mario Cuomo, who defeated Koch in the primary and became governor, later named William D. Cotter, the editor of the Syracuse paper, to be head of the State Energy Office.)

Koch's decision to run for governor marked the turning point of his almost uninterrupted good relations with reporters. As he notes in his 1984 book, *Mayor,* after his announcement to run "the reporters felt they had been taken. They had never believed a politician before, but they had believed me when I said I was never going to run for any office other than mayor." The book itself, which became an instant bestseller, annoyed many reporters, some of whom were mentioned unkindly. The paperback version, published in 1985, exacerbated these bad feelings. In it, Koch added a chapter in which he explained that there was "a lot of envy involved" with those journalists who had reviewed the hardcover edition negatively. "This was, in many cases, their beat—politics in the City of New York, the fiscal crisis, the transit strike—and I scooped them."

Through this all, the one constant in supporting the mayor

was the *New York Post*. Speaking early in 1983, Rupert Murdoch described the role of the *Post* in persuading Koch to run for governor as "first-class journalism." Murdoch added, "We were only sorry that he didn't win."

On many occasions after his loss, Koch discounted the significance of the *Post*'s coupon drive and its draft-Koch movement. But I am certain, given Murdoch's importance to the mayor, that if the *Post*, like the Syracuse paper, had said, "Ed, please don't run," he would not have. (The mayor liked Murdoch; he also wanted his support. Once, after I had made a decision that displeased Murdoch, the mayor, in a rare fit of anger, scolded me and said: "Rupert is more important to me than anyone else.")

Through editorials, through behind-the-scenes maneuvering, and by erasing the distinction between news and editorial matter, many newspaper owners try to influence political races. Like Murdoch, some are blunt. In 1977 John P. McGoff, who headed companies that ran eight daily and forty weekly newspapers, fired two of his Michigan editors after they refused to run articles on page one that were critical of President Carter. One article began: "President James Earl Carter condones promiscuity—affairs with other women—for the male staffers who work for him." The second quoted a psychologist as predicting that Carter was "grooming wife Rosalynn for the Vice Presidency in 1984."

Other papers are more conventional in their attempts to affect the outcome of political contests. They use the editorial pages. In the same sense that Koch could not have been mayor without the *Post*, Daniel Patrick Moynihan could not have been elected senator without the support of the *Times*. In 1976 Arthur O. Sulzberger, at the last minute, exercised his prerogative as publisher of the *Times* and overruled his cousin, John Oakes, who ran the editorial page, throwing the editorial support of the paper to Moynihan, who narrowly defeated Bella Abzug, Oakes's choice for the Democratic nomination to the United States Senate. Sulzberger recalls: "John Oakes was very unhappy that I called the shot that way and, indeed, 'disassociated' himself from the decision." At a victory party, Moynihan brought out an apron bearing the famous promotional slogan of the classified employment advertisements of the *Times:* "I Got My Job Through *The New York Times*."

Although they both helped elect candidates, Murdoch and

Sulzberger are judged by different standards. Sulzberger's strong endorsement of Moynihan was viewed by critics as being in the mainstream of American journalism, while Murdoch's efforts on behalf of Koch and other politicians were not. Yet Moynihan enjoys an exceptionally good press in the news columns as well as in the editorial pages of the *Times*, just as Koch and other politicians favored by Murdoch do in the *Post*. What distinguishes Murdoch from Sulzberger and from most other owners is that he is open, almost brazen, about his politics. That is not to endorse Murdoch's approach; it merely is to say that he is more transparent about his personal biases.

"We are advocates," he said in 1983, "and we expect to have no difficulty in identifying where our loyalties lie." He makes it no secret that he uses news columns to help politicians he supports, and readers of his newspapers should hardly be surprised to find that political coverage is sometimes slanted. In 1980 the *Columbia Journalism Review* said that the *New York Post* "is no longer merely a journalistic problem. It is a social problem—a force for evil." But it strikes me as hypocritical that the *Times*, which is less straightforward about its support of Moynihan (or John V. Lindsay in his first term as New York's mayor in the late 1960s), generally escapes criticism, while the *Post* is condemned for its vigorous support of certain politicians.

Murdoch is a throwback in the way he uses the *Post* to advance his political ends. The *Post* was founded in 1801 by Alexander Hamilton and other Federalists after they had lost power. Until the Civil War, papers like the *Post* dominated American journalism. They were for the most part partisan operations associated with political parties. The press was full of propaganda and contained undisguised *ad hominem* attacks. Although that stridency was somewhat modulated, the great news proprietors at the turn of the century were still politically active. "Rupert Murdoch's *Post* would look like a tame pussycat compared to the press of 70 years ago," observed Hodding Carter III, the columnist and press critic. "But in an institution that increasingly looks like a Rotary Club meeting, Rupert Murdoch is a sign on the right of what is needed across the board."

Quite understandably, Murdoch has been castigated by those who suffer at his hands. In the 1977 primary campaign, the incumbent, Mayor Abraham Beame, became so exasperated that before the primary he issued this statement, which would be considered intemperate even for a politician of feisty disposition, and Beame was known for his solemnity: "I am particularly saddened to see a fine old newspaper like the *New York Post* corrupted into a sensationalist rag by an Australian carpetbagger. He came here to line his pockets by peddling fiction in the guise of news. As a self-acclaimed kingmaker, the man from Down Under has openly used his publications to wage political war and engage wantonly in character assassination. No New Yorker should take Rupert Murdoch's *New York Post* seriously any longer. It makes Hustler magazine look like the Harvard Review." (Beame lost the primary, but time heals most wounds, and he has since attended breakfast meetings sponsored by the *Post*.)

Just as understandably, Murdoch has supporters among those whom his papers treat well. The first time Koch ran for mayor, in 1977, was shortly after Murdoch had purchased the *Post*. In a seven-person field, Koch was an underdog. Murdoch supported him enthusiastically, and Koch has often said that he would not have been elected without the *Post*'s editorial support.

Koch reciprocates when he can. In 1980, the *Post* sought the Pulitzer Prize. The *Post* had run frequent editorials and articles in favor of stricter gun-control legislation, a position endorsed by the mayor. At the *Post*'s request, Mayor Koch nominated the paper for journalism's highest prize. This is in line with a dubious practice of the Pulitzer board that unintentionally causes politicians and news organizations to be more closely yoked than they should be.

Robert Christopher, administrator of the prizes, says entrants are encouraged to have "prominent people" recommend them for the awards. But while this gives a politician a chance to ingratiate himself with a publication that covers him, the process is something of a charade because, according to Christopher, "in general I think it is safe to say that their impact is quite limited unless the writer (the politician) can and does make a case that the story or stories he is praising have had demonstrable impact, such as exonerating an improperly convicted criminal, significantly assisting in getting legislation passed or something of the kind." With its sustained campaign, the *Post* undoubtedly had a "demonstrable impact" in getting New York's tougher gun-control legislation enacted. But it did not win a prize; it did not come close. The Pulitzer jurors are prominent editors and reporters, most of whom frown on the *Post*.

Murdoch's influence, if sometimes underestimated, is also sometimes misunderstood. It was by Harold Evans, who was installed in 1981 and fired a year later as editor of the *Times* of London, another Murdoch purchase. He had ample reason to be furious with Murdoch, but he let his good judgment be obscured in his book, *Good Times, Bad Times:* "If the British Establishment had been hostile to Murdoch, the New York one was murderous. . . . Murdoch was also excoriated everywhere for what he was doing to the Post as the 'hands-on' chief editor. 'Headless Body in Topless Bar' was the style, the ultimate parody of the macho tabloid. Everyone's distaste for the Post's salivation over crime, gossip, sport and Wingo (the Post's equivalent of Bingo) was made tolerable by their certainty that he would fail because the New Yorker was more sophisticated than the sex-ridden and credulous Londoner. . . ."

In New York, and I suspect in London as well, there are many Establishments. And while certain New Yorkers clearly have been "murderous" to Murdoch, others surely have not. Under his reign, circulation has nearly doubled to close to a million. That says as much about New Yorkers as it does about Murdoch. He has openly flouted the present standards of American journalism, and he has done so with the tacit acceptance of the power structure of New York City, which consists of elected politicians, union leaders, real estate developers, bankers and civic leaders. Perhaps their approval is based as much on fear as on respect, but in a relatively short time—less than a decade—he became a major figure in New York and in the country.

By the time Koch was reelected in 1981, it had become extraordinary to witness the homage being paid the *Post* by politicians, even those whom it had once attacked. The day after the election, Murdoch sponsored a breakfast that was attended by just about every politician who counted in the city, including some whom Murdoch had vigorously opposed. This event also gave the *Post* a marked advantage on that day's news. Reporters from other news organizations attended the gathering, but they faced the galling prospect of including the line "politician so-and-so said this at a New York Post breakfast" in their stories. (This was particularly annoying to the *Times*, which generally ignores the *Post*, mentioning it as little as possible.) For the past several years, Murdoch, with the help of Howard Rubenstein, a shrewd public relations operative, has continued these breakfast forums. They are regularly attended by up to a thousand civic leaders, union officials, businessmen and politicians—the same crowd that vies for the best tables at the Inner Circle show. In a predictable bit of self-praise, the *Post* calls these breakfasts "the city's most prestigious arena for serious civic discussions."

Like Harold Evans, Michael O'Neill had good reason to be upset with Murdoch. He was the editor of the *New York Daily News* when the *Post* made serious inroads into its circulation. In reviewing Evans's book in *The St. Petersburg Times*—a paper that in its scrupulous orthodoxy and its unwavering adherence to the notion of ethical journalism is about as far removed from the *New York Post* as can be imagined—O'Neill shows a much clearer understanding of Murdoch than does Evans. Murdoch, he said, is "an old fashioned power merchant whose private political agendas, even more than his sex and sensation journalism, make him a public concern." O'Neill places Murdoch in context. "Like Hearst, Murdoch puts his newspaper to personal use. He runs roughshod over journalistic rules whenever it suits his purpose. He loads propaganda into his news columns to boost his political friends and intimidate his foes. And out of sight, away from the headlines, he is constantly laying down his own underground power cables to governors, mayors, prime ministers and presidents."

Murdoch, who had cultivated an image of well-mannered shyness, has begun gradually to emerge. In 1982 he was honored as the Communications Man of the Year by the American Jewish Congress—a highly respected organization—"for his role in the struggle to maintain a free and outspoken press." The honorary chairmen of the event made an impressive list: Israel's Ambassador Yehuda Z. Blum, New York Governor Hugh L. Carey, then-lieutenant governor Mario Cuomo, senators Alfonse D'Amato and Daniel P. Moynihan, and the U.S. ambassador to the United Nations, Jeane J. Kirkpatrick.

In the *Post*, to mark this occasion, there was a picture, half a page wide, of a smiling Murdoch with Senator Moynihan and Howard Squadron, the president of the American Jewish Congress. Squadron, who presented the award to Murdoch, also happens to be Murdoch's longtime lawyer in the United States, a fact that was omitted in the thirty-paragraph story that accompanied the picture. It was the longest story in the paper that day, or almost any other day. In fact, the whole event smacked of being a setup to bolster Murdoch's reputation. He was the first recipient of the award, and it was not presented in the three years since. (None of those who have been proposed after Murdoch, said a spokesman for the American Jewish Congress in 1985, "were deemed appropriate.")

In his speech, Murdoch sounded closer to more conventional publishers as he spoke about the role of the press: "Newspapers must speak out resolutely and responsibly on the great issues of the day and give voice to the national conscience or that voice will become severely and dangerously muted. And it must to a large extent address those issues which most concern its readers, whether they be local crime, taxes, Mayor Koch or the Yankees."

For many years, when questioned by reporters, Murdoch was unavailable or would respond with a simple "no comment." But in the winter of 1984, when he became involved in a fight for control of Warner Communications, he suddenly became quite accessible. It suited his purpose then to come across as a sincere, polite executive. True to the perception that he is not bound by ordinary journalistic conventions, he borrowed a page from the politician's book and set up a "negative research" team in charge of digging up dirt on his opponent, Steven J. Ross, chairman of Warner, who was resisting Murdoch's takeover attempt. A *Post* editor and two reporters were assigned to find out whatever they could about the company and its chairman. They lied about their assignment. They told people whom they interviewed that they were working on a story for the *Post*. In fact, their material was used by Murdoch's lawyers.

Murdoch did not capture Warner but did profit by $40 million on his stock purchases. (He cleared another $40 million later in the year when he failed to gain control of the St. Regis Corporation but again profited on stock purchases.) In the midst of the Warner takeover battle, Murdoch was the subject of a glowing cover story in *Forbes*, an influential financial magazine. The *Forbes* profile of Murdoch was reprinted in the *Chicago Sun-Times*, yet another paper that Murdoch had just purchased.

Forbes magazine gushed: "To a degree that few people, least of all his fellow journalists, yet understand or even want to admit, Rupert Murdoch is an authentic heir of some great publishing figures of the past, of William Randolph Hearst, of Henry Luce, of Joseph Pulitzer, of Britain's Lord Beaverbrook . . . those who think Warner is 'too big' for Murdoch simply do not understand the man." The article ends with the prediction that "by the time Rupert Murdoch retires to his Australian farm in the 21st century, his current vulgar image will have faded, and he will be regarded as a sage who followed opportunity where it led and put together a global empire in what may be the 21st century's greatest industry, communications."

In contrast to this encomium, Murdoch's rival in Chicago, the *Tribune* (which, in a neat piece of symmetry, is the flagship property of the company that owns the *Daily News*, Murdoch's rival in New York City) began its own profile: "Editors of the Western world hate him only slightly more than Cain hated Abel."

■

New York City is a cultural, financial and fashion center. It is an international city, and local politics is only one of many stories that occupy the attention of journalists. In Washington, by contrast, the business of the city is government, and that is what the reporters—several thousand of them—cover.

Martin Tolchin, a reporter for *The New York Times* who covered the Lindsay administration in New York and went on to cover government in Washington, explains it this way: Mayor John Lindsay "conveyed the feeling that if you were anyone, you would be a Wall Street lawyer or stockbroker. In addition, it is rare for New York reporters to socialize with politicians." By contrast, he said, those with important political positions in Washington seek contacts in the media as readily as journalists look for sources among officials.

Journalists and politicians belong to one community and they often share the same values. More frequently than elsewhere, they are interchangeable—a former government official may become a columnist, while reporters often enter government service. At the top of the Washington journalistic structure is a well-educated elite. They are the columnists, the bureau

chiefs, the celebrity journalists who appear on television pub-
lic-affairs shows—those who shape opinion. But in Washington
even the outsiders are important, for they may become insiders
one day.

The advice of the late Edwin A. Lahey, the Washington bureau chief for the Knight newspapers in the late 1950s and
1960s, was probably the most practical for journalists. Lahey
advised young reporters to "pee on your source's leg at least
once a week," recalls his colleague Philip Meyer, who now
teaches journalism at the University of North Carolina at
Chapel Hill. Lahey would say those words to Meyer often. "I
think he kept saying it partly to remind himself, because he
was a very warm, convivial guy with many close friendships."
Lahey knew Felix Frankfurter, Arthur Goldberg, Robert Kennedy and other decision-makers socially. The danger that
Washington correspondents will become too friendly with politicians has been aptly—if ironically—described by I. F. Stone:
"You begin to understand there are certain things the public
ought not to know."

Withholding the news from the public is only one of the many
activities that reporters in Washington engage in which they
should be embarrassed about. In 1983 Mary McGrory, the
Washington columnist, commented: "Scratch a scribe in this
town and you will find a campaign manager. The candidate has
no more seductive, nay irresistible, gambit in wooing the press
than asking, 'What do you think I should do?' " ("Scratch a
journalist and you find a reformer" is how Leo Rosten put it
nearly half a century earlier in his study of Washington journalists.) In a 1984 study for the now defunct National News
Council, Charles Bailey, a former editor and Washington reporter at the *Minneapolis Tribune*, observes, "More reporters
and editors and producers than want to admit it have, on one
occasion or another, given free advice to public officials. Such
advice is sometimes sought, sometimes unsolicited; either way,
the donation, especially if not placed on the public record,
raises ethical questions."

In an acerbic article in *Washingtonian* magazine in 1983,
Henry Fairlie, the British journalist, condemned the "pious
self-advertisers and self-seekers" in the Washington press
corps who devote their energies to television appearances and
command up to $10,000 for a single lecture. "The very profes-
sion that should be the acid, relentless critic of the affluence

and cynicism of Washington is now the most ostentatiously affluent and cynical profession in the city," he said.

It is hard for Washington journalists to maintain their distance. A lot of the problem revolves around eating. "I was invited to a high power dinner party before I even knew I was going to be transferred down here," recalls Martin Tolchin. Reporters covering Capitol Hill have access to the same dining rooms as congressmen. The annual Gridiron Club dinner in Washington, a magnified version of New York City's Inner Circle dinner, features skits in which politicians are satirized. *The Washington Post* commented on the 1983 dinner: "Competition was keen among reporters and the news organizations they work for to bring as guests the most glittery government uppity-ups."

The dinner gives the reporters an opportunity to show off in front of their bosses, and the owners have a chance to hobnob with government officials. For many years, Henry Z. Urban was the low-key president and publisher of the *Buffalo News* and its predecessor, the *Buffalo Evening News*. In a column on the occasion of Urban's retirement, in 1983, Murray B. Light, the editor of the paper, wrote, "And I am certain that one of Urban's proudest days was in March 1975 when he sat for five hours next to President Ford at the head table of the prestigious Gridiron Dinner in Washington. He received that coveted spot the year Lucien Warren, then head of the News Washington Bureau, was president of the Gridiron Club."

None of this does much to inspire confidence in the adversary relationship that journalists reflexively point to as their prime function and a prime reason for their receiving special treatment in the Constitution.

The temptations that reporters, especially in Washington, feel to participate in politics and policymaking are felt by owners as well. Though owners are not hamstrung by the ethical restrictions that bind reporters, they can set a bad example for those who work for them. Many people who grew rich and powerful in the media have been in politics, and conversely, many politicians have had media connections.

Joseph Pulitzer was a member of Congress for a brief period. Warren Harding still owned the *Marion* (Ohio) *Star* when he was elected President in 1920. In that race, Harding defeated another Ohio publisher, James Cox, who had served as governor for three terms. Lyndon Johnson made a fortune in broadcasting, as did the Tafts and the Buckleys. In Texas, William P. Hobby, the lieutenant governor, was also president of the Houston Post Company until the family sold it in 1983. The Knowlands in Oakland, the Chafees in Providence and James Cox's heirs in Atlanta owned newspapers and had family members who served in national political roles.

Some owners and publishers have preferred to be kingmakers. Henry Luce, of *Time* magazine, whose wife, Clare Boothe Luce, served in Congress, took much of the credit for Dwight Eisenhower's nomination in 1952; and in California the Chandler family, the owners of *The Los Angeles Times*, were important Republicans and early and ardent Nixon supporters. In 1972, Francis L. Dale, then publisher of *The Cincinnati Enquirer* (who went to *The Los Angeles Herald Examiner*), served as chairman of the Committee to Re-elect the President, President Nixon's campaign committee.

In the 1950s and early 1960s, *The Washington Post*'s publisher, Philip Graham, played a behind-the-scenes role in American politics which had rarely been equaled and had far greater consequences than an endorsement by his paper. (In those years, the *Post* had no consistent policy on endorsements. In 1952 it came out for Eisenhower. In 1960 it avoided endorsing a candidate. But the official biographer of the paper, Chalmers Roberts, notes that "given Herblock's biting anti-Nixon and pro-Kennedy cartoons as well as laudatory editorials and articles, *Post* readers had no doubt as to the paper's choice.") Graham was a man of great influence in Washington politics and a trusted confidant of national leaders. He was one of the principal go-betweens in forging the Kennedy-Johnson ticket in 1960.

In his biography of the *Post*, done at the request of Katharine Graham, Philip Graham's widow, Roberts, a longtime *Post* reporter who had retired, notes that Philip Graham's friendship with Lyndon Johnson preceded the publisher's friendship with John Kennedy. In 1956 Graham had sketched out for Johnson what Johnson later, as president, privately described as "the basis for the Great Society programs." In *A Thousand Days*, Arthur M. Schlesinger, Jr., says that Graham saw in Kennedy "another man of power; and he was captivated by Kennedy's candor, detachment and intellectual force." Because of his friendship with both men, Graham found himself in the role of matchmaker, persuading Kennedy to pick Johnson and then persuading Johnson to accept.

Accompanied by the columnist Joseph Alsop, Graham visited Kennedy during the 1960 convention to urge him to choose Johnson as his running mate. This meeting was not reported on in the *Post,* although *Post* executives, editors and reporters knew of it, and by any definition, it was news. The role played by Graham appeared in print for the first time in Theodore White's *The Making of the President, 1960,* which was published in 1961. Graham disagreed with White's account and gave him a detailed memorandum, which was published after Graham's death as an appendix to *The Making of the President, 1964.*

Graham felt that Kennedy was already predisposed to picking Johnson. At the request of Alsop, Graham wrote, he "urged Kennedy to offer the Vice Presidency to Johnson. He immediately agreed, so immediately as to leave me doubting the easy triumph, and I therefore restated the matter, urging him not to count on Johnson's turning it down but to offer the VPship so persuasively as to win Johnson over." Perhaps Kennedy was predisposed, but Graham also wrote that he was often on the telephone with both Kennedy and Johnson and that he shuttled messages back and forth between them. On at least two occasions, he noted that he had to wade through "a solid jam of press people" on his mission.

Did any harm come of this relationship? Here is Chalmers Roberts's observation in his book: "As a publisher, Graham personally was much too close to the Kennedy administration and too protective of it. That, coupled with a sympathetic attitude toward the President by some on the paper who wrote about his administration, resulted in far less critical reporting and editorializing than should have been the role of the capital's leading newspaper."

The relationship of the *Post* to Kennedy was mirrored in an equally close relationship between Kennedy and a member of the staff of *Newsweek,* which had the same ownership as the *Post.* (In 1961 The Post Corporation had acquired *Newsweek,* in which another public servant, Averell Harriman, a former governor of New York and onetime presidential hopeful, was an important minority stockholder.) *Newsweek* enjoyed the benefits of the close friendship between the president and Benjamin Bradlee, Kennedy's Georgetown neighbor in the late 1950s, who was then a reporter in *Newsweek*'s Washington bureau and now is executive editor of the *Post.*

Conversations with Kennedy, a book of reminiscences and

conversations that Bradlee had with the President (he had taken notes and saved them for a decade before writing about them), was published in 1975. In it Bradlee describes groping "for the answer to a question that has plagued Washington journalists since the birth of the Republic: What is the dividing line between friendship and professionalism? Closeness brings the access that is essential to understanding, but with closeness come potentially conflicting loyalties." Bradlee wisely understood that while Kennedy valued his friendship, "he valued my journalism most when it carried his water."

In those years Osborn Elliott was editor of *Newsweek*, and in his memoir, *The World of Oz*, published in 1980, he writes, "Bradlee was a special friend of Jack Kennedy, and some second-thinkers have since charged that this closeness led *Newsweek* to bend too sympathetically toward the people and policies of the Kennedy regime. I didn't believe so then, and I don't believe so now. On the contrary, we editors in New York were forever challenging Bradlee with just that nasty supposition, and he was constantly pressed to justify stories in ways he would not have been had his friendship with Kennedy not been so well known to all."

What made Bradlee's reporting so valuable to readers was that he could provide glimpses that others could not. He could, as he recounts, give the "intimate details of the life and thinking of this remarkable man." What was missing from all this, of course, was a straightforward explanation to readers of the source of these insights. They came from a journalist, but a journalist who was also a close friend. Readers were entitled to know that connection in order to evaluate better what they read. Bradlee's reporting on Kennedy was filtered through rose-colored glasses. It was a glimpse by a journalist so close to his source that he could not be expected to be completely detached, a journalist who refers to the President as "this remarkable man who lit the skies of this land bright with hope and promise as no other political man has done in this century."

As an insider, Bradlee got exclusives. At a dance at the White House, Kennedy told him about the exchange of Gary Powers, the pilot of the U-2 reconnaissance plane shot down over central Russia, for Colonel Rudolph Abel, the highest-ranking Communist spy ever caught in the United States. No other reporters knew, but this information certainly could not wait for the next edition of *Newsweek*, a weekly. So, with the cooperation of Philip Graham, who was also at the party, Brad-lee dictated the story to *The Washington Post*, and it was the lead of the paper in its late edition.

More important than scoops, Bradlee's special access gave him what he describes as "a good understanding of who's riding high in Presidential esteem" and "early warning of subjects occupying the President's attention." In this context, the adversarial role of the press turns to mush.

The friendship proved mutually beneficial when the President wished to manage the news and leak an inside story with the assurance that it was in friendly hands. At a 1981 discussion at the University of Virginia on the presidency and the press, Charles Roberts, who had been the White House correspondent of *Newsweek* in the Kennedy years, recalled how he and Bradlee refuted a rumor that was damaging to the president. They were given unprecedented access to FBI files, and they collaborated on a *Newsweek* piece that put down what *Newsweek* called the "John's other wife" story—a widely circulated rumor that Kennedy had been secretly married to a thrice-married socialite before he married Jacqueline Bouvier. "The *Newsweek* story was far more effective than a White House denial would have been," said Roberts. In the story itself, *Newsweek* said as much. Kennedy, the story said, was "reluctant to issue a public denial for fear of giving it further circulation." The *Newsweek* reporters were given access to the FBI files on the condition that the President had the right of approval of what was written. In his book, Bradlee suggests quite properly that *Newsweek* erred in doing this story: "In effect, we were giving Kennedy what he later said he liked so much: 'the right of clearance.' This is a right all Presidents covet, but which they normally should not be given."

In those times, when journalists and White House officials were comfortable with each other, basic tenets of good journalism were often violated. There is a revealing footnote to that era in the chapter on "standards and ethics" in the current *Washington Post Deskbook on Style*. The chapter, which was written by Bradlee, says: "Many outside activities and jobs are incompatible with the proper performance of work on an independent newspaper. Connections with government are perhaps the most objectionable." In *The Powers That Be*, David Halberstam says that friends of Bradlee speculated that he wrote his Kennedy book when he did "to warn young journalists against the same course." (Bradlee dismisses this speculation. He wrote the book when he did, he told me in 1984, because that was the first opportunity he had after Kennedy's death.)

With Graham as its owner and Bradlee as its star reporter, it would have been only natural for *Newsweek* to enjoy an advantage in getting news from the White House. This was not necessarily so for President Kennedy was close to *Time* magazine as well. Halberstam notes that on the night of Kennedy's inauguration, Henry Luce and his wife sat in the imperial box with Kennedy's mother and father. In his book, Bradlee also comments on Kennedy's relationship to *Time*. This closeness enabled Bradlee to perform what amounted to low-grade industrial espionage. He recalls that "several times, when the editors of *Newsweek* felt they really had to know what *Time* had on its upcoming cover, I was able to get the answer from the President, and he was never wrong."

■

The ethical issues raised by the roles played by Graham and Bradlee during the Kennedy administration were not commented on until years later. In the 1980s there is a different climate in Washington, created, in part, by the central role of *The Washington Post* in the resignation of President Nixon. The press has been shown to be powerful, and this power has been accompanied by even greater public responsibilities. Thus, in the early 1980s, harder questions were asked about another journalist with a *Washington Post* connection, the columnist George Will, and his close relationship to Ronald Reagan. During the 1980 presidential campaign, Will helped coach Reagan for a crucial debate.

The press was again slow in picking up on a potential conflict, but once it did so, it perhaps was overly sensitive, for Will's transgression probably did not merit all the attention it received. Will was different from Graham, an owner, and from Bradlee, who had been a reporter. As a columnist, he is more of a polemicist, a pamphleteer. Should the same rules apply to him as apply to reporters or to owners? Just as deft columnists like Jimmy Breslin or Mike Royko or Art Buchwald inject humor into what they write and are given latitude to make up characters and dialogue, so too does a political columnist have greater leeway than a political reporter in expressing his views.

Will, a columnist for *Newsweek* who has a newspaper column

syndicated by the Washington Post Writers Group, made no secret of the fact that he was close to Reagan. Late in the fall of 1980 he gave a dinner party welcoming Reagan to Washington. (Katharine Graham attended; shortly after, she gave a party for the Reagans, and Will attended that.) In January 1981, just before the inauguration, Will wrote in *Newsweek:* "We all have our peculiar tastes. Some people like Popsicles. Others like Gothic novels. I like politicians. . . . Friendship between journalists and politicians offends persons who consider a mean edge the only proof of 'candor' in writing about politicians. . . . The idea that only an 'adversary relationship' with government is proper for journalists pleases some journalists because it seems hairy chested, and because it spares them the torture of thought."

A few months earlier, immediately following the Carter-Reagan debate, Will, in the role of ABC television commentator, was asked his reaction to the debate. Will was introduced by Ted Koppel, who said, "George, it is my understanding that you met for some time yesterday with Governor Reagan, and I'm just wondering what you know of his game plan and how you think his game plan worked out tonight."

Will commented that Reagan had performed like a "thoroughbred." What was not stated—though it should have been —was that Will had played a direct role in coaching the candidate for the debate. Nor was it mentioned that before the coaching session Will was shown some briefing papers that apparently had been taken from the Carter campaign—although Will said later that the papers he saw were so innocuous "it wasn't an incident that registered on the screen."

Will's role in the debate rehearsal had been noted in two books—Jack Germond and Jules Witcover's *Blue Smoke and Mirrors* in 1981 and Lou Cannon's *Reagan* in 1982. It was raised again in the spring of 1983 after the publication of Laurence I. Barrett's *Gambling With History*, which mentioned in passing that Reagan's aides had seen in advance briefing material that Carter's forces were using to get him ready for the debate. Barrett's book had been out for several weeks without creating a great stir. Then, a few columnists, including Jody Powell, who had been Carter's press secretary, asked in their columns why no attention had been paid to what became known as "Debategate." ("It was amazing that the Reagan people would engage in such skulduggery in the aftermath of Watergate," Powell, who clearly had an axe to grind, wrote in his 1984 book, *The Other Side of the Story*. "But the initial reaction of major news organizations was even more mind boggling: a collective shrug and yawn.")

A secondary effect of Barrett's book was to spark a debate over the role of columnists. Just what role a columnist should play eludes even columnists. In the wake of the controversy, various journalists offered these comments:

• David Broder, a columnist and reporter for *The Washington Post:* "For the privilege of being political journalists, we accept certain inhibitions. One of them is forsaking the role of political activists—or strategists."

• Jack Germond and Jules Witcover, political columnists: "You have to wonder . . . what is wrong with the old morality stipulating an arm's-length distance between the press and the people it covers."

• Joseph Sobran, a conservative columnist: "The American reporter is not a neutral umpire, but, rather, one of the players."

• Max Lerner, a liberal columnist: "As columnists, our province is power. . . . Is it any wonder that, now and then, we fantasize ourselves in the seats of the men we study? . . . Almost forty years ago, in the campaign of 1944, Judge Sam Rosenman—FDR's chief speechwriter—asked me to send him a draft for a speech. I walked on air while I wrote it, I sent it off, and was chagrined only because Roosevelt used so little of my draft. . . . A human being doesn't become a political castrate just because he writes a column."

In *The Washington Post*, Will defended himself: "The relation of columnists to politicians can be different from that of a straight news reporter. Walter Lippmann, Arthur Krock, Joseph Alsop, Charles Bartlett and others have had various relationships from Woodrow Wilson on. All journalists have political views—who would want journalists who do not?—and those views influence their journalism, sometimes in ways unseen even by themselves. Columnists, of course, are different. Concerning their views they are as secretive as steam calliopes." (Walter Lippmann, a name invoked often by Will and other columnists, played a minor role in Kennedy's 1960 inauguration speech; he suggested that Kennedy refer to the Soviet Union not as the "enemy" but as an "adversary." Ronald Steel, in his biography of Lippmann, notes that Lippmann praised the speech in his column as a "remarkably successful piece of self-expression" that "exemplified the qualities which the world has come to expect of the President.")

Later, in a letter to Dennis Ryerson, then editorial page editor of the *Columbian* in Vancouver, Washington, Will offered a partial and quite appropriate mea culpa: "Given today's expectations (which are particularly intense regarding someone who comes into the living room not only in the newspaper, but also via television), I shall not again come as close to a political campaign as I did in 1980." Will later joked about his role. He included this banter in his conversations following the 1984 election: "Someone called me after the first debate and asked, 'Did you coach the President?' I said, 'When I coach him, he wins.' "

Will's involvement with Reagan in 1980 was a sideshow—a misjudgment on his part, not a misdemeanor. He should not have done what he did, but once having coached Reagan, much could have been avoided had he fully—and humbly—disclosed his role.

In high dudgeon, and before Will had a full opportunity to explain his role in the 1980 campaign, the *New York Daily News* overreacted and dropped his column, one of eight newspapers to do so. Its editorial, citing a "violation of journalistic ethics," concluded: "Will's column has appeared occasionally in the *Daily News*. It won't anymore." Nine months later, in the spring of 1984, the *News* reinstated the column. There was no editorial explaining the paper's change of heart. In an interview, James G. Wieghart, then the editor, said, "It was never my intention to ban it forever."

In the fall of 1984, that same editorial page carried an endorsement of Ronald Reagan for reelection. It is an assumption of American journalism that it is perfectly proper for newspapers and broadcasters to endorse candidates. It is also an assumption that individual reporters (and, to a lesser degree, columnists) would be wrong in publicly endorsing or working for a candidate. It is an informal Hatch Act—the law that forbids federal employees to engage in political activities. It is further assumed that readers understand that the endorsement by the paper or radio or television station in no way influences the way candidates are covered in the news pages. Rupert Murdoch, John McGoff and the late William Loeb of the *Manchester Union Leader* in New Hampshire are among con-

temporary owners who have openly ignored the separation between endorsements and coverage in the news pages.

Nor have some highly regarded journalists accepted the wisdom of endorsements. "It would be great with me if the paper
didn't endorse," says Benjamin Bradlee of *The Washingon
Post*. He thinks endorsements are especially "awkward" in
local elections, where the *Post* wields greater clout. "When we
endorse a mayor, for instance, in the middle of a race here, the
other candidates say to our reporters, 'What the hell, you've
already made up your minds who you're for.' They don't understand the subtleties, and I don't think readers ever believe it
when you talk about this separation of powers. They say, 'You
mean to tell me you yourself couldn't write an editorial if you
wanted to?' "

Grist for public cynicism about endorsements has been provided by the Newspaper Guild, the principal union that represents reporters in this country. In October 1983, more than a
year before the presidential election, and long before the first
Democratic primary had been held, the guild, without polling
its 31,000 members, endorsed Walter Mondale. When there
were complaints, the guild leadership, which had endorsed
Democrats before, defended its action by saying that not to
endorse a candidate would be admitting a double standard—
allowing the privilege of endorsing to owners while denying it
to employees acting collectively. Charles Perlik, Jr., president
of the guild, said the "basic question raised that's bothering
some of our members is not that they weren't polled but
whether newspaper reporters and editors have any business
endorsing candidates at all."

In a letter to Perlik, Francis X. Clines, the guild shop stew-
ard of *The New York Times* bureau in Washington, said that
guild members "protest and disassociate themselves from the
highly compromising endorsement" of Mondale. Many *Times*
staff members, including Clines, cover politics; in his letter,
Clines pointed out that the Guild should have thought first "of
its members, whose fairness, actual and perceived, is ever at
stake in covering the full field of candidates." Perlik's defense
was that "if a reporter is not compromised by the arbitrarily
determined editorial positions taken by his employers, surely
his integrity and objectivity are not impaired by the democrati-
cally espoused positions of his union."

However, the practice of endorsing by newspapers in national elections seems gradually to be withering away. In the 1984 election, many of the nation's major dailies—*The Wall Street Journal, USA Today, The Los Angeles Times, The Baltimore Sun* and the *Dallas Times Herald*—did not endorse candidates.

Perlik wants *more* endorsements—from the reporters' union as well as the papers. It would be better to have fewer. In announcing to its readers that it would no longer endorse presidential candidates, *The Baltimore Sun* said its decision rested on its belief that the best way to serve its readers is to remain independent, "provocative and plainspoken": Instead of endorsing candidates, the editorial said, "we will do what we do best—which is to critique the candidates, day after day, on the basis of their performances and values." Abiding by the same rationale, reporters and their union should also shun endorsements.

Publishers are businessmen, and most of them, like most business executives, are Republicans. It comes as no surprise that newspapers endorsing presidential candidates overwhelmingly support Republicans.

During the 1984 presidential election, one publisher, George Measer, who runs the Bee newspapers—eight small weeklies in the Buffalo suburbs—went beyond merely endorsing the Republican candidate. He organized "Newspaper Friends of Reagan-Bush." In defense of this, he said: "As a businessman, I have the same rights to support candidates of my choice like every other citizen whether I'm selling apples, potatoes or newspapers."

Measer is free to do as he wishes, of course, but what he overlooks is that the press is not just any business. Newspapers and broadcasters have been granted Constitutional protections, because the founding fathers felt that a vigorous and independent press was essential to let people know what government was doing.

It is best that journalists—including publishers—maintain an arm's length distance from government. George Will is a columnist, not a campaign strategist. The Newspaper Guild represents reporters who cover candidates, not reporters who promote candidates. And George Measer is a journalist first and a businessman second.

5. "FROM MOTIVES HIGHER THAN MERE GAIN": WHAT MAKES BOSSES DIFFERENT

I particularly enjoin upon my sons and my descendants the duty of preserving, perfecting and perpetuating The World Newspaper, to the maintenance and publishing of which I have sacrificed my health and strength, in the same spirit in which I have striven to create and conduct it as a public institution, from motives higher than mere gain. . . . .
— The will of Joseph Pulitzer, who died in 1911

If the purpose of a university is to have a lot of students, then the university that has the most is the best. If the purpose of a newspaper is to make a lot of money, then the newspaper that makes the most is the best. If, however, the purpose of universities and newspapers is the same, to the extent that both should aim at public enlightenment, then largeness and profit become irrelevant.
— Robert Maynard Hutchins, "Freedom of the Press," 1948

What I and people of my kind expect is to be allowed to live our lives in decent privacy. I own newspapers, but I don't like them. I regard them as a constant menace to whatever privacy we have left. Their constant yelping about a free press means, with a few honorable exceptions, freedom to peddle scandal, crime, sex, sensationalism, hate, innuendo, and the political and financial uses of propaganda. A newspaper is a business

out to make money through advertising revenue. That is predicated on its circulation and you know what the circulation depends on.
— Harlan Potter, the owner of several newspapers, in Raymond Chandler's *The Long Good-Bye,* 1953

What you have in a one-paper town is a privately owned public utility that is constitutionally exempt from public regulation, which would be a violation of freedom of the press.
— A. J. Liebling, "Do You Belong in Journalism?" *The New Yorker,* 1960.

Those who run newspapers and broadcast stations have a dual role—that of corporate citizen and that of journalist, and they often try to operate under different standards than those that govern reporters. Political endorsements have been a staple on newspaper editorial pages—although the practice seems to be diminishing; reporters are permitted no such latitude. In Knoxville the editor served on the local parking authority, while he forbade a reporter from sitting on a nonpartisan school board.

Sometimes, in order to distinguish between the corporate entity and the publication itself, a newspaper will go to almost absurd lengths. This happened when *The New York Times* decided to help celebrate the anniversary of a park that is located near its headquarters.

In May 1984 Bryant Park, in midtown Manhattan, was celebrating its one hundredth birthday. In recent years, the park, named in honor of the poet William Cullen Bryant, who was also editor of the *New York Post,* has fallen on hard times. Although it abuts the New York Public Library, a site of heavy pedestrian traffic, the park has defied repeated attempts to make it a place where the public could come to relax. Instead, it has served as a refuge for drug dealers and derelicts. Several months before its one hundredth anniversary, however, plans to redevelop the park were announced on the front page of *The New York Times.* A huge glass restaurant and a cascading fountain would be added to the park. The plan was controversial in that the park would be partially managed by private interests. The details were still being worked out, and the one hundredth birthday party would be more a celebration than a news event.

The New York Times, whose headquarters is three blocks from Bryant Park, has long taken a keen interest in this and other New York parks. Parks were long a passion of Iphigene Ochs Sulzberger, the daughter of Adolph Ochs, who purchased the nearly bankrupt paper in 1896, the wife of Arthur Hays Sulzberger, who was the publisher from 1935 to 1961, and the mother of Arthur Ochs Sulzberger, the current publisher. It was only appropriate that the *Times* decided to hold a party with supporters of the park. The invitation read: "The New York Times and the Bryant Park Restoration Corporation invite you to celebrate the 100th anniversary of Bryant Park. Join Mayor Edward I. Koch and Parks Commissioner Henry J. Stern and other special guests in welcoming a new era in the revitalization of this historic park and have a piece of birthday cake."

However, when the event actually occurred, there was a barely perceptible but nonetheless significant change in the sponsorship. On posters announcing the party, the co-host was listed as The New York Times Company, the parent corporation of the newspaper. After the original invitation had been sent out, some staff members of the paper were embarrassed to discover that the newspaper itself was involved. The original invitation was reprinted in the *Village Voice*, a weekly paper that regularly attacks, among others, the *Times* and the mayor. The propriety of a newspaper's sponsoring such an event was questioned. It is highly unusual—and undoubtedly unwise—for newspapers to sponsor events at which mayors are the main attraction. But it is not unacceptable for the corporate parent to do so. (The *Times* sent a reporter to the event, but there was no story the next day.)

This illustrates a basic paradox. Journalists are supposed to be impartial observers of their communities, but they work for businessmen who are free and, some say, obligated by a sense of civic duty to contribute to these same communities. "Among the tasks assigned to me as publisher is the task of helping community causes of all sorts which improve the quality of life for our citizens," said Francis L. Dale, the publisher of the *Los Angeles Herald Examiner*, after he received an award in 1984 for helping to bring the Olympic Games to Los Angeles. "To perform in such a fashion is in the highest tradition of journalism and certainly consistent with the good corporate citizenship practiced by the Hearst Corporation." (In March 1985, Dale resigned as publisher to become commissioner of the Major Indoor Soccer League. He did so, he said, as part of a deliberate career policy of changing jobs every seven or eight years.

"A manager is a manager," he said. "Modern professional managerial techniques apply to whatever the product is.")

In the long run, after all, a newspaper or a television station survives on the basis of its customers. Yet it is more than slightly hypocritical for certain activities of reporters to be routinely proscribed, while the top executives, who decide what is published, are often not bound by any rules. Reporters can be scrupulous, even monkish, in their desire to avoid conflicts, but if the owners wish to use their publication for their private ends, their view will prevail, and reporters must bear the consequences of what the publisher has done. When I was at the *Times*, I was well aware of which judges and lawyers were friendly with the publisher, and I was also aware of his special interest in such issues as the rehabilitation of Times Square and the First Amendment. I do not doubt that, just as the *Times* gives more coverage to the city's parks than may be warranted, so too does it saturate its readers with coverage of First Amendment issues and with stories on the possible renewal of Times Square, which got its name because the newspaper once had an office there. (In a 1984 editorial, the *Times* called Times Square "the town square of New York and in some ways of the nation.")

Policies regarding community involvement vary among newspapers and television stations. Rarely are executives governed by the same rules that apply to their staffs. In response to a questionnaire I sent, James I. Houck, managing editor of the *Baltimore Sun*, said: "Editors and reporters cannot serve on corporate or community-related boards, such as school boards. What the publisher does is his own business." It is the view of Benjamin Bradlee, of *The Washington Post*, that editors and members of the business side of a publication would be better off not joining any civic groups or clubs. He belongs to none, and he would be just as happy if newspapers wrote a check to charity instead of sponsoring charity drives.

At *The Dallas Morning News*, officers of the company are not permitted to participate in politics or attend political rallies, receptions or dinners. They must also refuse invitations to sit on bank, insurance and utility boards. Yet Joe M. Dealey, the former publisher of *The Dallas Morning News* and now chairman of the board of its parent company, A. H. Belo Corporation, maintains that a newspaper has a vital role in boosting its community. In a speech in 1983 at the University of Texas, he told graduating journalism students that "it is necessary for that newspaper to give real evidence to its living being by taking an active role in community affairs beyond the mere remarking on such and such condition or project. To do this requires that employees to an extent reasonable and practical get out in the hustings and rub elbows with persons involved in important and worthwhile civic endeavors such as needed hospital capital programs, Red Cross drives, the United Way, the arts etc. It is even better when the owners and operators take on major responsibilities in these efforts. . . . This sort of essential dynamism places the newspaper in the forefront and greatly tends to diminish thinking that it sits merely as a judge of affairs or tally counter of results."

Media enterprises are generally more inclined to let senior editors and management participate in civic activities than to let them sit on the boards of corporations. Just about every newspaper and television station takes some civic role. It is good promotion—it keeps the name of the paper or call letters of the station before the public. And, it is presumed, it makes for a better community.

The range of these endeavors is broad. Publications and broadcasters sponsor charity drives, sporting activities and cultural events. Since often they are major real estate owners, they are concerned with city planning and urban renewal. Executives serve on the boards of schools and universities.

In New York, Warren Phillips, chairman of Dow Jones & Company, which owns *The Wall Street Journal*, and Arthur O. Sulzberger, of the *Times*, sit on the board of Columbia University—an institution often in the news. The relationship of the *Times* to Columbia is especially close, and it is resented by some educators who have complained that their schools receive short shrift in the news pages of the *Times*.

In Chicago, Stanton R. Cook, publisher of the *Chicago Tribune*, has been a director, vice chairman and chairman of the board of directors of the Federal Reserve Bank of Chicago. Those positions are more than honorific. The board of directors can change the reserve bank's discount rate and provides information about regional economic conditions to help formulate the country's monetary policy. The board can significantly alter the course of events—events that Cook's newspaper should be covering rigorously.

When I asked Cook whether his active role in the community created problems for the news staff of the *Tribune*, he referred me to James Squires, the editor of the paper. "Generally speaking, I think it's terrible for publishers to be active corporate citizens," said Squires. "But in this specific case, I don't have too big a problem. Cook has all kinds of involvements. He is the chief executive officer of a television station, and of the company that owns the Chicago Cubs. He's active in promoting a world's fair for Chicago. If he were in the building, actively impacting on policy, it would be a problem. But he's not. I do not deal with him on a day-to-day basis. I control the editorial policy. I am in effect the publisher. And I belong to nothing, only to the American Society of Newspaper Editors and the American Quarterhorse Association."

In New York, the *Daily News*, which is owned by the Chicago Tribune, sponsored a "Save the Lady" promotion, raising money to help pay for the restoration of the Statue of Liberty. The effort was reminiscent of the campaign undertaken by Joseph Pulitzer a century earlier to raise $100,000 to finance the construction of the pedestal of the statue. "The World is the people's paper, and it now appeals to the people to come forward and raise this money," an editorial in Pulitzer's *World* said in 1885.

In the summer of 1984, the *Daily News* took on a second major community commitment and served as the lead corporation in the annual campaign to find summer jobs for poor teenagers. The program is sponsored by the New York City Partnership—a coalition of business and civic leaders. The paper carried many articles about this, including one of questionable news value telling how President Reagan sent a telegram to the then editor of the *Daily News*, James Wieghart, praising the newspaper and the New York City Partnership "for setting such a high goal" in finding jobs. The *News* was so pleased with its recruiting efforts that in the fall of 1984, its publisher, James Hoge, said it was exploring the idea of continuing the jobs program year-round.

The problem with all this is that a newspaper in this position may be less rigorous, or at least give the appearance of being less rigorous, in doing what newspapers should be doing—monitoring and investigating, for example, whether money for the Statue of Liberty restoration project is misspent, or whether the job program has in fact met its goal, or whether the New York City Partnership, which is involved in some controversial projects, is performing as it should.

What might be regarded as proper—indeed honorable—conduct in any other type of corporation can undermine (or at least appear to undermine) the editorial integrity of a newspaper or television station. In 1978 a group of Florida newspaper and television-station owners, acting as corporate citizens, contributed $180,000 in order to defeat a referendum item calling for the legalization of casino gambling in Miami Beach and other nearby resort communities. The best-known figure of the pro-gambling forces was Jim Bishop, the author and syndicated columnist, whose articles appeared in *The Miami Herald*. He served as chairman of the statewide steering committee of "Let's Help Florida." The opposition was led by Alvah Chapman, president of the *Herald*. He feared that the introduction of casinos into the Miami area would be a threat to the area's economy and therefore an equally serious threat to the future economic well-being of the *Herald*, a highly profitable member of the Knight-Ridder chain.

Eugene Patterson, of the *St. Petersburg Times*, which made a $25,000 contribution, said this issue "transcended ordinary politics" and was really "an ethical argument for the soul of the state." He said that he "would hate to think newspapers are neutered as citizens by a pacifist mentality when rape is threatened." Richard Wolfson, executive vice president of Wometco Enterprises, the parent company of WTVJ in Miami, which also gave $25,000, called it a "once-in-a-lifetime issue."

In a statement in 1978 to the National News Council, John McMullan, then the executive editor of the *Herald*, said, "There is no question in my mind that such media contributions not only lowered our credibility but created a distracting spinoff issue." In a statewide pre-election opinion poll taken by the *Herald*, most of those responding felt that newspapers that contributed financially to the referendum campaign could not be fair in their news columns. In its ruling, the National News Council warned of the dangers of direct participation of news organizations in controversies they cover. While it concluded that coverage by *The Miami Herald* had been fair, it also said it was too extensive and amounted to overkill. On election day, casino gambling lost overwhelmingly.

Just as exceptions often swallow up the rules that govern the conduct of reporters and just as owners are frequently not governed by the same rules as their employees, so, too, different standards apply to those who own and run small publications. "While proprietors of large papers can remain aloof from traffic on the street, those who run smaller papers find that much harder," says Elwood Wardlow, assistant director of the American Press Institute, a teaching and research organization outside Washington which is funded by publishers.

In smaller communities, editors and owners are intimately involved with what is going on around them. A survey conducted in 1981 showed that editors in smaller cities tend to be more active in civic affairs than their big-city counterparts. They serve more frequently on boards of colleges, hospitals and charities and on the local chambers of commerce.

William Allen White, the legendary editor of the *Emporia Gazette*, was an unabashed booster of Emporia, Kansas—and he also was a censor of bad news. In a 1911 editorial, he wrote: "There is an office rule not to print details of local divorce suits, statutory assaults and other local stories in court and out involving the sex question. . . . Details of murders, hangings, suicides, sex crimes, highway robberies, burglaries, and crimes of violence generally should be suppressed under the police power of the state. They are bad for public morals, and a newspaper that prints such things inveterately should be declared a nuisance. . . ."

In small towns, many readers are at least as interested in knowing about one another as in knowing about the outside world. The local newspaper's primary function is that of community bulletin board. It reports births, deaths and scholarship winners, town board meetings, installations at the VFW and speeches given at the Kiwanis. In small papers, especially weeklies, the editors and owners are more likely to be acquainted with those whom they cover. For them, the news is less abstract. It is natural that smaller papers wish to help out local businesses, which also often happen to be advertisers.

For example, in a 1983 issue of the *Reporter*, a weekly in Walton, New York, in a news column adjacent to an advertisement for the Imperial Restaurant, there was an article on the renovations that had been completed at that building. There was a picture of the new entryway with this caption: "From a newly-paved parking lot one now may enter Walton's Imperial Restaurant under a new canopy to a new entrance. Foyer includes a large hanging area for coats." A weekly in a neighboring town, the *Hancock Herald*, ran a picture of the Delaware Land Office in the spring of 1984 with a caption explaining that the real estate firm had a new "outlook" on Hancock as a result of "thermo-pane windows installed on the first floor in the front to replace the old windows which had become leaky." The office is run by a frequent advertiser.

On most large publications, the business and news sections are supposed to be divided like church and state. It is wrong for advertisers to be treated favorably in the news columns merely because they advertised. But intrusions into editorial independence nonetheless happen with regularity.

Just before he left his job as chairman and chief executive of the *Dallas Times Herald* in 1984 to become president of *USA Today*, Lee Guittar recalled that he made a big mistake with the Dallas paper by giving editorial independence to the real estate section. In 1977, when he came to Dallas, he told me that he "was surprised to discover that the editorial copy in the real estate section of both Dallas newspapers was prepared by writers in their respective advertising departments." Furthermore, "the amount of 'editorial copy' devoted to a particular builder depended on that builder's advertising schedule." Guittar changed this, and the paper substituted original news coverage. As a result, its share of real estate advertising dropped from parity with the *Morning News*, its competitor, to just about 25 percent of the market. Reader surveys indicated that they did not seem to notice any difference in the new section. And, even worse, said Guittar, "I had anticipated some industry recognition for what we were trying to do. It never came."

Late in 1983, Guittar said, the practice of having the advertising department write "news stories" was resumed.

What is acceptable for a small weekly in Walton or Hancock should certainly not be the standard for the Dallas newspapers or *The New York Times*. As of December 1985, The New York Times Company owned thirty-five other newspapers, mostly dailies in smaller southeastern cities with neither competition or unions. Different standards are applicable to these papers, many of which employ part-time staff members and unpaid stringers. The *Gainesville Sun*, with a daily circulation approaching fifty thousand, is a staunch patron of local arts, just like the flagship of the company, *The New York Times*, with a circulation approaching one million. The Gainesville paper contributes to the local theater, and it goes one step beyond, by helping to produce some of the plays, which are invariably praised by its reviewers. Such behavior would be inappropriate for *The New York Times*, whose drama critics' reviews often determine the success or failure of a Broadway show.

In small towns, the old publishers were generally a permanent part of a local power structure, and their allegiances were to their towns rather than to abstract principles of journalistic ethics. With the growth of newspaper chains—by 1982, 155 chains controlled nearly three-quarters of the country's seventeen hundred dailies—that has changed. Like the executives in William Whyte's *Organization Man*, the new publishers identify not so much with their geographic community as with the corporation that employs them.

Richard Reeves, in *American Journey*, retraced the steps of Alexis de Tocqueville. In his travels, Reeves, a former political reporter for *The New York Times*, found, "The old publishers and editors bought out and moved out by Gannett and other chains all across the country were often stupid, lazy, biased, or dishonest. Sometimes they were all those things and worse. Neuharth [Allen Neuharth—the chairman of Gannett] was essentially accurate in saying that his chain 'improves' the papers it buys—at least in the sense of making them more professional. But the old-timers had a stake in their communities that would not be shared by upwardly mobile strangers." Gannett, the largest of the chains, owns ninety newspapers.

To show the mobility of Gannett executives, Reeves referred to an article in *Gannetteer*, the company magazine. In 1981 it ran a feature on Gary Watson, then thirty-five years old, who was about to become publisher of the *Rockford* (Illinois) *Register Star* after three years as editor of the chain's papers in Springfield, Missouri, and before that, three years as editor of the Gannett paper in Boise. The angle of the feature story was that Watson was going home—he had grown up in Rockford and had once worked on the paper.

"But hometown boy or not, Watson would be a failure if he stayed long back in Rockford," said Reeves. "The idea was 'up or out.' If he succeeded in Rockford—success being defined as meeting Gannett's projections for a fiftieth straight quarter of record profits—Watson would be moved up in the Gannett empire, perhaps to Cincinnati, to Wilmington, Delaware, to San Bernardino or El Paso. It didn't matter where; it's all Gannett."

In the spring of 1984, *Gannetteer* again carried a story about Watson. He had been named president and publisher of *The Cincinnati Enquirer*. Other news executives who were promoted had followed similar career paths. Michael Coleman, forty-one years old, was named publisher of the Rockford paper. He had been president and publisher of *The Saratogian* in Saratoga Springs, New York, since 1980. Before that, he had been an editor at the *Times Herald* in Port Huron, Michigan, for five years. Gary Stout, thirty-nine years old, was named president and publisher of *The Commercial-News* in Danville, Illinois. He began his Gannett career as publisher of the *Little Falls* (Minnesota) *Daily Transcript* in 1980, and became publisher of the *Fremont* (Nebraska) *Tribune* in 1982. There were eleven other executives promoted along with Watson, Coleman and Stout. None had stayed for more than a few years in one community.

Some enlightened community involvement is necessary for a newspaper or broadcast station—but not so much so that it becomes an uncritical booster and not so much that it loses its critical detachment. Such involvement is rooted in civic duty. For example, many newspapers and broadcasters are properly concerned about the poor and homeless, and many run campaigns such as *The New York Times*'s Neediest Cases Fund. Another—and probably better way—of discharging this responsibility—is merely to make a substantial donation, and then publish stories (which a paper should be doing routinely anyway), prodding private charities and the public authorities to act and then publish follow-up stories that monitor the performance of those agencies.

There is no question, though, that being a profit-making business brings on its own set of problems for news executives. In the late 1970s, when American Express attempted to purchase McGraw-Hill, Harold McGraw, Jr., a grandson of the founder, wrote an open letter telling American Express that it "lacks the integrity, corporate morality, and sensitivity to professional responsibility essential to the McGraw-Hill publishing, broadcasting and credit-rating services relied upon by so many people." As part of McGraw-Hill's defense, Lewis Young, editor-in-chief of *Business Week*, the most successful McGraw-Hill publication, argued, in a memorandum made public, that being part of a conglomerate would be dangerous, that "American Express would taboo certain story subjects, such as the troubles in the entertainment credit card business," that even if there were such coverage "our readers wouldn't believe what we published, thinking it was biased in favor of the magazine."

Ultimately, McGraw-Hill stayed independent, but Young's expression of journalists' uneasiness with conglomerates overlooked the fact that *Business Week* already was part of a large corporation whose primary, though not exclusive, business was communications.

There are built-in tensions between what Young referred to as the "professional responsibility" essential to a media enterprise and the need to make money. The tensions between making a profit and the public service that the media perform are part of the crosscurrents of pressure that bear down on newspapers, magazines and broadcasters. They have many different constituencies, beyond the consumers of news, to whom they must answer. These different constituencies may have interests other than the quality of the news. With television, federal regulators must be satisfied. Newspapers do not have that burden, but like television stations they have to cater to advertisers. Publicly held companies must meet the demands of shareholders, who wish a reasonable return on their investments.

The very nature of corporate governance leaves publishers and station owners open to possible conflicts—or to the appearance of conflicts. They sit on boards of companies that their reporters must cover, and executives of companies that are involved in newsworthy events sit on their boards. In the early 1970s publishers sat on the boards of Ling-Temco-Vought, Allied Chemical, American Motors, McDonnell Douglas, R. H. Macy, General Foods, American Airlines, United Air Lines and Pan American.

Although it is nearly impossible to know precisely, it appears that these executives sit on fewer boards these days; at many organizations they are prohibited from serving on corporate boards altogether. Nonetheless, they still are active in the corporate world. In 1984 Richard D. Simmons, president and chief operating office of the Washington Post Company, was a director of Union Pacific Corporation. Daniel B. Burke, president of Capital Cities Communications, an aggressive broadcasting and publishing company, served as a director of Avco Corporation, Consolidated Rail Corporation, Palm Beach Incorporated and St. Regis Corporation. The Capital Cities's chairman, Thomas Murphy, served on the boards of the General Housewares Corporation, Johnson & Johnson and Texaco. Franklin Murphy, chairman of the executive committee of the Times Mirror Company, owner of *The Los Angeles Times* and several other newspapers, sat on the boards of the Ford Motor Company and the Bank of America.

At Gannett, in 1984, Allen H. Neuharth, the chairman, president and chief executive officer, was a director of Marine Midland Banks. On the Gannett board were Rosalynn Carter, Walter A. Fallon, retired chairman of Eastman Kodak, Julian Goodman, retired chairman of the National Broadcasting Company, and Meredith Brokaw, owner of the Penny Whistle Toy Boutiques in New York City, and wife of Tom Brokaw, the NBC anchorman. In 1985, Howard Baker, who had just retired as majority leader of the United States Senate, joined the board.

At *The New York Times*, in 1984, Richard Gelb, chairman of the Bristol-Myers Company, had been a director of the *Times* for ten years, a fact that business reporters for the *Times* cannot possibly be unaware of when they write about his company. John Akers, president of IBM Corporation, joined the board in 1985. When I was a reporter for the *Times*, Cyrus Vance was on the board of directors. During three of those years, 1974 to 1976, he was president of the Association of the Bar of the City of New York, a group whose activities I covered. To be sure, the city bar association, which was then particularly active in lobbying for changes in the court structure, is a major New York institution, and its positions on issues are traditionally listened to. But I was surprised at what easy access Vance had to the *Times*'s editorial board—access, I suspect, that would have been harder to achieve had he not been a director of the company.

While it would be silly to advocate doing away entirely with "outside" directors for newspapers (outside directors are those with no day-to-day connection to the paper) merely to preserve the notion of absolute independence, large newspapers could go a long way in quieting fears of potential conflicts by disclosing more fully what business relationships their executives and board members are engaged in. I am not suggesting that newspapers each day become like stock prospectuses, in which all potential conflicting information is disclosed. But an article from time to time alerting readers to the relationships would be helpful.

A newspaper's or a television station's being part of a diversified company is fraught with conflicts and potential conflicts, and from time to time owners have failed to prevent them. Until a few years ago, the papers in Jacksonville, Florida, were owned by the Jacksonville-based Seaboard Coast Line Industries, which, among other activities, runs railroads. In the newsroom, reporters spoke openly of certain sacred cows and routinely advised one another not to write stories that might offend the railroad management. The standing joke was that in Jacksonville "cars run into trains," and not the other way around. (The new owner, the Morris Communications Corporation, is a vigorous community booster. In each city where Morris owns a paper—Amarillo and Lubbock in Texas, and Savannah and Augusta in Georgia—the paper has run promotional series on the advantages of the city. After publication, the series frequently is reprinted and distributed to government agencies seeking to promote the city.) A situation in Wilmington, Delaware, was similar to that in Jacksonville. Until 1978, when Gannett purchased the daily papers, they were controlled by the du Pont Company. Periodic disputes centered on whether news embarrassing to the du Pont interests could be published.

Newspapers and broadcasters run a serious risk if they are parts of conglomerates. They become part of just another big business, and it becomes harder to justify their claim to special protection under the Constitution. The Founding Fathers gave the press its special constitutional protections not as a license to make money but, rather, because they felt that a vigorous and independent press was necessary to let people know what government was doing. But the bigger and more diverse a company, the better the chance it will have business dealings with the government. There are regulations and licenses, tax benefits and mergers that need government approval. Seeking favors and tax breaks from the government is not compatible with the press's primary function—watching over the government.

■

The potential for ethical problems is magnified as many news-gathering organizations move far afield from gathering the news. The path taken by the owners of the sole surviving newspaper in Oklahoma City shows just how far publishers can branch out.

Edward King Gaylord, the publisher of *The Daily Oklahoman*, was a civic leader who agitated for Oklahoma statehood, which was granted in 1907. Gaylord had bought a part of the paper in 1903, when Oklahoma City, with a population of 10,000, was still a frontier town, and he was its publisher until his death in 1974 at the age of 101. During the early 1930s, when train service was cut dramatically, he established a company-owned trucking line, Mistletoe Express, to deliver newspapers across the state. The trucks no longer do that, and now the trucking line carries commercial freight in the Southwest. During these years, Gaylord's company, Oklahoma Publishing, purchased broadcast properties.

In the 1960s Oklahoma Publishing continued to diversify, forming the Publishers Petroleum Company, an independent oil company now active in gas and oil exploration in Oklahoma, Texas and Kansas. Since the mid-1970s it has been buying ranchland, much of it around Dallas. Its holdings in Colorado include a gold mine and Greenland Ranch, seventeen thousand acres that parallel the interstate highway between Denver and Colorado Springs, a rapidly growing area. In 1980 the company, which by then owned seven television stations, bought "Hee Haw," a syndicated country-and-western music television show. The show is taped at Opryland, a country-and-western theme park and convention center outside Nashville and the home of the Grand Ole Opry. In 1983, when Opryland was put up for sale, the Oklahoma company purchased it for nearly $300 million.

Oklahoma City is a large, growing city, which had a population in 1980 of 400,000, and *The Daily Oklahoman* has a circulation of 225,000. The city depends on oil exploration and therefore experiences jolts of prosperity and bumps of poverty. It is not particularly well served by its newspaper, whose publisher and editor is Edward L. Gaylord, the son of Edward King Gaylord and the head of the Oklahoma Publishing conglomerate.

For example, the paper, with vast resources at its command, barely scratched the surface in its coverage of the biggest business story in at least a decade in Oklahoma—the collapse of Penn Square Bank, a local bank with headquarters in a shopping center. Penn Square went under the Fourth of July weekend in 1982, setting off a national banking scare that is still being felt. Many of the leading citizens of Oklahoma City—who with Gaylord make up the city's social and business establishment—were directly involved in the failure of the bank. But little of this was reported in Oklahoma City. Coverage was far superior in the *Tulsa Tribune* and in many out-of-state papers. With all the wealth of its parent company—or perhaps because of this wealth—the Oklahoma City paper disserved its community.

Oklahoma Publishing is a privately held company, and when I asked Gaylord, who retains the title of editor of the newspaper, what percentage of the revenues are contributed by the newspaper, he replied: "Sorry, we are a private company—no reports to the public." Until quite recently, private ownership was the rule among newspapers. Now, all of the ten newspapers with the largest circulation are owned by public corporations. However, most of these publicly owned companies are still dominated by a single individual or family—like the Graham family of *The Washington Post* or the Sulzbergers of *The New York Times*.

In the annual survey that *Forbes* magazine does on the 400 richest people in America, Edward Gaylord is listed as the richest man in Oklahoma in 1985, and, with a net worth of at least $600 million, he is one of the forty-five richest individuals in the country. In the 1985 survey, as in previous years, the dominant sources of wealth were real estate, oil and media properties, and Gaylord benefited from all these businesses.

The *Forbes* list is studded with people with media connections. Some built their fortunes on broadcast or cable or newspaper businesses. Others made their fortunes elsewhere, and then used them to acquire communications properties. In all, more than 15 percent of the 400 richest Americans have fortunes derived from media enterprises.

Among the wealthiest people in America in 1985 were Samuel I. Newhouse, Jr. and Donald E. Newhouse of the Newhouse chain (a combined fortune of $2.2 billion); John W. Kluge, who runs Metromedia, which sold seven television stations to Rupert Murdoch in 1985 ($1 billion); Barbara Cox Anthony and Anne Cox Chambers, the surviving daughters of James Cox, the unsuccessful 1920 Democratic Presidential candidate who in 1934 founded Cox Enterprises, now based in Atlanta ($950 million each); Walter Annenberg, publisher of magazines, including *TV Guide* ($875 million); Jane Bancroft Cook, the granddaughter of Clarence Barron, who built up *The Wall Street Journal* and *Barron's* ($525 million); O. Wayne Rollins of Atlanta, who controls Rollins television stations ($500 million); Richard Mellon Scaife, who inherited part of the Mellon fortune and built up a small newspaper chain in California and Pennsylvania ($500 million); Joe L. Allbritton, who owns a chain of newspapers and five television stations ($450 million); and Oveta Culp Hobby, who sold the *Houston*

Post in 1983 but retained ownership of a Houston-based broadcast group ($400 million).

People worth more than $150 million—the cutoff point to make the list of the top 400—include:

• William C. Cox, Jr. and Jane Cox MacElree, who are great-grandchildren of Clarence Barron, of *The Wall Street Journal* and *Barron's;*

• Frank Batten of Virginia Beach, Virginia, who runs Landmark Communications;

• Malcolm A. Borg, owner of the *Bergen Record* of New Jersey and four television stations;

• Helen K. Copley of the Copley newspaper chain;

• Marshall Field V and Frederick W. Field, who sold the *Chicago Sun-Times* in 1984;

• Robert Guccione, publisher of *Penthouse* and other magazines;

• Robert S. Howard, who bought a South Dakota daily after World War II and now owns nineteen daily newspapers and a television station;

• Stanley S. Hubbard, who runs a broadcasting company based in Minneapolis–St. Paul ("We don't make money," Hubbard said in an interview in *Forbes* in 1983. "We're just public servants, struggling along.");

• John H. Johnson, publisher of *Ebony, Jet* and other magazines;

• James L. Knight of the Knight-Ridder newspaper chain;

• Patrick J. McGovern of Nashua, New Hampshire, publisher of computer newspapers and magazines;

• August Meyer, who owns Midwest Television, Inc., based in Champaign, Illinois;

• William S. Paley, the longtime chairman of CBS who now serves on its board;

• Roy Hampton Park, a cofounder of the Duncan Hines cakemix business who now runs twenty-seven daily newspapers, seven television stations and sixteen radio stations from Ithaca, N.Y.;

• Generoso P. Pope, Jr., owner of *The National Enquirer;*

• Donald W. Reynolds of Fort Smith, Arkansas, founder of the Donrey Media group;

• Edward W. Scripps of Charlottesville, publisher of small daily newspapers;

• William Ziff, Jr., publisher of technical magazines.

Descendants of William Randolph Hearst are on the list. So are heirs of Harry Chandler, who gained control of *The Los Angeles Times* at the end of the last century. Not on the *Forbes* list but still extraordinarily wealthy, according to the magazine, are the heirs of the people who built up the *Chicago Tribune*, the *Detroit Evening News*, the McClatchy newspaper chain (based in Sacramento), the Minneapolis newspaper, *The New York Times*, the *San Francisco Chronicle*, the Scripps-Howard chain and the Spokane newspapers. Other multimillionaires include the Horvitz family of Cleveland, which owns five newspapers plus cable television interests; the McGraw family, which controls McGraw-Hill; the Pulitzer family, whose wealth is based on the *St. Louis Post-Dispatch* and television stations, the Wolfe family of Columbus, owners of the *Columbus Dispatch* and broadcast properties, and the Block family, which owns newspapers in Toledo and Pittsburgh.

These people could easily spend some of their vast fortunes to improve their coverage (which well might have the effect of increasing their audience). But there is little evidence that this routinely happens, and it seems that many media owners are in business merely to increase their profits instead of serving the public.

In a speech at Yale in 1984, Arthur Ochs Sulzberger of the *Times* complained that the "average reader" does not seem to understand that "our function is to serve as the eyes and ears of the public." Rather, he said, "we are often perceived as merely another form of big business—in business to make money just like everyone else—and our service to the community goes unperceived." Sulzberger, whose company earned record profits in 1984, acknowledged that it may be "our own fault" that the public views the media this way. His concern echoes that of another major publisher.

"We must do a better job of explaining the media as a business operation," Katharine Graham, chairman of the board of the Washington Post Company, said in a speech in 1983 at the University of Georgia. "What is not clearly perceived by the public—and even, on occasion, by our own people—is this: Financial success is not a luxury in today's world, but a necessity. Quality costs money. The cost of maintaining an overseas bureau, for example, has risen from $60,000 a year, when I first joined the business 20 years ago, up to $200,000 today. More important, financial strength is the foundation on which the independence of the press is built. It gives us the ability to pursue the news, no matter how unpopular, costly or even dangerous that might be."

Graham, whose family fortune is estimated by *Forbes* at $350 million or more, is right, of course, to say that the independence of a newspaper is crucial. Her commitment to quality is exemplary. Foreign news bureaus are obviously important, but there are relatively few of them outside the networks, the news magazines and a handful of newspapers, including *The Washington Post.*

But Graham's argument in favor of financial success is less convincing because there are so many people in the media business who are not merely successful but fabulously wealthy. These people could improve their coverage by having even more foreign bureaus—or more science reporters or City Hall reporters. Or they could pay higher salaries and attract better minds to journalism. In this regard, news executives should be guided by the same set of obligations that the best journalists adopt for themselves—reporting the news fully, even if that means restrictions and sacrifices in their personal lives.

Making a profit—even a comfortable one—is hardly evil. What is particularly ominous about the broad diversification of media conglomerates and the disproportionate wealth of media owners is that it gives press critics as diverse as Warren Burger, the Chief Justice of the United States, and Mary Cunningham, the business executive, opportunities to construct arguments that undermine the constitutional pedestal on which the press stands.

Burger gave his view of the press in a concurring opinion in a 1978 case called *First National Bank of Boston* v. *Bellotti,* in which the court struck down a Massachusetts statute forbidding corporations to spend money to publicize their views on a political issue, such as the graduated state income tax.

Burger wrote that "making traditional use of the corporate form, some media enterprises have amassed vast wealth and power and conduct many activities, some directly related—and some not—to their publishing and broadcasting activities." Executives of media corporations, he said, are no "more virtuous, wise or restrained in the exercise of corporate power" than executives in other fields. He noted that companies owning newspapers, news magazines, television stations, book publishers and newsprint plants employ the same "corporate form" used by other types of businesses. He said that "large media conglomerates" had no special claim on constitutional liberties, including First Amendment rights of free speech. Therefore he said he would refuse to endow what he called the "institutional press" with special privileges based on the Constitution's guarantee of press freedom.

This same argument, stripped of its intellectual shine, is made in *Powerplay*, a peevish book by Mary Cunningham, who felt victimized by the press, first as assistant to William Agee at the Bendix Corporation and then as his wife and co-strategist when Bendix unsuccessfully sought to acquire Martin Marietta. In her 1984 book, she says: ". . . what is perhaps unique about the press, and therefore worthy of critical note, is that it is the only institution in this country today that is not held accountable by any other authoritative body. No one in government, business or even the clergy dare to criticize it for fear of the repercussions. . . . Perhaps, I'd feel a little more comfortable if the press—especially the less responsible element in it— would just admit to being a business. I know that doesn't sit well with those in the profession who prefer to duck behind slogans about serving as the watchdog for First Amendment freedoms. But despite these noble objectives, they are still in business—with profit-and-loss statements—just like any other commercial concern. A more honest appraisal of their profession would show that they live and die by the same rules of business as everyone else. . . . If it's 'true,' that's nice, but if it 'sells,' that's even better."

Early in 1985, in *The Wall Street Journal*, Mary Cunningham's complaint was presented more forcefully by Hodding Carter III, a onetime newspaper editor and owner who has become a columnist and press critic:

"Profit margins that are double the industrial average, laws providing special protection and exemptions, monopolistic or semi-monopolistic positions, courts that have vastly expanded press freedoms and the definition of such freedoms: What is the press crying about? If anyone has the right to complain, it is Joe Citizen, who has to wonder how such insulated and powerful baronies, their owners or headquarters so often far-removed from their products' effects, can be made more responsive to his concerns and criticism, more accessible to his point of view and rebuttal.

"But there is another question that arises in this day of 'bigger and better' newspapers and of the overarching reach of television. It is whether the affluence of newspapers and television is being used to improve the supposed point of the enterprise, which is the delivery of news that makes the world around us more understandable. It is whether the industry as a whole is not so dominated by those acutely sensitive to its business necessities that it will slight the mission for which it was given constitutional protection."

If the media behave just like any other businesses, they will be treated like other businesses, and soon they will be regulated like them. Of course, newspapers and broadcasters need to earn profits in order to survive. But there is a difference between reasonable profits that enable a newspaper like *The Washington Post* to staff foreign bureaus and profits that accumulate at the expense of hiring more reporters. Too few papers and broadcasters operate—as Joseph Pulitzer instructed his heirs—"from motives higher than mere gain." Public service —the reason that newspapers and broadcasters have been granted constitutional protection in the first place—requires sacrifice, and a slavish preoccupation with profits makes sacrifice unfashionable.

Part II

THE TECHNIQUES OF JOURNALISTS

6. BEING THERE: JOURNALISTS AS EYEWITNESSES

Sometimes I smoak a Pipe at Child's; and whilst I seem attentive to nothing but the Post-Man, over-hear the Conversation of every Table in the room. I appear on Sunday nights at St. James's Coffee-House, and sometimes join the little Committee of Politicks in the Inner Room, as one who comes there to hear and improve. My Face is like-wise very well known at the Grecian, the Cocoa-Tree, and in the Theatres both of Drury-Lane and the Hay-Market. I have been taken for a Merchant upon the Exchange for above these ten Years, and sometimes pass for a Jew in the Assembly of Stock-Jobbers at Jonathan's. In short, where-ever I see a Cluster of People I always mix with them, though I never open my Lips but in my own Club.
— Joseph Addison, *The Spectator*, March 1, 1711

All the reporters in the world working all the hours of the day could not witness all the happenings in the world. There are not a great many reporters. And none of them has the power to be in more than one place at a time.
— Walter Lippmann, *Public Opinion*, 1922

Gallagher, what'd you expect? I'm a reporter.
— Sally Field, the reporter in the film *Absence of Malice*, after Paul Newman discovered she was wearing a hidden microphone, 1981

Those people who love sausage and those who love investigative journalism should not watch either being made.
— Don Shelby, WCCO-TV, Minneapolis, 1984

In 1983, KMTV, the NBC affiliate in Omaha, Nebraska, won an Alfred I. du Pont/Columbia Award for a series on the shabby care provided at a facility for the mildly retarded and the mentally ill in McClelland, Iowa. At one point earlier in this century, every county in Iowa had a "poor farm" where the old and friendless wards of the county were sent. This arrangement slowly evolved so that by the 1970s these government-run institutions became custodial homes for those mentally retarded people who did not need nursing service yet were incapable of making their own way in life.

The McClelland facility, ten miles northeast of Council Bluffs, housed forty-five residents, most of whom were men between sixty and seventy years old. Except for a few newspaper articles about personnel and budgets and physical improvements, the McClelland facility had been largely ignored by the local media.

This is not an area of the country where investigative journalism would be expected to flourish. The region's principal paper, the *Omaha World-Herald,* is a nondescript paper extolling provincial chauvinism. Omaha is a major livestock market and meat-packing center. Across the Missouri River is Council Bluffs, Iowa, which also has a newspaper, the *Daily Nonpareil.* With a weekday circulation of 19,000, the *Daily Nonpareil* is a paper of such modest means that it had no photocopying machine in its newsroom when I visited in late 1983. The paper reflects stolid midwestern values. A framed editorial in its offices reads: "Speak your truth quietly and clearly. . . . Listen to others. . . . They too have their story."

Council Bluffs has no television station of its own; instead it is served by the three highly competitive stations in Omaha, the nation's seventieth largest market. The CBS outlet has traditionally been the leading station in Omaha, with the city's two other stations, KMTV and KETV, fighting for second place. It is in this sort of market that highly ambitious and driven reporters come to make their mark and then leave. Gene Greer, the reporter who won the du Pont award, came from a station in Boise and went on to Seattle.

It was not any of the television stations that broke the story about misconduct in the McClelland home. Rather, it was the *Daily Nonpareil* that had the exclusive in March 1982. In a short article, the paper disclosed that a former employee of the facility had told of instances where residents were made to stand in hallways for long periods of time as punishment, slapped in the face repeatedly and forced to go without proper clothing in cold weather.

The fact that it was the newspaper that carried the initial story was brought to the attention of the du Pont jurors—who included Fred Friendly, former president of CBS News, Elmer Lower, former president of ABC News, and Osborn Elliott, dean of the Columbia Graduate School of Journalism—after the award had already been made to Gene Greer. In an agitated and highly unusual letter, journalists at KETV, the station battling KMTV for the second spot in the Omaha market, asked that the award be withdrawn—not only was KMTV merely following up a newspaper story, but more seriously, the letter said, "To let it stand as it is would be like allowing Janet Cooke to keep the Pulitzer Prize." They said that the methods used by Greer and his "I" team (a shorthand for Investigative Team, but there is an unmistakable suggestion of "eyewitness" as well) were "both unethical and repugnant." The staff members at KETV accused their competitors of "bullying patients, barging in with cameras rolling, forcing confrontation for its own sake, and creating controversy when it was not necessary."

The KMTV crew had indeed entered the facility with its camera rolling. On the air, listeners could hear the crew being told by a nurse, "We can't have anyone in here—I'm sorry." Then Greer's voice is audible over the din: "But we insisted." The camera stayed glued on the administrator, Phillip Sherbon, who shielded his face, blocked the way of the cameras and implored: "Please turn the cameras off."

The segment continued with Greer speaking: "In an effort to make the residents inaccessible to us, the staffers quickly herded them into a basement area beyond our reach. But they missed one. We talked with her."

A second letter was dispatched to Columbia University, this one from David Richter, county attorney of Pottawattamie County, where McClelland is located. He called the reporting "inaccurate, prejudicial to the interests of the residents, yellow journalism to the exponential function of nine, and borderline legal, at best." He attached the report of a local grand jury that was critical both of the home's administrator and of the television station. The grand jury found that Sherbon and his wife were blameworthy and therefore should be fired. The report also specifically attacked KMTV's coverage for violating the right to privacy of the home's residents.

In a gracious letter of response to the complaining reporters, Marvin Barrett, then the director of the du Pont program, declined to withdraw the award, and noted: "It is our belief that on occasion the rights of people in custody are better served by exposing their grievances and mistreatment rather than respecting a privacy which is of more concern to a secretive bureaucracy than individual inmates of public institutions."

Joe Jordan, who had supervised the "I" team and was the station's acting news director when I visited him late in 1983, justified the unannounced entry into the home—the ambush with camera rolling—because it was meant to "correct a greater harm." He said his station used this technique sparingly, and this time it was used only after the reporter was given eyewitness accounts by a resident of physical abuse and beatings at the facility.

The story was first telecast on KMTV on March 4, 1982, three days after details appeared in the *Daily Nonpareil*. "We used the Council Bluffs paper as a tip sheet," said Jordan. "A print reporter writes what he saw, a camera is our tool. Until we took cameras into the home, the magnitude of the problem was not apparent. When we did the story, the whole thing broke open. We forced authorities in Council Bluffs to move."

Stu Nicholson, a reporter with the rival station and an organizer of the letter of protest, disagreed with this assessment and said the investigation of the McClelland facility was under way well before the KMTV report aired. Two years after, he reflected on the episode. "It gave investigative reporting a bad name, at least in Omaha. For a year, I would go to the Council Bluffs courthouse and get the hairy eyeball like you wouldn't believe." Nicholson asked that his station set up an investigative unit; he said he was turned down.

■

The footage from Omaha was certainly dramatic, but it raises hard questions of whether the results justified the means. The ambush interview is only one of many controversial techniques used by aggressive reporters. Other durable—and sometimes dubious—techniques used by both print and television journalists include the secret taping of the unwary, the reconstruction of an event long after it happened, reporters' misrepresentation of themselves and the use of undercover reporters. At times, these techniques may do as much to distort truth as to reveal it.

Reporters use these techniques to try to overcome a fundamental limitation of journalism. Rarely are they eyewitnesses, rarely are they in a position to observe precisely what it is they are reporting on. They may watch a parade, or attend a highly manipulated event such as a press conference, or cover a speech that probably has been ghostwritten anyway. On occasion, they may be in a position to witness a battle or watch a man set himself on fire. But ordinarily, reportage suffers from the absence of direct observation.

The reporter does not see the murder, the hit-and-run accident, is not sitting in the mayor's office or in the boardroom or at the lunch table when the key decisions are made. A newspaper reporter is often told about the accident or the government decision in a telephone conversation with someone who quite probably was not an eyewitness either. The need to "be there" is magnified on television, which requires visual support for its stories. Don Hewitt, the executive producer of CBS's "60 Minutes," the show that popularized such techniques as the unannounced visit and that has served as a model for young investigative journalists in cities such as Omaha, argues against using secondhand information: "Which is the more honest reporting—taking the word of people who said this happened to them, or going out and showing it happen?" Hewitt often makes the argument that print journalism is outmoded: "What has to make reporters unhappy, and I would be unhappy if I were still in print, is if they go out and work their asses off on a story, and find out that people who read their story had seen it closer up than the reporter did; they were there. Television has taken them there."

The desire for verisimilitude also accounts for the proliferation of "Eyewitness" news programs on television, but there is an air of artificiality to these shows because viewers are rarely eyewitnesses to anything very special. "Live shots," made much easier by satellite technology, are overused at those local stations with enough money to afford it. More often than not, in search of immediacy, the reporter comes on the scene after the newsworthy event is over. The live shots show people milling around at the scene where an accident occurred, or a traffic jam that resulted from the accident, or an empty room in which an important decision was made hours earlier.

Day in and day out, what journalists are left with is the need to reconstruct what happened from bits of evidence. In trying to establish truth this way, reporters operate under severe handicaps. They lack the detachment and perspective of historians, the precise techniques of scientists, and the most rudimentary tools of law enforcement: subpoena power to compel testimony or the production of documents and the authority to wiretap or to lawfully search a stranger's premises.

Some journalists try to convert these restrictions into benefits by rationalizing that they are above the law. "Entrapment applies only to prosecutors," says Bob Greene of *Newsday*. "Entrapment has nothing to do with what we do. It is not a moral concept. It is a legal concept." By law, a person who is "entrapped"—or encouraged by law enforcement officials to commit a crime he was not otherwise predisposed to commit—is excused from culpability. Using Greene's rationale, many reporters have gone undercover, used false identities and set up "sting" operations, with none of the procedural safeguards that society requires of its police.

A prosecutor or policeman needs a warrant to tap a telephone, but a reporter and camera crew can use hidden microphones and cameras with virtual impunity. By using these techniques, reporters may achieve a "better" or clearer rendition of reality in that the subject of a story is behaving naturally, but mostly these are unacceptable shortcuts.

There is not much difference in motivation between a reporter who ambushes the subject of an interview because he is *convinced* his target has done something wrong and an overzealous police officer who takes a convenient suspect into the rear of the station house and subjects him to the third degree in order to get a fast confession. Such improper police behavior would render the confession inadmissible at trial. There are no such procedural checks on the behavior of reporters.

■

In the past several years, journalists have begun to examine more carefully some of the techniques and procedures they use. The consensus at a meeting of investigative newspaper and television journalists who met in Miami in the spring of 1984 was that they have become *too* introspective.

"Ethics to me is a lot of crap," said Donald Thrasher, a producer of ABC's "20/20." "The only ethical thing to me is using common sense." Much of the convention, which was sponsored by Investigative Reporters and Editors, was devoted to a discussion of the propriety of ambush interviews—and that was too much time in the minds of many veteran journalists in attendance. Marion Goldin, then of ABC news in Washington, D.C., said she was getting "awfully bored" by the discussion of hidden cameras and ambush interviews "year after year." "Give something a bad title—like ambush—and you've gone a long way to discrediting it."

Geraldo Rivera, who resigned from ABC's "20/20" in 1985, said that the ambush had fallen "by the wayside." It is "worthless, in most cases," he said, "to confront an executive in the parking lot who we know won't comment. It is not fair." (Three years earlier, in a segment that caused great controversy, Rivera, with cameras rolling, surprised a Chicago landlord whom Rivera suspected of arson as he came out of a restaurant, bombarded him with hostile questions and got a somber denial of guilt.)

Despite Rivera's rhetoric, the ambush seemed to be a favorite among television's investigative elite as late as 1984. Less than thirty minutes before Rivera spoke, a television news series in which ambush interviews played an integral part was awarded IRE's highest prize. Bruce Bowers of WSOC-TV in Charlotte, North Carolina, won for a series on improper moonlighting by Charlotte's chief of park police, who subsequently resigned. In the series, Bowers used documents that had been stolen specifically for him by a disgruntled employee. He made use of a hidden camera and a hidden microphone. He also twice confronted the police chief with camera rolling. Bowers had made no appointment to see him; and on the air, the police chief, who said he was too busy to speak, looked terrible. At the convention, Bowers explained why he did not try to call ahead for an interview: "I did not make an appointment because of the type of person I thought he was." The award was presented by James Polk, an investigative reporter for NBC-TV, who described the series as a "model" of investigative journalism.

Certainly, not all journalistic techniques are as controversial as the ambush interview, but many of the practices and strategies taken for granted by journalists raise troubling questions. Journalists engage in daily deceptions. They fake taking notes or lull the subject of an interview by not taking notes and then run to the bathroom to write things down. They appear to be sympathetic—nodding their heads, saying yes, smiling all the while, in order to tease out information. They deceive their subjects by telling them they are interested in one thing while they are really interested in another, or they deceive them by making them think they don't know very much when in fact they know a lot. They overhear conversations and write about them. They read memoranda upside down that are on someone's desk. If that desk is unattended, they may go one step further and photocopy the document or walk away with it. That way, the reporters have the "real" evidence.

In a piece of mischief designed to underscore how unscrupulous reporters can be, Larry Speakes, President Reagan's chief spokesman, planted two phony documents on the desks of aides in the White House press office late in 1983. One document proposed moving the press corps to another location; the other suggested that Reagan announce his candidacy for reelection during halftime of a New Year's Day football game. Two reporters "bit like snakes" into the false documents, Speakes reported. One removed a bogus document, and both inquired about the authenticity of the information in them.

An extreme position of how far a reporter can go in pursuit of a story was staked out several years ago by Robert Scheer, the reporter who became a celebrity after he conducted one of the most famous interviews of the century. In 1976 he coaxed Jimmy Carter, then a candidate for president, into saying in a *Playboy* magazine interview how he had "committed adultery" in his heart "many times."

A couple of months after the interview was published, Scheer appeared at a panel discussion of journalists, where he was asked how far a reporter should go to check out the facts behind a public official's statement. Scheer's reply was bracing, but disturbing, in its candor. Scheer told the audience that "politicians try to prevent you from knowing what's going on because that's how they survive. And they have lots of people employed to help them. The journalist's job is to get the story by breaking into their offices, by bribing, by seducing people, by lying, by anything else to break through that palace guard."

In the textbook *Investigative Reporting*, David Anderson and Peter Benjaminson establish a standard for reporting that assumes that good reporters must behave unethically. They declare that "many fundamental techniques of investigative reporting involve actions some would label dishonest, fraudulent, immoral, and perhaps even illegal." A bit later, they caution: "A reporter should never resort to questionable methods if the information can be obtained in any other way." But caution has its boundaries: "In those cases which are difficult to judge, most reporters tend to err on the side of dishonesty to obtain the information. The underlying assumption is that society has more to gain from an accurate, thorough reportage of events than it has to lose from the discomfort of the corrupt." The textbook, which is still in use, was touted by its publisher, Indiana University Press, as "a definitive work, of enormous value to working journalists as well as to students and their teachers." It appeared in 1976, a post-Watergate year in which investigative journalism was enjoying great acceptance.

It is not clear how many investigative reporters use the techniques advocated by Scheer or by the authors of the textbook. "I'd say most do not endorse such methods," says Steve Weinberg, executive director of Investigative Reporters and Editors. In nearly two decades as a successful investigative reporter covering law enforcement and government in Washington and New York for *Newsday*, *Newsweek* and *The New York Times*, Anthony Marro says he "never impersonated, never stole, never cajoled, never browbeat." "How could I?" asks Marro, a shy man with an occasional stammer who is now managing editor at *Newsday*.

■

Much of what journalists do that is ethically suspect is not illegal—it does not violate a specific statute. For example, there is no statute against lying. There is no statute against entrapment by a journalist. There is no statute against the ambush interview. In Iowa the grand jury found fault with the Omaha television station, but it did not formally accuse it of breaking a law.

But even when journalists *do* break the law in pursuit of a story, they rarely have to live with the legal consequences of their lawbreaking. To this extent they are above the law. Geraldo Rivera made his reputation in the early 1970s by uncovering appalling conditions at Willowbrook, a vast facility for the mentally retarded in Staten Island that housed more than five thousand patients. Using a stolen key, Rivera and a camera crew entered one of Willowbrook's buildings one morning. Inside, they saw bedlam. Patients, smeared in their own feces, were screaming and fighting with one another. They were abused by the people who were supposed to care for them.

Rivera's narration was unsparing: "This is what it looked like. This is what it sounded like. But how can I tell you about the way it smelled? It smelled of filth, it smelled of disease, and it smelled of death."

At a panel discussion years later, Rivera, himself a lawyer, explained how he and his crew had criminally trespassed to get the story. "Yes, I violated the law," Rivera said. "It was a question of balance. I stood ready, willing and able to suffer the consequences. I stood ready to be prosecuted." But Rivera was not prosecuted, as he knew he would not be. He was a hero. "Our position commanded the moral high ground," he said. He possessed what is known as "jury appeal": After what he disclosed, no jury would convict him; knowing this, no prosecutor with any sense of self-preservation would dare bring a case against him. What Rivera found at Willowbrook had an enormous impact. But there is a danger that his lawbreaking has become a standard for reporters pursuing petty and insignificant stories.

In an influential and often-cited article that appeared in the *Columbia Law Review* in December, 1976, Alfred Hill of the law faculty at Columbia notes that "our law is replete with instances in which conduct ordinarily deemed tortious or even criminal is fully legitimated by circumstances that bring into existence a privilege." He then argues that "the First Amendment requires that the communications media be allowed investigative methods that are somewhat offensive, and that in cases of relative public importance they must be allowed a greater degree of offensiveness than in others." This is hardly complete, but probably it is as economical a formulation as there is on the outer boundaries of reporting.

An earthier—and more pragmatic—explanation of a journalist's techniques was offered several years ago by Robert Sherrill, an iconoclastic longtime White House correspondent and accomplished muckraker. "Trying to decide in the abstract how far a reporter should go is about as futile as parents trying to decide how far their daughter should go," Sherrill wrote in the *Columbia Journalism Review.* "When the passions are up and the story is tempting, any reporter . . . is likely to do whatever the moment seems to call for. No good reporter is honest all the time, and it's silly to pretend otherwise. The ethical difference between a reporter's accepting stolen information (for example, the Pentagon Papers) and actually stealing the information is so slight as to be of little consequence: it is simply the difference between being a thief and being a fence."

Generally, courts have held that a publication or television station that obtains stolen information is exempt from prosecution and is perfectly free to use the information once it has it. The Pentagon Papers that Sherrill refers to were something more than just another purloined document. They consisted of forty-seven book-length "top secret" documents. In printing portions of these documents, the decision facing *The New York Times* was whether to publish classified material that dealt with a war that was still going on. It was not a decision made lightly. The lawyers for *The New York Times*, Herbert Brownell, an attorney general of the United States in the Eisenhower years, and Louis Loeb, who had been the paper's longtime general counsel, told the editors not to publish, warning that publication could set in motion successful legal action by the government under the Espionage Act. Their advice was ultimately not followed, they resigned from the case, new lawyers were hired, and the *Times* won the legal action, but only after publication had been enjoined for several days.

The journalistic fraternity looked kindly on the *Times*, which was awarded a Pulitzer Prize in 1972 for meritorious public service. However, Columbia University's trustees, who then officially approved the award, issued a statement expressing "deep reservations" over the awarding of prizes to the *Times* and to Jack Anderson, the columnist, who had obtained access to secret government documents made during the Indo-Pakistan War of 1971.

With the benefit of twelve years' hindsight, even Henry Kissinger, the President's National Security Adviser at the time the Pentagon Papers were published, gave the *Times* his qualified blessing. In an interview published in *American Heritage* magazine in 1983, he deplored the media's trafficking in stolen information, but he said: "I do not think the media should censor themselves with respect to information that has come their way, provided they did not commit the act of theft or get somebody else to steal a document. I would regret that, I think it would be wrong. But if somebody takes a document and gives it to them, however ill I think of the thief, it is not the media's responsibility to police themselves in that regard."

Like Geraldo Rivera's breaking into Willowbrook, the publication of the Pentagon Papers was a special circumstance in which the ends justified the means. Publishing the Pentagon Papers, which influenced the way Americans viewed the Vietnam War, is one matter; adopting as a general principle the view that journalists are free to make use of stolen material is quite another.

■

It is inevitable that in their search for the spontaneous and the unrehearsed, journalists jeopardize the rights and privacy of others. Sometimes they go too far. When more than two hundred U.S. servicemen were killed in the terrorist attack in Beirut, the homes of the victims were surrounded by reporters and camera crews seeking to record the families' grief. In one instance, a CBS News crew taped the actual moment when Marine officials arrived to report the death of a young corporal to his family in Rhode Island.

In contrast, there are times when people's right to be left alone legitimately succumbs to a newsworthy event. On August 17, 1981, the son of the managing editor of the *Spokane Review*, the afternoon paper in Spokane, Washington, was sentenced to life plus seventy-five years for committing four rapes. (The conviction was subsequently overturned on appeal.) Later that day, a woman struggling with policemen was photographed by a staff member of the morning paper, the *Spokesman-Review*. She had just driven her car into the river, and she appeared to be drunk, disoriented, and angry. The woman, editors learned shortly after, was Julie Twyford, the lawyer whose client had just been sentenced in the rape case. She was charged with negligent driving and driving while under the influence of intoxicants. Her photo appeared on page one, and the paper, the *Spokesman-Review*, was criticized for sensationalism, and for trying to destroy the career of a young lawyer.

In a column in which he persuasively defended his decision to run the picture the way he did, Don Gormley, then managing editor of the paper, explained the criteria that he used: ". . . it is a splendid news picture. It has action, emotion, composition and a strong focus of attention. And it tells a story, better than words could possibly do. . . . It is clearly news. A driver zipping off a bridge into the Spokane River is not a common occurrence. When the driver then struggles with police, that makes it a little better story. When the driver turns out to be a public defender in a widely publicized and important trial, the story gets more compelling. Let it happen on judgment day for her client and it becomes very touching. It was a really rotten day for Julie Twyford. . . . The picture was made in a public place of a public incident. The information in the picture and the cutline was accurate."

It is hard to quarrel that Julie Twyford was a legitimate subject of news—even though the criminal charges were subsequently dropped. The position of Clarence Arrington, another reluctant newsmaker, is more ambiguous. Early on Sunday, December 3, 1978, he received a phone call from a friend who told him his picture was on the cover of *The New York Times Magazine* to illustrate a story on the black middle class. (In the picture, Arrington, a financial analyst in Manhattan, is walking briskly along the street, and he is clearly recognizable, although his name is not used.) Arrington was shocked, because, as he claimed later, he did not even know his picture was being taken. The lead article in the magazine described black middle-class aspirations and the failure of middle-class blacks to continue to press for the needs of lower-class blacks, a thesis that Arrington found repugnant. He sued.

The principles of the law of privacy were not totally settled in this area, and Arrington's case moved up through the state court system. At the New York Court of Appeals, the state's highest court, he was told he could not prevail against the *Times* because his picture appeared in connection with the news-gathering process. But almost as a consolation prize, the court said he was permitted to pursue his suit against the free-lance photographer and the photographer's agent, because they were engaged solely in commerce. The Court of Appeals was clearly troubled by the result and seemed to be saying that while the state law was against Arrington, fairness was on his side. He appealed to the United States Supreme Court, which, in 1983, refused to entertain his appeal against the *Times*, which, because it is wealthy, was clearly a more desirable defendant for Arrington than the photographer or his agent.

Incidentally, the *Times*, which views itself as a guardian of the First Amendment, failed to cover this lawsuit until the Supreme Court reached its decision, and then it devoted only a paragraph to its victory. This is odd given the seriousness— even near hysteria—with which some publishers viewed this case. At one point, after the ruling of the state Court of Appeals, Cravath, Swaine & Moore, a conservative and prestigious Wall Street law firm, submitted a highly charged friend-of-the-court brief asking the court to reconsider its decision. The firm, which was representing CBS, *Time, Newsweek,* the Gannett chain and others, went so far as to predict that if free-lance photograhers could be held liable if they failed to obtain the consent of their subjects "some of the publishers who depend on the these photojournalists might have to leave New York, others, severely to curtail their use of illustrative material." That, said the law firm in its brief, would lead to a situation where "the press will not operate freely and the public will not be as informed." Eventually, the state legislature, heavily lobbied by the media, nullified the state court's ruling. That was not covered in the *Times* either.

There is something unpleasant about taking advantage of unwary bystanders like Clarence Arrington. He was wronged, even though there was no legal remedy to correct it. The free-lancer who took the photo, Gianfranco Gorgoni, said afterward: "I feel I am for Arrington, in a way, because of the contents of the article." But the photographer said he disapproved of the lawsuit and would have resorted to the concept that lawyers call self-help: "If it had been me, I would have gone and punched the writer." In contrast to Arrington's assertion, the photographer insisted that Arrington saw the photograph being taken, and had he wished, he could have objected and the photographer would have stopped shooting.

All this took place in the open. Many of the most questionable techniques used by journalists in their quest to be eyewitnesses rely on stealth, secrecy and deceit.

A. A. Dietemann was a disabled veteran who claimed to be a doctor. He was later labeled by a judge as a practitioner of "simple quackery." In 1963 two reporters from *Life* magazine visited him in his California home, which he also used as his office. One reporter, who did not disclose her identity, described imaginary symptoms of cancer, saying she had a lump on her breast. The reporter told how Dietemann immediately diagnosed the problem: "He began beating that wand and rubbing me. He finally decided I had butter poisoning because I ate rancid butter exactly eleven years, nine months and seven days ago. That poison settled in my leg, causing the lump in my breast. He gave me some clay pills for it." Unbeknownst to Dietemann, the reporter was wired to transmit the conversation to a car, where another *Life* employee was recording it, along with law enforcement officials. While Dietemann talked, the woman reporter's companion, who was actually a *Life* photographer, secretly snapped pictures. After the photo spread and 400-word article were published, Dietemann was convicted of practicing without a license. But he sued *Life* for invasion of privacy, and won at trial.

In 1971, his claim was upheld in an opinion by Judge Shirley Hufstedler of the United States Court of Appeals for the Ninth Circuit. In her opinion, the judge pointed out that a person should not be required to take the risk that what is heard and seen in one's house will be transmitted by photograph or recording to the public at large. Judge Hufstedler also disagreed with the magazine's contention that concealed electronic instruments were "indispensable tools" of news gathering. Investigative reporting, said the judge, "is an ancient art; its successful practice long antecedes the invention of miniature cameras and electronic devices. The First Amendment has never been construed to accord newsmen immunity from torts or crimes committed during the course of news gathering. The First Amendment is not a license to trespass, to steal, or to intrude by electronic means into the precincts of another's home or office. It does not become such a license simply because the person subjected to the intrusion is reasonably suspected of committing a crime."

Hufstedler's opinion has been widely cited; nearly identical language was used by the highest state court in Florida in 1977 when it upheld a state statute that makes recording of telephone conversations illegal without prior consent. The Florida Supreme Court said: "Hidden mechanical contrivances are not indispensable tools of news gathering. The ancient art of investigative reporting was successfully practiced long before the invention of electronic devices. . . . "

The controversy over the taping issue is an unusually resilient one, even though by all accounts it should have been settled a long time ago. The Federal Communications Commission insists that parties to a phone conversation across state lines must be aware their words are being taped. There are two ways to do this: either by use of a beep tone or simply by telling the other party you wish to make a recording. A dozen states besides Florida prohibit or otherwise curb the secret taping by one party to a telephone conversation. From a survey I conducted and from others I have seen, the prevailing view among editors in those states in which secret taping is legal is that it should not be done, even though the gap between their pronouncements and the practices of reporters is wide.

The reasons for taping are clear. It makes for a better record, a more accurate version of events. So why not just routinely tell the other person? Journalists offer many reasons why they do not. They wish to insure themselves against a person who may later complain about being misquoted by producing that person's actual words; they do not wish to telegraph their moves to the interviewee, who may then be put on guard; or they wish to tape someone suspected of wrongdoing who would never consent to a taped interview. Journalists argue that if people engaged in unlawful or undesirable conduct are told they are being recorded, they will not speak candidly. The tape offers convenient corroboration beyond notes and the memory of the reporter, both of which can be highly fallible.

"It is more difficult to disavow a tape than it is a story that is backed only by a reporter's notes," says Frederick Taylor, executive editor of *The Wall Street Journal*. He disagrees with the policy at the *Journal* that forbids taping phone calls without first telling the other party that it is being taped. "Taping a phone call is like taking notes," says Taylor. He suggests there is some hypocrisy in opposing secret taping. Without the other party's knowledge, Taylor says, reporters will take shorthand on the phone, will take notes on a word processor, which is almost silent, and without telling the other party will put another reporter on an extension line to serve as a witness. His point is well taken, but the way to eliminate the hypocrisy is not necessarily to permit secret taping. It is just as easy for the reporter to disclose to the other party that he is taking notes on a word processor or that a second reporter is listening in.

The reasons against secret taping are compelling. There is something unsettling about taping. It is akin to photographing the unwary and to using a concealed tape recorder in a face-to-face interview. A person who knows his comments are being recorded may choose to phrase them differently—or even not make them at all—from the way he might in an unrecorded conversation. It comes down to a question of expectations. Knowing they are talking to reporters face to face, people do not expect to be taped unless they see a tape recorder. Similarly, on the telephone, they do not expect a conversation to be recorded unless they are told so.

At many newspapers, including *The New York Times*, secret taping used to be common. For most of the time that I was reporter there, I sat near the rear of the block-long newsroom with reporters working on larger projects who had less day-to-day responsibility for stories. Telephone induction coils were attached to several phones. The devices attach to a tape recorder like a microphone. Conversations at the *Times* were recorded secretly in spite of a policy forbidding it.

This policy, however, was hardly well advertised. I do not recall it ever specifically being mentioned in the six years I was there. I only became aware of it several years after I left the newspaper, when, in connection with the survey I conducted for this book, I was sent a memorandum issued by A. M. Rosenthal, the same day the *Times* broke a front-page story on secret taping conducted by Charles Z. Wick. Rosenthal's memorandum read:

"The story about the taping of telephone calls in the paper of December 28th, prompts me to issue a reminder of what has long been a *Times* policy:

"We do not make any tapes of telephone calls without informing the person at the other end of the line."

Then, a month later, Arthur Ochs Sulzberger, the publisher of the *Times*, in a sensible amplification of that memorandum, issued another written statement:

"Recent reports in the press of the surreptitious use of tape recorders leads me to restate and emphasize the policy of The New York Times Company on the use of such machines.

"It is the policy of The New York Times Company not to record either business or news telephone conversations by an electronic device unless we have the clear agreement of the other party prior to the conversation.

"This policy is one of common sense and courtesy. It is not intended to limit the use of tape recorders in face-to-face interviews when the party being interviewed agrees to the recording, or in press conferences where the speaker is 'on record.'

"While taping of conversations without the other party's prior approval is a crime in Florida, it is a discourtesy everywhere. We wish to conduct our business only in a highly ethical way."

■

What these memoranda do not say is how often secret taping leads to trouble. In June 1983, CBS News suspended George

Crile for having recorded a brief, off-the-record telephone conversation he had with former Secretary of Defense Robert S. McNamara without McNamara's knowledge. Crile said he was unaware of the written CBS regulation prohibiting such taping. In an interview, he also said he knew it was legal to tape calls secretly in New York and that it was a "reasonably widespread practice." Asked why he had recorded the conversation without telling McNamara, Crile said: "I was simply trying to get as accurate a record of his remarks as possible." Crile said he had feared "it might have been inhibiting" to tell McNamara that he was using a tape recorder.

The tape was made in the course of putting together "The Uncounted Enemy: A Vietnam Deception," the 1982 documentary that accused General William C. Westmoreland and other officers of manipulating figures on enemy troop strength during the Vietnam war.

After the show appeared, in a cover story entitled "Anatomy of a Smear: How CBS News Broke the Rules and 'Got' Gen. Westmoreland," *TV Guide*, in May 1982, attacked the CBS documentary, charging that the network had disregarded evidence that might have contradicted its conclusions. That story prompted the internal CBS investigation in which Burton Benjamin, CBS News's senior executive producer, concluded that ten of CBS's own standards had been violated in preparation of the broadcast. The flaws including taping an interview twice with the same person to elicit a more dramatic response, the "coddling" of sympathetic witnesses, editing an interview so that replies to several questions were combined into one answer and making insufficient efforts to interview those disagreeing with the thesis of the program. "The pity of it, the pity of it— had all the rules been followed, it would have been just as good a broadcast," said Benjamin, shortly before his retirement late in 1985.

Both co-authors of that article have left *TV Guide*. Sally Bedell went to the *Times*, and Don Kowet expanded the article into a book, with a title that shimmers with double meanings— *A Matter of Honor*. It was published in the spring of 1984, just about a year after Crile had been suspended. In connection with it, Kowet committed some of the same journalistic sins of which Crile was accused. Shortly after it was published, he released portions of a telephone interview with Howard Stringer, then a senior editor, later the executive vice president, of CBS News, which took place just after the disputed program was broadcast in January 1982. The interview was taped by Kowet without Stringer's knowledge (in violation of the policy of *TV Guide*), and key parts of it were "off the record"—a journalistic shorthand understood to mean that the reporter pledges not to reveal that the conversation even took place. This conversation was subpoenaed after Kowet's book was published, and Kowet surrendered it, demonstrating the dangers for a news source holding an off-the-record conversation—and on the telephone at that.

In this incriminating conversation, Stringer said: "As you may have gathered, we have our own suspicions about George Crile anyway." Speculating about whether Crile might have taken shortcuts in the documentary, Stringer says, "I should have known I wouldn't get fair journalism off him." In the tape, Stringer repeatedly emphasized that his remarks were "off the record." The tape ends with Kowet saying to Stringer, "Well, thank you for this conversation, even if it is off the record." Kowet turned over that and three dozen other tapes to Westmoreland's lawyers. He said he did not resist the subpoena, as is standard practice among journalists, because CBS had strongly criticized his book as being inaccurate, distorted and false.

CBS had not responded to the initial *TV Guide* article. But it changed tactics with Kowet's book and hired an outside public relations consultant, John Scanlon, the same consultant who effectively promoted the movie *Absence of Malice*. "Our concern," said Scanlon, "was to make sure the book was not considered the permanent record." In his effort to undercut the book, Scanlon interviewed past and present CBS employees and found "almost, without exception, that Mr. Kowet's portrayal of meetings and conversations differs significantly from the recollections of the people who were, in fact, there."

Scanlon cited Kowet's report of Mike Wallace, the lead correspondent of the documentary, telephoning A. M. Rosenthal of the *Times*, regarding a damaging critique of the documentary that appeared on a segment of "Inside Story," the public television show that examines the media. "Let me state unequivocally that on no, repeat no, occasion have I ever phoned Abe Rosenthal on any matter having to do with that broadcast or its aftermath," Wallace wrote in a letter to Hillel Black, an executive at Macmillan, Kowet's publisher. Rosenthal also denied that the calls were made. In response to this, Kowet, who had attributed the conversation to "a CBS source," said that Wallace refused him an interview and that he did not check his account with Rosenthal.

CBS did an effective job in showing that Kowet was guilty of journalistic misconduct and of sloppiness similar to that which Kowet accuses CBS of committing. In search of evidence to support his thesis, Kowet improperly recorded an interview, and he reconstructed a telephone conversation that never took place. His motivation in doing this was the same as that of journalists who conduct ambush interviews or steal documents. He wanted to convey the impression that he was an eyewitness. He wanted "real" evidence, but by overreaching and engaging in dubious practices, he fatally undercut the credibility of his own reporting.

7. BEING SOMEONE ELSE: JOURNALISTS WHO MASQUERADE

There is no place in journalism for the dissembler; the distorter; the prevaricator; the suppressor; or the dishonest thinker.
— The Oregon Code of Ethics for Journalism adopted by the Oregon State Editorial Association, 1922

The risk of being overheard by an eavesdropper or betrayed by an informer or deceived as to the identity of one with whom one deals is probably inherent in the conditions of human society. It is the kind of risk we necessarily assume whenever we speak.
— Justice William Brennan, dissenting in *Lopez v. United States*, 1963

C arla Cantor, a young reporter starting her second year at the *Daily Record* of Morristown, New Jersey, sought to talk to the brother of Deirdre O'Brien, a New Jersey waitress who had been stabbed to death in December 1982. She went about this in a straightforward way, asking for the interview; She was unsuccessful. Eight months later, there was another sordid murder in Morris County. A twenty-four-year-old go-go dancer was stabbed to death, and this time, according to court records, in her attempt to add depth and color to her story, Carla Cantor apparently resorted to means that were less than straightforward.

She says that she told the stepfather of the dead go-go dancer that she was a reporter but did not tell anything to the mother, whose native tongue was not English. The family of the dead woman disputed this and said Cantor had told them she was "from the morgue" in an attempt to obtain personal information about the victim. Cantor was prosecuted for impersonating a government official, and a local judge found that she had violated a New Jersey statute that forbids someone from posing as a government official. At the very least, based on the testimony at the trial, Cantor was aware at an early point in her interview that the dead woman's parents misunderstood who she was and that she apparently did nothing to correct this misunderstanding.

The article that emerged from her interview was full of chilling detail. It made good copy, and although not calculated to do so, it hurt the dead woman's family. It told of how the victim was born out of wedlock, how, according to her mother, she liked the "good times—wild crowds, drink and drugs," and how her mother had not seen her in the past three years. The most telling quote in her article, however, did not come from a family member but from an unnamed neighbor who spoke to the reporter on the condition that her name not be used: "Adele was the saddest child I knew. When other kids would get Good Humor bars, she would lick the wrappers."

At the trial Judge Aldan Markson found the story "artfully and manipulatively written; it was calculated to bring tears to the eyes of susceptible readers." As a witness, he said, Cantor appeared "naive, soft-spoken, shy, absent-minded and fearful." He found her "educated, able and intelligent." But "she was not a truthful witness," and Judge Markson fined her $500 and sentenced her to do thirty days of community work. (After her initial conviction, Cantor spent more than two years in an attempt to vindicate herself.)

Was the story worth doing? Clearly. A murder in a small community deserves a follow-up; and this story, no matter how painful to the victim's family, outlined the dark side of the victim's past and prepared the reader for what eventually developed in the case: The go-go dancer's death was ruled to be not a murder at all. Instead, it was determined that she was killed in self-defense. Could the story have been done without the reporter posing (as the judge determined she had done) or without her partially withholding her identity (as she herself conceded)? Most likely, yes. The victim's background could have been reconstructed using traditional reporting techniques —the searching of public records and interviews with friends, old acquaintances and neighbors (keep in mind the potency of the neighbor's quote in the article). It would have taken longer that way, but it is hard to see why a delay of a few days in and of itself would have been detrimental to the public interest.

From a purely practical calculus, the results gained from misrepresentation and posing hardly seem to warrant the risks. Pragmatism aside, there are fundamental reasons against masquerading. In the long term, posing mortgages the credibility of the press. The notion of truthfulness is so essential to journalism that it should not be trifled with. It is important that people know to whom they are talking, and impersonation undercuts an implicit trust between journalists and those whom they interview. Some stories will surely be harder to get if a reporter does not pose. Others will be impossible to get. But not so many as one might suppose.

In the context of the number of stories appearing each day, stealth or impersonation is used sparingly. Outright posing is generally condemned by today's editors, but this disapproval manifests itself more in word than in deed. When posing is considered in a written code, it is usually criticized. But few of the fifty largest newspapers ban it altogether. A survey in 1983 of television stations showed that undercover reporting was relatively common. More than a quarter of the 299 network affiliates in the top one hundred markets that responded said that in the previous two years reporters had gone undercover, representing "themselves as other than journalists." Another survey showed that two-thirds of journalists approved of the practice.

Still, most journalists feel there are limits to posing. Some will pose only in a public place as, say, a bartender. Some will not lie on an employment form. Others say they will not impersonate a policeman or anyone who is authorized to compel information. (Most likely, that impersonator would be subject to criminal prosecution, as Carla Cantor was.)

These distinctions, however, are often blurred. Bob Greene of *Newsday* draws a line on impersonation and says he would never pose as a policeman. Yet, with particular relish, he tells the story of how he and a colleague, in the aftermath of the drowning of Mary Jo Kopechne off Chappaquiddick Island in 1969, rented a black car, put an antenna on it to suggest they were policemen, wore black rain coats, went to a motel where the dead woman's friends were staying, and demanded to see the record of their toll telephone calls. "We never said we were cops," says Greene. "We never said we were reporters." If they had been asked who they were—and they were not asked —they would have answered: "People investigating Chappaquiddick."

This is passive deception, which occurs far more frequently than active impersonation. Greene and his colleague never misrepresented themselves. But they certainly tried to leave the impression that they were not reporters. The distinction between what Greene did and a reporter posing as a bartender is a fine one, but it is the type of distinction that journalists try to draw.

Probably the most elaborate and best-known recent example of posing bore fruit in a twenty-five-part series that appeared in the *Chicago Sun-Times* in 1978. The paper went one step beyond ordinary undercover work and engaged in the equivalent of a sting operation. For four months, the paper operated a bar —playfully called the Mirage—in order to document the day-to-day official corruption that plagued Chicago's small-business owners. Some reporters worked as bartenders while photographers worked from a hidden room, snapping pictures of payoffs. Payoffs of $10 to $100 were made to city inspectors so they would disregard health and safety hazards. Shakedowns by state liquor inspectors were observed. Tax fraud by accountants was uncovered.

In a book published shortly after the series ran, the two main reporters, Zay N. Smith and Pamela Zekman, explained their thinking as they prepared to go undercover. By owning a tavern, they said, "we could see how the system actually works." In their own eyes they would avoid technical entrapment. They interpreted this self-imposed mandate to mean that "it was all right to give somebody a chance to show off his normal talent for lawbreaking. It was not all right to nudge that person into committing crimes that were new to him." They distinguished what they would do from what they considered to be improper undercover work: "It would be an invasion of privacy if a reporter worked undercover, say, as a politician's valet or housemaid. But a tavern was a licensed public place."

There were other problems in conducting the investigation in a lawful way. In Illinois, any person who witnesses a crime is legally required to report it to the police. The Mirage team was in a quandary. "The Chicago Police Department was one of the project's potential targets," wrote Smith and Zekman. "The U.S. Justice Department and the FBI were pretty good at security, but neither was inclined to go along with newspaper investigations." Instead, they turned to the Illinois Department of Law Enforcement, and a deal was struck. The saloonkeepers would call up a friendly agent there and report any crimes. The agent would accept the information and protect the tavern's disguise. Another Illinois law forbade the secret use of sound-recording equipment without a court order. Therefore, the authors said, the *Sun-Times* team relied on "hidden photographers, multiple witnesses, and detailed memoranda for its documentation."

The reaction to the series was mostly positive. The story received national attention, in large part because the *Sun-Times* permitted the television show "60 Minutes" to join the scheme, and the undercover operation was shown on the television show as the first item after the 1978 Superbowl. It created a predictable stir in journalistic circles, and it won many prizes. The Chicago paper was expected to win the Pulitzer Prize in 1979, and a Pulitzer jury recommended that it receive the award.

But the *Sun-Times* was blocked from winning the prize by two prominent journalists sitting on the Pulitzer advisory board, which is the body that determines the winners. Objections were lodged by Benjamin Bradlee, executive editor of *The Washington Post*, and Eugene Patterson, who had once been managing editor at the *Post* and was then managing editor of the *St. Petersburg Times.* They argued that reporters needed to operate in the open. Patterson said the reporters should have interviewed bar owners. That, he said, "would have been the hard way to get the story." Several years later, speaking to an audience of students at the University of Florida, Patterson said he voted as he did because he "did not want other reporters to follow suit." At the time, Bradlee asked: "How can newspapers be for honesty and integrity when they themselves are less than honest in getting a story? We instruct our reporters not to misrepresent themselves, period."

Part of the reason the rejection of the *Sun-Times* entry came as such a surprise was that in prior years the Pulitzer board had often given its imprimatur to posing, signaling to thousands of journalists across the country that the premier award in journalism could be won if reporters showed enough ingenuity and courage in camouflaging the fact they were journalists. On at least four occasions in the preceding two decades, a Pulitzer Prize had been awarded to stories in which reporters posed:

• In 1961, Edgar May, a *Buffalo Evening News* reporter who exposed laxity and mismanagement in New York State's welfare services, had posed as a social caseworker.

• Ten years later, in 1971, William Hugh Jones, a *Chicago Tribune* reporter, posed as an ambulance driver to expose collusion between the police and private ambulance companies to restrict service in low-income areas.

• In 1974 William Sherman, a *New York Daily News* reporter, wrote a series in which, posing as a Medicaid recipient, he uncovered major abuses in the administration of Medicaid in New York City.

• That same year, *Newsday* carried a thirty-two-part series that followed the trail of heroin traffic from Turkey to France to the New York metropolitan area. Bob Greene was a member of the winning *Newsday* team. In France he impersonated a lawyer. (Ten years later, he said of his role in this series: "I lied. I cheated. I damn near stole. The result obviously was good. I'd do it again. Our fine sense of ethics diminishes in proportion to the importance of the story.")

The rejection of the Mirage series marked a change in the Pulitzer policy, and by the early 1980s, the message that the Pulitzer board looked on undercover reporting with disfavor had apparently spread. Robert Christopher, administrator of the prizes, said that relatively few entries based on undercover reporting had been submitted between 1981 and 1983. Two reporters—one for the *Los Angeles Herald-Examiner* who posed as an illegal alien in a sweatshop in 1981, the other from *The Wall Street Journal* who posed as a day laborer in 1983— were finalists in the competition, but neither won.

Even though it has lost the blessing of the Pulitzer board, posing seems still to be as entrenched among journalists as it has been for at least a century. An early impersonator was Nellie Bly, who rose quickly in journalism at the end of the 1800s at the *New York World* by engaging in a series of adventures. In the tradition of the intrepid participant-observers, she explored the depths of the ocean in a diving bell and went around the world in fewer than seventy-two days, beating the mythical record established by Phileas Fogg in Jules Verne's *Around the World in Eighty Days.* She gained admittance to Blackwells Island Insane Asylum in the East River off Manhattan (it is now Roosevelt Island) by posing as a madwoman, and she then exposed the filthy conditions inside.

In the late 1930s Dorothy Kilgallen, the energetic and hard-edged reporter and columnist for Hearst's *New York Evening Journal,* was based in Hollywood, and there she wrote a series of gimmick columns. In one of them, she tried to find out whether it was possible for a plain girl from Peoria—Mary Warren was her disguised name—to crash the formidable studio gates. To each studio guard, she repeated, "I'm Mary Warren from Peoria, and I'm looking for a job as an extra." Each time, she was referred to Central Casting, and then was turned down. In her column Kilgallen advised all the Mary Warrens from Peoria to stay and work at home, while nurturing the hope of being discovered there. "What was possible ten years ago in this town is no longer possible," she concluded about her rejection in Hollywood.

In the early 1960s Gloria Steinem first gained wide attention for an article she wrote for *Show* magazine: "I Was a Playboy Bunny." The article required her to lie repeatedly—about her age, her name and her background—and to pose. In applying for the job, she said she was twenty-four years old rather than twenty-eight. A supervisor came by and looked over the application. " 'You don't look twenty-four,' she said. *Well, that's that,* I thought. 'You look much younger.' I smiled in disbelief." Steinem let herself be flattered. Her undercover obser-

vations reveal a predictably unpleasant working environment.
The glamour that was promised in the advertisement that she
answered did not materialize. Some of her observations seem
particularly thin. She found that most of the customers
"seemed to be middle-aged businessmen"—a revelation that
hardly seems worth her going undercover to unearth. (In 1985
a television movie, *A Bunny's Tale*, based on her article, was
shown. In the film the seventeen days she spends working as a
Playboy Bunny radicalize her. In fact, she said, "It took me
longer in reality to reach that conclusion.")

Probably the most respectable, or at least the most defensi-
ble, use of posing, in terms of what can be accomplished, involves the investigation of what the sociologist Erving Goffman
called "total institutions"—mental homes, prisons, nursing
homes, boarding schools and monasteries. In this type of posing, the reporter masks his identity and is a participant-
observer.

Prisons appear to be the institutions most sought out by contemporary journalist-infiltrators. There are logical reasons for
this. They house the outcasts. They are forbidden places, that
ordinarily inquisitive reporters cannot plumb. They are often
dangerously overcrowded. How are prisoners treated? Are
there programs to help them? Or do prisons merely teach them
to be still more-hardened criminals? What causes disturbances
and riots? Few newspapers have a reporter exclusively assigned to cover prisons (I am aware of one paper, the *Jacksonville Times Union*, which has a reporter stationed near Florida's
death-row in Starke), and few reporters have much expertise in
penology. It is hard for them to get a fix on what is going on
inside.

In most jurisdictions, prison officials are willing to let reporters interview inmates, but these are often the model prisoners
—the best behaved and the most articulate—and these interviews can lead to a slanted Potemkin village portrayal of life
inside. In a 1974 opinion *Pell* v. *Procunier*, the United States
Supreme Court set limitations on what reporters could do inside prisons. Under the court's ruling, administrators need not
grant them interviews with specific inmates.

In the past several years, some administrators have allowed
reporters to masquerade as inmates to get an eyewitness view
from the inside. This has led to some good writing, and occasionally to shrewd insights. But overall the conclusions that
have been drawn rarely seem worth the effort.

In 1982 an ambitious examination of prison life was undertaken by a group of reporters at *The Arizona Daily Star* in Tucson. During the project, one reporter worked undercover as a guard, another as an inmate. Their assignments were authorized by prison officials, but their identity was kept secret from other guards and inmates. This was done, the paper said, so that "the Star could report more accurately and vividly about the conditions inside Arizona's prisons."

Ten days after the reporter, R. H. Ring, entered prison as an inmate, he was cornered in a stairwell and beaten by four other inmates because he refused to give one of them his belt. Six of his teeth were broken, and he suffered a bruise the size of a softball on his hip. (A photograph of him showing off the bruise accompanied his story.) He was sent back to Tucson later that night after he and prison officials decided that his safety was in jeopardy. Ring, something of an adventurer, had served a short period of time in prison a decade earlier, and he was anxious to do this assignment: "I wanted to see what prison was like, firsthand, to feel it and hear it and smell it and eat the bad food. . . . In a more professional stance, I told the appropriate officials that, to write an accurate news story on prison, I had to be there. No number of interviews with cons and guards would provide the same strength of reality." The result was a ten-thousand-word article, which lapses in and out of stream of consciousness. It bespeaks a rebellious reporter, and while powerfully written, it tells more about Ring and his feelings than about the prison. Such self-conscious writing seems to be the common failing of this genre of first-person undercover reporting.

At the end of 1983, a *Boston Globe* reporter went to jail for a week under an assumed name. The revelations in his five-part series did not seem to warrant an exception to the *Globe*'s policy prohibiting posing. The exception was made, said S. J. Micciche, the associate editor, so that a reporter could feel "what it was like for an ordinary, middle-aged man never in trouble with the law to spend time behind bars."

Richard Stewart, the fifty-two-year-old *Globe* reporter, wrote: "The court order looked official. It was phony. It was part of the deception to get me into jail as a 'legitimate' inmate without anybody knowing my true identity. For the duration of my jail term I would be Richard Leader, convicted felon. My address on the court order was in reality a vacant lot. Essex County Sheriff Charles Reardon had agreed to cooperate in the subterfuge. Grace, his assistant, was also enlisted in the plot. Reardon recommended that I use a phony identity so that neither inmates nor jail guards would know who I was. 'Otherwise you won't have a real experience. You won't be treated the same. . . .'

"Most Americans have no idea what life is like behind those high walls, barred windows and doors; most have no concept of the denigrating effect of the jail house, with its constant indignities, fears and frustrations. I would be their surrogate. . . ."

In the articles, expletives are deleted, a fitting touch for a family newspaper, but hardly in keeping with the search for what really happens behind bars. The series is well written, but it, too, contains its share of bland insights. Stewart found prison lonely, boring, claustrophobic and noisy, and he discovered that cigarettes were "the principal mode of currency." Surely he could have found this out through standard reporting.

The best part of the series is a recitation of an alcohol counseling session. Stewart notes: "When it was finally revealed that I was a *Globe* reporter, I returned to the group to assure them that I would not report on the sessions because of their confidential nature. They volunteered that I could use the material if I did not identify them by name." That suggests he could have used standard reporting techniques from the start to do the same story.

When he returned with the sheriff to reveal his identity to the inmates, he found no resentment. But "one inmate scolded me on the grounds that I did not bring to jail 'the same baggage the rest of us bring in here. So how can you write about it? You came in here with a carton of cigarettes, and you could buy a television set. Most of us come in here without a dime. You could leave any time you wanted to. There are guys who'll be here for years. You didn't do hard time.'

"That night, in my own bed with my own pillow, sipping a cup of tea while watching a color television set I could hear and see, I considered his words again.

"He was right.

"I returned home knowing that my friends and neighbors would not turn away from me. I would not be an embarrassment to my wife and children.

"I would not have to live the rest of my life with the burden of trying to conceal the fact that I was a criminal, a man with a prison record."

Once again in the Boston series, as in the *Arizona Daily Star* series, an experienced reporter demonstrates the severe limitations of undercover reporting. Capturing the reality of prison life is as elusive and difficult for the undercover reporter as it is for the reporter who identifies himself. But finding out what goes on in prisons is not impossible.

The Carson City *Nevada Appeal* came up with an unconventional—and aboveboard—approach: In 1982 it began carrying a weekly column, "Being There," written by Gerald Crane, who was not a reporter but a high school dropout serving a thirty-five-year sentence for kidnapping and bank robbery. He was at the Northern Nevada Correctional Center in Carson City. In a column in July 1984, Crane wrote: "We'd like to imagine riots are well planned by participants possessing a clear objective in mind. Of the several I have attended, all were the direct result of random events colliding. Because the casual chemical soup of prison changes its composition moment to moment, there is no way to anticipate the catalyst that will ignite the stagnant pond into boiling bog. Where there is a fire there need not have been smoke first."

Probably the best contemporary picture of prison life was contained in the official report of the state commission that studied the Attica prison riot and the bloody takeover by the New York state police. That commission had a large staff and subpoena power to force witnesses to testify, but many of the insights in its final report resulted from sensitive observation over a period of time and determined reporting.

For many years in the 1970s, without resorting to posing, the magazine *Corrections* gave a valuable look at the inside of prisons. Before it folded in 1983, the magazine dealt with a variety of topics—inmate capitalism, privately owned prisons, pretrial diversion, the problems of transsexuals in prisons, preventing suicides in prisons, inmate grievance procedures, the plight of retarded offenders, bail reform, the question of women guards working in male prisons, Vietnam veterans in prisons and the possibility that pastel walls prevent jailhouse brawls.

The magazine also carried a number of articles on individual facilities. An article in December 1980 on the mammoth County Central jail in Los Angeles concluded that most of the 5,000 inmates spent their days in idleness since the jail offered almost no programs. In December 1982 Bruce Porter, the director of the journalism program at Brooklyn College, used standard reporting techniques in writing about prison gangs in California. He spoke to officials, used public records and interviewed former gang members and those who knew gang members. Journalists can usually get at least as accurate a picture of prison life by interviewing convicts and ex-convicts as they can by posing as inmates who can walk out at any time.

Few, if any, newspapers will—or should—go into the kind of detail on prisons that *Corrections* magazine did, but what is necessary in thoroughly covering prisons—and other beats like prisons—is a long-term investment in manpower and dogged reporting. Posing is a shortcut that may be cheaper and may produce results faster. But, at its best, it can lead only to splashy "one-shot" stories.

The most common justification among editors for permitting reporters to pose is that, in limited doses, it is acceptable when there is no other way to ferret out an important story.

"I would limit role-playing to situations where the information to be gained is of *substantial* public interest, and when the information sought would not be available in the same form if reporters were required to use second-hand accounts," says John Seigenthaler, editorial director of *USA Today* who is also publisher and editor of *The Tennessean* in Nashville. In 1984 the policy of the McClatchy newspapers in California, according to Frank McCulloch, then the executive editor, "emphasized our distaste for posing but pulls up just short of forbidding it under any circumstances."

Sissela Bok, who in her book *Secrets* expresses undiluted dislike for clandestine reporting, suggests it may be permissible when no other means of probing a particular problem is available. Once it is determined that there is no alternative to subterfuge, she says, newspapers, "knowing that such means are morally questionable," must "then ask themselves whether their goal warrants the use of such methods." That kind of analysis, though, does not provide much guidance. A journalist will invariably argue that the goal is a worthy one.

Most of the time, there is an alternative to posing. "We stopped the practice," says Eugene Patterson of the *St. Petersburg Times*, who had been instrumental in blocking the granting of the Pulitzer Prize to the Mirage series. "We reserve the right to resume it if a specific case arises wherein an important public interest can only be served by disguising a staffer. But such cases will be rare indeed. We pay a price in lost credibility each time we sneak. Hard work and burnt shoe leather can produce the facts the old-fashioned way—cleanly."

At NBC, misrepresentation is permissible only in "isolated and infrequent situations where, for example, failure to conceal one's identity would make it impossible to investigate and disclose an impropriety of major significance." At ABC, reporters "should not disguise their identity or pose as someone with another occupation" without the approval of management. In its production standards, CBS says: "In approaching individuals or organizations for interviews or coverage, misrepresentation should be avoided. Misrepresentation is unnecessary and in any event, candor on the part of the reporters and producers most often would better achieve the purpose." The drafters of the standards leave room for an exception—"when there is clear reason to believe that an improper activity could *otherwise not be reported.*"

What sometimes happens, though, is that journalists skip over the tough intermediate steps and reach the "last resort" justification too hastily. In fact, most stories where impersonation has been used and the "last resort" justification has been cited could, with some ingenuity and hard work, have been done without posing.

For example, in 1979, the Strand, a large, cluttered book store on the edge of Greenwich Village in Manhattan which is well known for selling new volumes at sharp discounts, sent out a letter soliciting copies of books from reviewers. One of these letters was passed along to an executive of the Gannett chain, who happened to be chairman of the Professional Standards Committee of the Associated Press Managing Editors Association (APME). The editor was upset, and a reporter with *The Rochester Democrat and Chronicle*, a Gannett paper, was assigned to do a story on the bookstore for the Gannett News Service. He was sent to work at the store for fourteen days.

In an editor's note that accompanied the article, the undercover approach was never really justified. "We had to do it from the inside to be effective and accurate," was the only explanation given at the time by Richard B. Tuttle, the Gannett executive who was chairman of the Professional Standards Committee of the APME.

In Rochester, the article appeared on a Sunday in early August 1979 at the top of the front page. There were three sidebars to boot, thus deluging newspaper readers in Rochester with a story of far more interest to the paper's executives than it possibly could have been to upstate New Yorkers. (The editor's note, in fact, said the articles would be part of a report to the APME's October convention that year.)

The story, by Michael Cordts, began: "In private transactions with a New York City bookstore, reporters across the nation have been pocketing thousands of dollars by selling complimentary copies of books sent to their newspapers." Cordts said ten newspaper book reviewers had "admitted" selling copies to the bookstore. In his story, Cordts told how he had confronted reviewers with his knowledge that he had seen crates bearing their return addresses at the bookstore.

If indeed as many reviewers were selling their books as the story claimed, it seems that a lot of phone calls strategically placed around the country would have led to the same result as the undercover reporting. The likelihood is that some reviewers would have lied on the phone and that others would have confessed. It is unethical for reviewers to sell copies of books that were given to them, but it is hardly the worst transgression committed by journalists. The articles in the Rochester paper overplayed a rather trivial matter. (Many newspapers forbid their reviewers from profiting personally on the sale of books. Often, they will auction off review copies and donate the proceeds to charity.)

The Strand continues to do a flourishing business in selling reviewers' copies. In 1985 the store still advertised that it had "tens of thousands of new reviewers' copies"; earlier, in an interview, Fred Bass, the president of the store, said he received thousands of reviewers' copies a week—more copies than ever. Cordts's article, he said, actually had helped his business.

Another example of pointless posing occurred in Albuquerque. With braces on her teeth and dye on her prematurely graying hair, Leslie Linthicum, then a twenty-four-year-old reporter for the *Albuquerque Tribune*, took on a false identity and became someone else. Without the knowledge of administrators and teachers, she entered Eldorado High School, the city's largest school, as Leslie Taylor, a seventeen-year-old senior transfer student. She signed her false name to documents—an identification card and a class schedule. In a five-part series, she found that teachers were scorned by students and did not do much work. Some students drank whiskey in their cars and used drugs.

Late in 1983, Ms. Linthicum wrote for the Journalism Ethics Report of the Society of Professional Journalists, Sigma Delta Chi: "The editors and I wanted an untarnished picture, one not colored by the public relations interests of school officials or the self-consciousness of teachers and students. To get a true picture, we decided, I could not identify myself as a reporter. The announcement would have altered their behavior—and the story, we thought. . . . The initial decision to misrepresent myself was made with little hesitation and was never regretted, even though negative reaction to the method was swift and vehement. Espionage usually is not a newspaper's job, and to violate trusts and perhaps even laws requires a commitment that a story is significant. This was one. Students, teachers, parents and school administrators reacted with shock and anger, not to the meat of the articles but to the ethics of the method. They felt violated, intruded upon and tricked into trusting an individual who lied for no good purpose. The purpose and outcome, though, were worthy and thus justified the method, I am convinced."

Again, hers were hardly astonishing disclosures. The conclusions that she reached were obvious ones; it hardly seems necessary to assume a guise to show that teenagers can be ill-mannered, lazy and rebellious.

Some newspapers that prohibit the type of posing engaged in by Michael Cordts and Leslie Linthicum permit reporters to mask their identity or merely to withhold mentioning their occupation unless questioned.

At *the Denver Post*, Tim Kelly, the managing editor in early 1984, said that while posing is "judged on a case by case basis, a reporter is not permitted to deny he's a reporter if questioned." At the *Seattle Times*, James B. King, the editor, reports: "Years ago we allowed a reporter to be hired as a nurse's aide in a nursing home suspected of fraud and poor treatment of patients. We had been barred from inspecting the facility. I'm not sure we would do the same again. We have, however, allowed reporters to not identify themselves unless asked. If asked, they are instructed to identify themselves."

The New York Times takes an unambiguously hard line in forbidding journalists to misrepresent themselves. "I don't believe in journalists' masquerading," said A. M. Rosenthal. "I don't think it is illegal. But I don't think it is in the spirit of the First Amendment." But the *Times* permits reporters to mask their occupation and behave as ordinary members of the public when covering consumer stories, such as reviewing restaurants. (Mimi Sheraton, who had been the longtime restaurant reviewer, occasionally wore wigs and other disguises; her picture was posted in kitchens in some of the city's better-known restaurants.)

There are other occasions where the lack of disclosure works well enough. Reporters do not wish to disclose their identity immediately so that they can more accurately get the "feel" of a situation. In the summer of 1983, Philip Shenon of the *Times* wrote a diary about three days he spent in a welfare hotel. In *Winners & Sinners*, an internal publication of the *Times*, Shenon was properly credited for his ingenuity and was asked to share his techniques in getting the story. "Don't reveal yourself too soon," he said. "I feared that the hotel management would learn about me from some gossipy tenant and throw me out. For most of the first day and a half, I just wandered around the hotel, watched the tenants and observed their living conditions. I began my interviews late in the afternoon of the second day. I always identified myself as a *Times* reporter. People were usually willing to talk; by then, many were used to seeing me in the hotel. There is another advantage to remaining incognito for a time: you don't have to worry what events are being staged for your benefit. I wore a Walkman, which often sparked conversation. The young kids kept pulling the earphones from my neck to listen to the music. As they listened, I talked to their parents."

In other special instances, lack of full disclosure may be acceptable. For many years, Nicholas Gage was an investigative reporter for *The Wall Street Journal* and *The New York Times*. He left the *Times* in 1980 to devote himself full-time to writing a book about his mother, Eleni, and how she had died. The book became an obsession. As if he were an actor in one of the great Greek tragedies, he embarked on a successful search to find his mother's killer. She had been executed in 1948 by Communist rebels during the Greek Civil War. The book was a huge success, and Gage became a hero among Greek-Americans.

In the spring of 1984, when I was teaching at the University of Florida, Gage spoke to a group of 150 or so Greek-Americans in a crowded, windowless room. He spoke about Greece and about the book. The audience was attentive and well informed.

"I used all the techniques I have learned over two decades," he said in a barely audible monotone. He said that he had taped all interviews, some secretly, and once, when he confronted his mother's murderer, a gun was hidden in the back of his pants and a tape recorder was hidden in a sock. ("As an investigative reporter," he writes in *Eleni*, "I had used this mini-recorder many times when interviewing criminals and informants.") In gathering material for the book, he did not fully disclose his intentions. He told people he was a Greek writer doing a book on the civil war, and he gained valuable material from former guerrillas who thought Gage was sympathetic to them.

Eventually, Gage did not kill his mother's assassin: "I realized my mother had made me, and she had not made me a killer," Gage told the Florida audience. In his quest he violated all sorts of journalistic rules. But in contrast to his investigative reporting at *The Wall Street Journal* or the *Times*, his book is really not a piece of conventional journalism at all. It is a first-person adventure and, in a sense, a journal. He records a personal mission of such intensity that in his mind he was prepared to kill. In this context he could hardly be bound by the rules of journalistic ethics.

In Florida he said: "As Tom Goldstein, a former colleague at the *Times* can tell you, you have to tell the truth, but nothing says you have to tell the whole truth." But there are great problems with adopting his advice as a general rule.

It is a deception when a reporter pretends not to be one. At Chappaquiddick, Bob Greene of *Newsday* was careful never to say what he was, but he wanted others to think that he was a law enforcement agent. The distinction between active posing and passive deception is subtle. Benjamin Bradlee of *The Washington Post*, who vehemently objected to the posing in the Mirage tavern series, takes the view that it is not always necessary for a reporter to identify oneself as a reporter. At the *Post* it is all right for reporters to dress and act like someone else as long as they do not give another identity or say they are not reporters.

For example, in 1983, in an account of how men from the streets of Washington seek work in the fields of North Carolina, Neil Henry posed as a destitute drifter "with a scraggly beard" who carried with him a social security card for identification along with a notebook and a *Washington Post* press pass. Some of his companions knew his real identity. In another series in the *Post*, in 1984, on how easily drugs could be smuggled into a prison near Washington, a *Post* reporter did not disclose her identity. The reporter, Athelia Knight, sat silently on a bus that was headed for Lorton Reformatory to observe ways in which marijuana and other illegal drugs were surreptitiously brought into the facility. She said about the bus ride, "I must have seemed like just another woman with a husband or boyfriend locked up."

In defending the two series, Bradlee told me: "I see a really seminal distinction between planning any kind of a deception, however much the end might seem to justify the means, and embarking on a project where your occupation as a journalist is not advertised.

"In the first instance the journalist is actually posing as someone else, be it a bartender or be it a doctor or whatever. In the second instance there is no pose. There may be no sign around the reporter's neck, but at no time did Neil Henry or Athelia Knight lie."

Yet, it is by no means certain that the reporters needed to mask their identity to come up with these stories. In his series Neil Henry came up against the same problems that the reporters in Boston and Arizona who posed as prison inmates faced. There is a real question of just what he was observing. At one point, Henry self-consciously says, "Having come to North Carolina without a change of clothes, and having neither the means nor opportunity to acquire another set, I was ughsome, foul-smelling, and exhausted." But, of course, this was make-believe, since Henry was, in fact, a reporter and could, had he wished, easily have acquired another set of clothes.

The larger problem with stories like this is that they rely exclusively on the integrity of reporters. Bradlee says his reporters do not lie. But it is asking a lot of readers to accept this as a general rule, since readers know that some reporters sometimes lie. At trial, under oath, Carla Cantor said that all she did was fail to reveal to the dead go-go dancer's mother the fact that she was a reporter. The judge did not believe her.

The question of credibility was also at the heart of an undercover story by Agnes Palazzetti, a veteran reporter for the *Buffalo Evening News*. In 1981 she wrote a story on how getting caught for shoplifting can be "a traumatic and terrifying experience." The headline was: "Posing as Shoplifter Works Too Well." The overline to the headline bore this message: "Embarrassed Reporter Learns a Lesson." But the headline is misleading. She did not merely masquerade as a shoplifter; she *shoplifted,* and when caught she claimed she did so because she was a reporter.

In her first-person account, Palazzetti wrote how she sought to test out the rather tepid hypothesis that retail stores do not have the proper security or enough sales personnel to curb shoplifting. "In order to learn exactly what shoplifting is all about, this reporter, working outside of the boundaries of truly ethical journalism, decided that after almost 30 years' experience as a reporter, I would find out if what had been written on shoplifting was really so. I didn't even tell my editors, because I knew they wouldn't allow me to break the law for a story."

Perhaps not, but after she did so, they ran her story, and played it prominently. Palazzetti recounts: "Eventually, it dawns on you, you're being arrested and you are not being believed—at least by some. One feeling is more bewildering than the other, but finally you sort it out and realize that all of this nightmare will make an even better story." Eventually, she was released from custody.

Palazzetti's explanation of her arrest is limp, and there is absolutely no evidence that she was not in fact shoplifting and would have said nothing had she not been caught. The reader cannot independently know if the reporter is telling the truth. A newspaper needs the trust of the reader, and one of the problems of selective posing is that this trust is undermined.

■

A common thread runs through many of the stories where reporters pose or fail to disclose their identities. They wish to take the law into their own hands, or at least to help law enforcement—which they sometimes view as inefficient.

This was the case at the *Miami Herald,* which did a major series on drugs in South Florida schools in 1982. Illegal drugs are a serious problem in Miami. In the early 1980s three-quarters of the cocaine and three-quarters of the marijuana that entered this country did so through Florida, according to Stanley Marcus, United States Attorney for the Southern District of Florida. The *Herald* is an aggressive paper, deeply concerned about its community, and it wants to do something about curbing drugs. In the fall of 1983, the *Herald* stepped beyond the normal role of a newspaper as recorder of events on its news pages. Along with the Junior League of Miami, a local television station and a group called Informed Families of Dade County, it sponsored what an advertisement called a "media campaign" —"EPIDEMIC: South Florida Fights Drugs."

A year earlier a team of reporters from the paper had spent two months preparing a major series of stories in which they explored the drug culture in south Florida high schools. Initially, the editors were going to have youthful-looking reporters buy drugs in school yards to show how easy it was. The paper had no intention of letting the local prosecutor, whom the ranking editors distrusted, know of their plans. In early March the paper was poised for the mass buy. (I know this because I had informally applied for a job there and was spending part of an afternoon with three top editors. Our conversation was interrupted when they held a conference call with one of the newspaper's outside lawyers to talk through the story a final time. Several months after this, I discussed the incident with an editor at the *Herald* and was authorized to write about the private conversation.)

At the paper, the policy is to discourage active posing, but there had been instances where it has been allowed, says Pete Weitzel, the current managing editor, "where there was no misrepresentation, simply no representation as a reporter." Ultimately, the undercover buys in the drug series did not happen. "We decided it was not wise," says Weitzel. "We initially thought we would make purchases, verify they were drugs, then write our stories. It raised all the obvious questions. Suppose someone got arrested? There are real problems in aiding and assisting, of witnessing a crime, in gathering a story."

Reporters did not pose, but they dressed like high school students to blend in with their surroundings. The main story that was finally published focused on a young man named Rob Cappello, the son of a former policeman. He was brash and a braggart, and he is quoted directly and extensively, and was the only offender identified by his full name. At the time, he was eighteen years old, just beyond being protected by Florida's juvenile offender laws. He was the only person the reporters talked to who was eighteen. The article said that he sold about thirty marijuana cigarettes a morning from his territory, which was pinpointed unambiguously in the article. He was dealing boldly, in plain view, and had no right to expect privacy. Pictures of him were snapped by a photographer hiding behind a bush.

He knew he was talking to reporters. They had identified

themselves. He was also naive, and the reporters said afterward that Cappello probably was not aware that the reporters were witnessing all that was happening or that what he said would be quoted directly in the paper. When they chatted with him, the reporters did not take notes. After a conversation, they rushed to their car to take down what he had said. The reporters did not pose. They disclosed their identity, but they still were being deceptive, and even though Cappello was a wrongdoer, their deception undercut an otherwise fine story. The day the story ran Cappello did not show up at school. He never returned.

The *Miami Herald* stopped short of stepping over into the domain of law enforcement. Other journalists have not. Sometimes, as in the Mirage series, journalists set up a sting operation. In its guidelines, ABC acknowledges that in some "exceptional circumstances" it will sanction cooperation with police. "These involve occasions when ABC News is invited to accompany and observe police in undercover or 'sting' operations."

But this approach can result in a reporter's becoming a willing pawn of law enforcement. In 1982 Danny Garcia, a reporter for *The San Antonio Light*, posed as an illegal alien to experience, according to an editor's note, "the real-life ordeal of an illegal alien crossing into the United States."

Posing as a Mexican, Garcia infiltrated an operation that smuggled aliens into the United States. He floated across the river from Mexico in a tire tube. (He wrote of this experience: "I had been overcome by a feeling of terror, fearing that I would either drown or be robbed by my crossers. But at the same time, those fears had been outweighed by a strange sense of fascination. 'So this is what it's like. *This* is what it's like to be a wetback,' I thought to myself.") Eventually, he was caught by "La Migra"—the U.S. Border Patrol—on the way to San Antonio with a group of real aliens. He was then charged as a co-conspirator in the trafficking of undocumented aliens.

His role was an ambiguous one. He told his arresting officers that he was really a reporter. They didn't believe him. Then, he wrote in his story, he "explained to the officers that I would provide information if they helped protect my cover." They still did not believe him. But the reporter felt secure for he knew that he "had already implicated a major smuggler in an organized felony offense." The charges against him were eventually dropped. Garcia had taken on the role of informant for the government, just as Chere Avery had done in the investigation of the city commissioner in Fort Myers. That is a role a journalist should never wittingly play. A journalist is paid to write stories, not assist the government.

One of the obvious dangers of reporters' posing as illegal aliens, as prisoners, or as prison guards or of their taking on the role of law enforcement agents is that others may then use this as a pretext to pose as journalists. There is no way of knowing how common this "reverse-posing" is, but examples are cited with sufficient frequency to suggest that this subterfuge is employed often. This undercuts the ability of journalists to do their job.

Lyndon H. LaRouche, Jr., a sometime presidential candidate, is a shadowy figure possessing an unwholesome ability to manipulate the media. Members of his highly disciplined organization have often disguised themselves as reporters representing well-known media outlets in order to gather information and gain access where they might not otherwise be accepted. LaRouche's politics swing from the far left to the far right, and the fringe group he leads has remarkable staying power. In 1984 he ran for president as the head of the Democratic National Policy Committee, an intentionally misleading name because it has nothing whatsoever to do with mainstream Democratic Party politics. His group used to be the U.S. Labor Party, and it was no friend of labor.

At the A.F.L.–C.I.O. convention in 1983, a LaRouchite who pretended to represent *Business Week* was barred. "Our experience with the LaRouche group has been entirely negative," said Murray Seeger, director of the department of information of the A.F.L.–C.I.O. "We, by tradition, operate an open policy in dealing with the media. At our 1983 convention, for instance, we granted press credentials to American newspapers and magazines ranging from the Communist Party's Daily World to *Forbes*, 'the capitalist tool.' We admitted representatives from East Germany and the Soviet Union. Only those from the LaRouche publications—'New Solidarity' and 'Executive Intelligence Review'—were barred automatically.

"The reason for that unusual position is that the representatives of these publications do not meet the barest minimum standards of journalistic behavior. The same persons who purport to be reporters are also pamphleteers and salesmen for the various LaRouche products. They agitate. Since President Lane Kirkland is one of the targets for their abuse, LaRouche representatives come to our meetings and hand out their papers or slap stickers on meeting room walls in the early morning hours when the rooms are empty." Seeger said that he has been approached by "Atlantic Business Week" and "other pseudo publications" and traced the telephone numbers to LaRouche headquarters.

In the fall of 1984 LaRouche lost a $150 million libel action he brought against NBC because it had characterized him as the extremist leader of a political cult. Instead, the jury awarded damages to NBC, which had countersued. A main contention in the countersuit was that LaRouche followers had tried to sabotage an NBC interview with Senator Daniel P. Moynihan. They impersonated network reporters and called his office to say that the interview had been canceled. Patricia Lynch, an NBC producer who testified at the libel trial, wrote extensively about "LaRouchian trickery" in an article in the *Columbia Journalism Review* in 1985. Asked for comment about the practices described in the article, LaRouche denied personal knowledge of a 1981 incident in which one of his followers was accused of impersonating a newsmagazine reporter. He declined to talk about other incidents, and he then went on to say: "I do know that the liberal press uses undercover press practices that are abhorrent and beneath description."

Even more serious than the activities of LaRouche's followers are the occasions when law enforcement officials cloak themselves in the wrappings of reporters. In the late 1970s, officers from the Public Disorder Intelligence Division of the Los Angeles Police Department would sometimes show up at news conferences at the Los Angeles Press Club wearing civilian clothes and taking notes, and in 1978 members of that unit were caught posing as a television crew in order to videotape spectators and speakers at a city council meeting on a nuclear power plant. That same year Utah police attempted to arrest a man by posing as reporters from *The Los Angeles Times*.

In 1981, while pretending to be working for WCBS-TV, an investigator hired by the New York City Health and Hospital Corporation made videotapes of municipal hospital doctors who were on strike. He was collecting evidence to be used in a court action under the state's Taylor Law, which prohibits strikes by public employees.

That subterfuge, said Mark Lieberman, then a reporter for the *New York Daily News* and president of the New York Press Club, "poses a dire threat to the ability of honorable professional journalists to retain their credibility. Reporters must have the ability to gather information without the public feeling it is being duped or entrapped."

In 1983 deputy sheriffs in Portland, Oregon, induced a man to leave a barricaded shed by saying they were a television crew and wished to interview him. That same year, in Athens, Georgia, a United States marshal went to serve a summons on a member of an organization planning to hold a demonstration at the nearby Savannah River Plant, which produces fuel for nuclear weapons. In trying to identify the person to whom the court papers were addressed, one marshal said he was a reporter from Greenville, South Carolina.

Several months later, the Justice Department closed its inquiry of the incident by clearing the marshal. The department's Office of Professional Responsibility determined that the marshal did not engage in any "ongoing effort to masquerade as a reporter," but merely had "agreed that he was a reporter when another individual . . . suggested that he was." In its statement, the Justice Department unit said it was not aware that the marshal had violated any regulation or law. "His actions were limited in scope and undertaken to accomplish a bonafide law enforcement mission which he had been assigned."

A bill introduced in the Senate in 1983 would have set standards for Justice Department agents who impersonate reporters or others. That bill would have required that before an undercover operation involving impersonation of a reporter—or of a lawyer, doctor or clergyman—could be carried out, a determination would have to be made that there is "probable cause to believe that the operation is necessary to detect or prevent specific acts of criminality."

That legislation, which was never enacted, had been opposed by news organizations. In May 1984 John Seigenthaler of the *Nashville Tennessean* and *USA Today* and himself a former official of the Department of Justice, testified on behalf of several news groups that this legislation would "disastrously interfere with the independence and objectivity" of the press. "If the government infiltrates a news organization or impersonates a reporter, then that organization or reporter is the unwitting partner of the government," he said. "Once the news media becomes known as anything less than an independent chronicler of news and events, its vital role in the democracy is weakened." He said, "Once infiltration and impersonation are legitimized, the principle of independence for the news media is lost, the damage is done."

Posing, either by journalists or by others as journalists, leads to the erosion of boundaries between who has legitimate claim as a journalist and who does not. If reporters pose as others, it is only a matter of consistency that their moral authority to protest when others pose as journalists is undermined.

In May 1984, nine months after Carla Cantor, the New Jersey reporter, was accused of posing as a morgue employee, six young people were arrested at a "smoke in" staged at the town green in Morristown to protest laws forbidding the use of marijuana. They were passing around a substance that they said was marijuana, but was in fact an herb. (Under the state's "look-alike" law, a substance need only look like a forbidden drug, and therefore these arrests were apparently valid.) A "cameraman" and an "interviewer," who wore T-shirts and windbreakers that said they were from Channel 6, "New Jersey Morning News," covered the demonstration. There is no such station. The cameraman was a deputy sheriff, the interviewer an assistant county prosecutor. (By posing as television journalists, they reaped the benefit of having ready evidence on videotape.) In New Jersey there is no statute forbidding police officers to pose as news gatherers.

After the arrests, David Corcoran, the president of the New Jersey chapter of the Society of Professional Journalists, Sigma Delta Chi, recalled Carla Cantor's conviction. In view of that case—then under appeal—he said, "it comes with particularly bad grace for law enforcement to do the same thing."

But he missed the point by half. Cantor's conviction for impersonating a government official gave the law enforcement officials the very pretext they need for doing so.

Part III

THE STANDARDS OF JOURNALISTS

8. AN OCCUPATION, NOT A PROFESSION

The events happening in the world are as open to all men as the air or sunlight.
— Justice Owen Roberts of United States Supreme Court, dissenting in *Associated Press* v. *United States*, 1945

If anyone who wrote anything could call himself or herself a journalist, the results would be ludicrous. Imagine, Betty Ford writes her autobiography. Is she a journalist? Julia Child pens a cookbook. Is she a journalist? The court writes a decision. Is [the judge] a journalist? The Appellate Division, in a written decision, affirms (or, heaven forfend, reverses) that decision. Are those august jurists journalists? Reductio ad absurdum.
— Justice Sybil Hart Kooper of New York State Supreme Court, distinguishing between the legal rights of journalists and book authors as she refused to quash a subpoena served on an author, December 1978

Many fine men are to be found among butchers, but a certain brutality is inseparable from being a butcher; it goes with the profession. It is worse to be a journalist. . . . If I were a father and had a daughter who was seduced, I should not despair over her; I would hope for her salvation. But if I had a son who became a journalist and continued to remain one for five years, I would give him up.
— Søren Kierkegaard, *Journals and Papers*, 1846

I don't think it is necessary in this day and age for someone to have covered arson, robbery, murder and mayhem on the streets of New York and Chicago to qualify as a journalist.
—Ed Hookstratten, defending the choice of his client Phyllis George as co-anchor of the "CBS Morning News," December 1984 (Ms. George lasted only eight months on the show.)

The casual switching of roles—reporters in the guise of illegal aliens or of prison guards, and law enforcement officials impersonating reporters—forces an examination of what distinguishes journalists from other citizens.

In July 1983, the *New York Daily News* printed a photograph of a man leaping to his death from the Empire State Building. The dramatic photograph was not taken by a staff member but by a tourist with an Instamatic. Fees from its sale exceeded $4,500. "I'm excited to say the least," said the amateur photographer, Genaro Martinez, in an article in the *Daily News* a week after the picture appeared on the front page of the newspaper, "and my wife Linda, is just ecstatic."

All it really takes to sell a news picture is a camera, some luck in being at the right place at the right time and the resourcefulness to find a buyer. Martinez's glee at making money calls to mind one of the least appealing traits of journalists— the fact that its practitioners prosper at the expense of others. But was Martinez a journalist for a day?

The question of who can legitimately claim to be a journalist is not readily answerable. A lawyer is someone who goes to law school for three years and passes a bar examination and pays a license fee. It does not matter if he chooses to hang out a shingle and open an office; even if he does not, he still can call himself a lawyer. I am a law school graduate and a member of the New York bar. I have never practiced law, but I am still considered a lawyer. Sidney Zion, a predecessor of mine at *The New York Times*, practiced law in New Jersey in the 1960s before turning to journalism. He, too, has remained a "lawyer." But after he left his reporting job at the *Times*, and after *Scanlan's Magazine*, where he was an editor, ceased publication, there was a real question of whether he was still a journalist. Zion's status became a central issue in the stories about the person who was identified as having leaked the Pentagon Papers to the *Times*.

On a Wednesday evening in late spring in 1971, Zion went on a radio talk show in New York and said Daniel Ellsberg was the source of the leak. Zion is a man with many friends in public life and in journalism, but some people are rubbed the wrong way by his irreverence, braggadocio and occasional name-dropping. After his disclosure, he was instantly shunned by many journalists who felt he had betrayed the *Times* and other journalists by identifying a confidential source—although by then Ellsberg's identity was a poorly kept secret and was about to become widely known anyway, according to Sanford Ungar's *The Papers & The Papers: An Account of the Legal and Political Battle Over The Pentagon Papers*. By the time Zion went on radio, Ungar said, "the word was out" that *Newsweek* had already found Ellsberg for an interview and that the *St. Louis Post-Dispatch* would report in its edition of Thursday that Ellsberg was the source for the Pentagon Papers.

But Zion was first, and after his disclosure, he was no longer welcome in the *Times'* building and was ostracized at Sardi's, the restaurant that served as a canteen for many *Times* reporters and editors.

A couple of weeks later, *Women's Wear Daily* published Zion's first-person defense: It was a great scoop, said Zion, and "what bedeviled the reporters—and, as I later was to learn, many people outside the media—was the fact that I wasn't working for a paper or a TV station." More than a decade after the incident, in 1982, in his book *Read All About It!* Zion recalled a conversation he had with A. M. Rosenthal of the *Times*, once Zion was forgiven by the paper's top editors and was no longer a pariah. "You had every right to break it," Rosenthal told Zion. "But you put your finger on it. You weren't working for anyone. That should have made no difference, only it did. I never thought of it until you wrote it [in *Women's Wear Daily*], but that was the real reason we all turned against you."

A journalist need not practice his craft every day. A journalist need not be paid for his work. Zion had a story; therefore, he was a journalist. At one level, you are a journalist if you say you are one and publish or broadcast—or try to—somewhere. There is no one to contradict you. As David Rubin, Peter Sandman and David Sachsman accurately note in *Media*, a mass communications textbook: "You become a journalist when you declare that you are one, and you remain a journalist as long as you keep declaring that you are one. It is hard to think of another occupation of comparable importance to society that exercises so little formal control over itself—no entrance requirement, no explicit code of ethics, no system for weeding out the incompetents and the scoundrels."

In the middle 1970s Congress attempted to define who journalists were, but ultimately it gave up. The attempt came as Congress considered drafting a federal shield law to blunt the effect of a 1972 Supreme Court decision, *Branzburg* v. *Hayes*. The Supreme Court had ruled that journalists, like other citizens, must testify before a grand jury about crimes they had witnessed. (In *Branzburg*, the court approved the "traditional doctrine" that "liberty of the press is the right of the lonely pamphleteer who uses carbon paper or a mimeograph just as much as of the large metropolitan publisher who utilizes the latest photocomposition methods.") After that ruling, several states enacted "shield" laws that generally protect reporters from being forced to testify unless the prosecution or defense can prove that the reporter's information is vital and relevant and that all other ways of getting the information have been exhausted. But the efforts in Congress to enact a national "shield" bill faltered, in large part because news organizations were reluctant to let it define who a bona fide journalist was. "There was a problem of definition of the 'press,' or the definition of a 'journalist,' " recalls Richard Schmidt, the general counsel to the American Society of Newspaper Editors. "There were fears expressed by many," Schmidt said, that a proposed shield bill "recognized only those who were employed directly by news organizations and did not cover free-lancers or others."

This problem of definition was one that William Frye, a freelance columnist, grappled with in court in 1983. Frye was sixty-four years old at the time and was close to retirement, but he was fighting for what he regarded as an important issue. He wished to be considered a "professional" so that he could qualify for an exemption from New York City's unincorporated business tax. The tax law was changed in 1971 to eliminate the professional exemption, but it was not until 1978 that Frye was dunned by tax collectors. Frye did not want to pay. At one point as many as 150 newspapers purchased his column on international affairs. By the time his case was first heard in court, in 1983, the number of subscribers to his biweekly column had dwindled to a dozen, some of whom paid as little as $8 or $9 for a column.

In its written brief to the Appellate Division of State Supreme Court in Manhattan—the state's second highest court—the corporation counsel of New York City said that Frye was not at the top of his field. If he were another Walter Lippmann, the brief said, then perhaps he would be entitled to a tax exemption. Frye lost and appealed to the New York Court of Appeals, the state's highest court.

At the oral argument, in May 1984, before the Court of Appeals, the name Walter Lippmann was invoked again. Stanley Buchsbaum, arguing on behalf of the city, said: "I don't think Frye rises to the level of Walter Lippmann."

He was interrupted by one of the judges, Sol Wachtler: "Isn't that terribly arbitrary? What is your criterion? Is professionalism like obscenity—'I know it when I see it'?"

Buchsbaum replied, "No journalist is a professional within the meaning of the tax law."

Frye was insulted by this. "It would be presumptuous to claim to be in the same category as such a giant," he told me. "But I don't think you have to be a Walter Lippmann to be a professional." Frye, a short, energetic man, was also irritated by the way he and the field of journalism had been demeaned by the lawyers for New York City.

In its brief submitted to the Appellate Division, the city cavalierly put down journalists in general: "References in common parlance to 'professional journalists' are like references to 'professional golfers' or 'professional tennis players.' To a large extent, the adjective is applied to show that they earn money for the performance of their activities. To the extent that it indicates that they perform at a higher level of proficiency, it is not unlike a reference to an extremely able automobile mechanic as a professional."

"Professional" has become a word so overused that much of its meaning has disappeared. Besides professional wrestlers, singers and football players, there are professionals who are licensed. In New York State, for instance, there are about two dozen types of licensed occupations, including doctors, dentists, masseuses, acupuncturists and engineers. In New York, certified shorthand reporters are licensed, while reporters for newspapers are not, and indeed cannot be licensed because the Constitution prohibits it.

The concept of the professional dates back to the Middle Ages—about A.D. 1200—when the word "profession" referred to the public vows made by a person entering a religious order. By the Renaissance, the word had come to mean an occupation in which someone *professed* to be skilled. The term was applied to the three "learned" occupations—divinity, medicine and law —because they adopted the institutional mechanisms of a profession—training, testing, and social responsibility.

In the Frye case, the Appellate Division had its own idea of professionalism. In ruling for the city by a three-to-two vote, the court found that Frye was not engaged in a profession: "He did not complete the course at a specialized school of journalism, nor obtain a degree therefrom. He does not have, nor is he required to have, a license to indicate that sufficient qualifications have been met prior to engaging in his occupation. Nor is he subject to any disciplinary body which has power to supervise his activities. There is no organized body of rules, standards of conduct or ethics to which he is required to conform. . . There are no recognized standards for entry into the field of journalism, and no agency which passes upon one's qualifications to be a journalist." This ruling, in August 1983, created surprisingly little stir in the press, which paid almost no attention to it.

Frye continued with his personal crusade, and with the help of Herald Price Fahringer, a well-known lawyer who also represented Larry Flynt and Claus von Bulow, he appealed to the State Court of Appeals. In his brief, he pointed out that the Court of Appeals had already held that an orchestra leader and a landscape architect were "professionals."

He also pointed out an apparent anomaly. In its shield law, New York State affords "professional journalists" the same right to privileged communication that is enjoyed by doctors, lawyers and clergy. In addition, Frye said, the United States Census Bureau considers journalists to be professionals, along with artists, architects, judges, librarians, social workers and social scientists.

New York City, which had not even bothered to send a lawyer to argue its case before the Appellate Division, crafted a much tighter argument before the Court of Appeals. The issue, the city said, had nothing to do with professionalism. Rather, the case dealt with whether the tax collector had exceeded his discretion in fashioning the regulations that Frye complained about.

In contrast to the lower court, the Court of Appeals generously acknowledged Frye's attainment of "pre-eminence in his field." But this was a pyrrhic victory, for the court said his level of accomplishment was not relevant. It chose to rule on a much narrower issue than the lower court. The issue, the Court of Appeals said, is "not whether in any sense of the word he can properly be referred to as a 'professional,' " but whether he fit the New York City tax collector's interpretation of one. The court concluded that he did not.

■

In order to practice, doctors must have a degree from an accredited medical school, architects must graduate from architecture school and lawyers must have law degrees. In the Frye case the Appellate Division noted that Frye had worked on the *Crimson*, the school paper at Harvard (Walter Lippmann, also a Harvard graduate, had never been invited to join it) but as impressed as the court was by this youthful accomplishment, this experience did not compensate for the fact that Frye had not taken journalism courses.

When Frye was in school, Harvard College offered no journalism courses. (It does not to this day.) In fact, very few schools did. Now, a great number of people in this country study journalism, or as some academicians prefer to call it, mass communications. Enrollment in three hundred undergraduate and graduate programs in 1984 approached 100,000, up more than fivefold from twenty years ago. But these numbers are somewhat deceptive in that up to half of these students study advertising and public relations. Only a handful of the undergraduates I taught at the college of journalism at the University of Florida in 1983 and 1984 showed the vaguest interest in becoming journalists.

Still, the journalism schools train most people now going into journalism. One recent study showed that nearly 85 percent of all beginning newsroom staff members came from journalism schools. These figures, too, are somewhat misleading, for those at the highest levels of journalism ordinarily have had a quite different background. Most of the best journalists in the country did not attend journalism schools at all, and some of the best were rejected from what is considered to be the country's premier journalism school—the Columbia University Graduate School of Journalism. Warren Phillips, who became managing editor of *The Wall Street Journal* when he was thirty years old and is now chairman of the board of Dow-Jones, its parent company, applied to Columbia and was rejected. (He currently sits on the board of trustees of the university.) Joe McGinniss, the author of *Fatal Vision*, applied in 1964 and was rejected. David Broder of *The Washington Post*, one of the country's foremost political reporters and analysts, did not get into Columbia either. He applied after receiving an undergraduate degree from the University of Chicago in 1947. "They told me that the Chicago B.A. did not satisfy their entrance requirements and I would have to take more undergraduate courses at Columbia or elsewhere before I would be considered," Broder said. "That ended it."

Despite their popularity, journalism schools still are in search of respectability. In 1938 Robert M. Hutchins, president of the University of Chicago, called them "the shadiest educational ventures under respectable auspices." Forty-five years later, in a booklet published by the Orwell Press, Irving Kristol, co-editor of *The Public Interest* magazine, was equally devastating:

"Now, of course, we have schools of journalism. Most publications these days—not all, thank God—recruit from schools of journalism. This means they are recruiting from the bottom 40 percent of the college population since, on the whole, bright students do not go to schools of journalism. . . . To the degree that the media recruit from schools of journalism, they are recruiting young men and women who don't think very well and who don't have the habit of thinking. When you go out and talk to young people in television, radio or newspapers outside New York (there the major publications can recruit the cream of this journalistic community), you find yourself facing a kind of invincible mindlessness."

His criticism is exaggerated, but even journalism educators recognize they have a problem. "The general state of journalism and mass communication education is dismal," concluded a 1984 report prepared by the faculty at the school of journalism at the University of Oregon and its then dean, Everette Dennis, who was also president of the Association for Education in Journalism and Mass Communication.

■

Journalism is not a profession in the traditional sense of the word. Nor is it pragmatically possible to consider as a journalist everyone who wishes to be one. At some novelty shops, press cards are available for $2.98, but the purchase of such a card certainly does not transform the buyer into a journalist. If there were not some limitations on who can gather news, then we would have the *reductio ad absurdum* alluded to in the decision of Justice Sybil Hart Kooper, who narrowly construed the definition of journalists, and said that not even book authors who were once daily journalists qualified for protection under New York's shield law. The judge turned to the definition in Webster's Third New International Dictionary, which says a journalist is one engaged in journalism, which is defined as "the collection and editing of material of current interest for presentation through the medium of newspapers, magazines, newsreels, radio or television." This definition seems needlessly narrow; one can as legitimately report through a book as in a newspaper. There have been fresh disclosures in Laurence Barrett's book on President Reagan, in Mayor Koch's book and in countless others.

There have to be restrictions, and it may be that about the only restrictions that affect journalists in a practical way are those relating to convenience. Not every reporter—staff member, free-lance or otherwise—can possibly squeeze into a press box at a football game, or into the congressional gallery or at a press conference at city hall in New York or at a political convention. After the invasion of Grenada, more than six hundred reporters, including many free-lancers and stringers, showed up on Barbados and tried to get seats on the press plane to Grenada.

The difficulty comes in deciding who should make the decision of who receives credentials. Sometimes this is handled by reporters themselves, as with those who decide who may be accredited for the Capitol press gallery. Sometimes accreditation is handled by an individual organization that is holding a convention—like the American Bar Association—or sponsoring an event such as the Olympics. Sometimes it is handled by police departments, and that unfortunately puts the government in the business of deciding who is a journalist.

Wherever there is accreditation, there are unhappy journalists; for example, even in sparsely populated Maine, where space is plentiful and news is not, a dispute over a proliferation of photographers erupted. In 1983 John Patriquin, president of the Maine News Photographers Association, said a necklace press card was necessary to identify photographers: "We are trying to maintain a standard where only real working photographers are involved in a news scene. A lot of amateur photographers are 'ambulance chasers' and we don't want news scenes overrun and spoiled by these people."

In May 1984 I went to the American Society of Newspaper Editors convention in Washington to listen to some panels of working journalists. I was told that I would have to pay $150 because I was not a journalist—I did not have credentials from the Washington Police Department, the Capitol press gallery, the State Department or the White House. I paid.

A key ingredient of the traditional professions is a system of licensing, and journalists almost uniformly reject this as an unacceptable encroachment by government. American journalists are generally critical of countries that, like those in Latin America, require journalists to get government licenses before they can go to work. The feeling is that licensing opens up the possibility of restrictive government regulation. Yet, in many cases in the United States, there is a kind of informal licensing in the form of credentials issued by police departments. The police are interested primarily in security and in controlling people at the scene of a fire or accident, but their cards often take on a greater significance.

In New York, for example, where space is limited and where there are plenty of people who call themselves journalists, the police department is quite tough about issuing press cards. In the early 1980s the department abandoned as unwieldy the practice of relying upon the advice of a committee of journalists in deciding who should be accredited. The department itself now decides.

The card enables the holder to pass police and fire lines and, like the various Washington press cards, has a significant secondary value. Whenever access to a news event is limited, a police card is routinely asked for. It is almost as if these cards possess talismanic powers. Shortly after the Shah of Iran had been overthrown, John Kifner, a *New York Times* correspondent, was sufficiently resourceful to use his New York City police press card to gain access to revolutionary tribunals in Iran.

To be eligible for a working press card in New York, an individual must be: "A full-time employee of a newsgathering organization covering spot or breaking news events on a regular basis such as robbery scenes, fires, homicides, train wrecks, bombings, plane crashes, where there are established police or fire lines at the scene." The working press card enables the individual to cross such lines at these emergency scenes and at public events of a nonemergency nature such as parades and demonstrations.

There are other, less prestigious cards issued as well by the New York police, including a card for free-lancers, who have long had a harder time than staff members in getting credentials. The police also issue a "press identification card." This card does not entitle the bearer to cross police or fire lines, but it does certify that the individual named on the card is employed by a "legitimate" news organization. (In the late 1960s and early 1970s, there were disputes about what that meant; and, predictably, members of the underground, alternative or radical press were denied press credentials.) This card is assigned to journalists who do not normally cover breaking news events. They include sportswriters, film and drama critics, fashion writers, financial reporters and music critics. This credential, according to the regulations, "is issued as a courtesy by the Police Department recognizing a need for official identification." The bearers of such cards are able to supply "proof" they are journalists if they are ever asked.

This scheme comes close to licensing, even though it is not called that. Many more people want to have cards than receive them. For some, the working press card is a badge of honor, and its denial is a serious snub. When I was Mayor Koch's press secretary, the publisher of a monthly magazine whose subject matter was not remotely close to falling within the police guidelines wrote detailed letters directly to the mayor every year, protesting vociferously the policies that denied him a card. He accused the mayor of playing politics in withholding a card from him. This was not in fact so; but given the arrangement in New York City, it is not inconceivable that a future mayor could either grant or withhold a press card, and that truly would be a dangerous licensing scheme.

■

In addition to licensing, another key characteristic of the professions is a code of ethics that can be enforced. Journalism has no single binding industry-wide code as there is in medicine and law; and those journalistic codes that do exist lack punitive provisions. Nonetheless, in the past decade or so, journalists have been busy adopting codes—both industry-wide codes and codes within individual news organizations.

This is part of a broader trend. Robert McKay, a professor at New York University Law School and an authority on legal ethics, has noted a rapid increase in codification of ethical standards since the late 1960s and early 1970s. Such traditional professions as law, medicine, engineering and social work have moved toward greater specificity in their codes.

Individual businesses and other institutions, mindful of the growing concern of the public and of government in the conduct of their daily affairs, have developed internal codes of conduct. Some, like the code of the International Business Machines Corporation, set out important ideals. ("Don't make misrepresentations to anyone you deal with" is an instruction in IBM's Business Conduct Guidelines. "If you believe the other person may have misunderstood you, correct any misunderstanding you find exists.") Most of these codes do no more than define generally accepted minimal standards. For example, door-to-door salespeople have had their own code of ethics since 1970, when the directors of the Direct Selling Association adopted a ten-page code instructing their membership not to "engage in any deceptive or unlawful consumer practice."

Some of the industrywide codes in journalism are as vague and inspirational as that of the Direct Selling Association. An early code was adopted by the American Society of Newspaper Editors in 1923, in the wake of the involvement of the editor of a Denver paper in the Teapot Dome Scandal. That code said, in part: "A journalist who uses his power for any selfish or otherwise unworthy purpose is faithless to a high trust." In the 1920s many individual newspapers adopted similarly high-minded guidelines. They also could be, by today's standards, prudish. The *Seattle Times* code said: "When it is necessary to refer to improper relations between the sexes, the limit permitted in The Times is some such statement as 'The couple were divorced,' or 'The couple separated,' or 'Various charges were made not considered fit for publication in the columns of The Times.' "

The second great push for codification among journalists began in the 1970s, following Watergate. After exposing wrongdoing in the highest places, the press began to examine itself more closely. In 1973 the Society of Professional Journalists, probably the largest organization of journalists, adopted a code whose language echoed the code adopted fifty years earlier: "Journalists who use their professional status as representatives of the public for selfish or other unworthy motives violate a high trust."

Despite the growing number of codes, there is still a deep-seated fear among many news executives and their lawyers that written codes will come back to haunt them in courtrooms. They feel that plaintiffs' lawyers in libel suits would misuse a written code by waving it at the jury. Eugene Patterson of the *St. Petersburg Times* feels it is enough for a paper to subscribe to the statement of principles of the American Society of Newspaper Editors. "By not writing a lot of stuff down, incidentally, we are limiting the contingency lawyer to one cryptic scrap of paper to wave before a libel jury he hopes to sway in his heated peroration," notes Patterson. That threat, I think, is exaggerated, and the trend is toward codification.

The three major television networks have codes, and in the past decade many of the country's largest newspapers and broadcasting stations have adopted codes or guidelines. In the survey I conducted of fifty of the largest newspapers in the country, thirty-seven responded; of those, twenty-seven had a written code of ethics or a written policy regarding conflicts of interest, or else were developing one.

Codes should not be oversold. No code of ethics will stop a reporter who is intent on lying or trading on inside stock market information. But codes can be useful, especially for young journalists, in setting out what situations represent conflicts of interest and what do not, in explaining what plagiarism is, and in setting forth an organization's policy on such subjects as posing, the use of anonymous sources, or the secret taping of conversations.

Without codes, says Louis Hodges, director of the Society and the Professions program at Washington and Lee University, "you're likely to have far worse behavior in the newsroom." Geraldo Rivera disagrees and thinks the code that governs him is a sham. At a conference of investigative reporters in 1984, Rivera set a bad example. He glibly commented: "Who reads it? It's 30 pages. It reads like an insurance policy." He hastened to add: "I'd get an 'F' in journalism school." (In the introduction to the 1982 edition of the ABC News Policy, Roone Arledge, president of ABC News, says: "It now becomes the obligation of every person employed by ABC News to read this guide, reflect upon what it means, remember what it says, and act accordingly. Being ignorant of our policies is as bad as consciously ignoring them.")

In September 1981 William Thomas, the editor of *The Los Angeles Times*, was asked his views of codes of ethics by David Shaw, the media writer for the paper. Thomas said: "We all know we're supposed to be honest. We all know we're not supposed to take free gifts from people who could be perceived as influencing what we do. . . . If you don't know . . . those things when you come here, then you don't deserve to be here. I don't like . . . codes of ethics . . . and other things like that which I think would look like we're denigrating the people we're handing them to. I don't like to be treated like a child . . . and that's what those codes of ethics seem to say to me. . . . It's insulting."

Just a little more than a year later, in November 1982, Thomas distributed a two-and-a-half-page code of ethics to the paper's editorial staff. In a letter to me, Thomas explained his turnabout: "In a nutshell, I changed my mind about an ethics code after one of our senior writers' meetings. The writers made it clear that, regardless of my views on the value of such a code, our reporters wanted one. So we made one."

The Los Angeles Times code is short, to the point and sensible. Staff members are told they cannot write for competing publications or take part in political activities they may be called upon to cover. In addition, "If a staff member has a close relative or personal friend working in a political campaign or organization, the staffer should refrain from covering or making news judgments about that campaign or organization."

On the question of whether to pay to cover events, the code says: "Staff members covering a sports or entertainment event can accept admission or preferred or press box seating. When attending an event upon which you will not report, but is judged by a supervisor to be useful to your work, pay the price and submit an expense report."

Its policy on gifts is:

"1. Shun gifts from news sources or subjects of coverage, except those gifts of insignificant value.

"2. Books or records received for review should not be sold by staffers."

As for junkets, ". . . within the bounds of common sense and civil behavior, staffers should not accept free transportation or reduced rate travel, or free accommodations or meals. Exceptions can occur in such areas as political coverage, when convenience or access to news sources dictate. Again: if there are any questions: ask."

In the study on journalistic ethics he completed for the National News Council just before it went out of business, Charles Bailey, a former reporter and editor at the *Minneapolis Tribune*, asked a rhetorical question: "Given all these existing codes and policies, and knowing that most journalists are already sensitive to the kinds of ethical problems these policies address, is anything more needed?''

His answer is yes. The gap between the admirable sentiments expressed in the codes and the way journalists actually behave is wide indeed. Consider, for example, the freebies and junkets. They continue to be unfortunate facts of journalistic life. For many, these fringe benefits are what make it pay to be a journalist. They supplement the modest salaries most journalists outside of major cities earn. (In 1983, a random sample of editorial personnel at daily and weekly newspapers, news magazines, news services and news departments of radio and television stations showed the median salary of a journalist to be $19,000.)

A look at how journalists were treated at the Super Bowl in 1984 amply suggests the difference between policies of journalists and their practices. In the third week of January 1984, the care and feeding of reporters were major concerns of both the National Football League and the city of Tampa. The football league was employing tightly controlled, sound corporate public relations. Tampa, a blue-collar city once famous for cigars, saw in the writers covering the event a medium to transmit their message about Tampa's progress as a commercial and tourist center. The local people did all they could to keep the out-of-town press happy.

About 2,500 reporters and editors received credentials to the Super Bowl as "working press," although it would be difficult to determine how many of these actually covered the game. Some credentials went to spouses or children or friends of reporters, while some journalists tagged along just to socialize. In the week leading up to the game, there was not much to report on. The attempt to equate football with war is probably most evident during the week that precedes the Super Bowl. Players and coaches employed images of injury and battle. Each team occupied a camp, which although not armed was surrounded by exceptionally tight security. Access to the players was limited to a very few, and the public, including journalists, was not welcome at the practice sessions. These drills were mostly designed for players to limber up, but—who knows?—a team may be working on a new play, and coaches, like good commanders, must be vigilant about spies. As is the custom of the NFL, only two pool reporters, who were selected to represent all other reporters, attended practice.

Their dispatches were ordinarily bland and uninformative.

At the end of one practice before the 1984 Super Bowl in Tampa, Tom Flores, the coach of the Los Angeles Raiders, was quoted in the pool report as saying, "It was a very physical practice, which shows you how important this game is." Not much news there. At the conclusion of another practice, Joe Gibbs, coach of the Washington Redskins, praised the security arrangements at the University of South Florida, where his team was quartered. "It's far better than it was in Los Angeles last year," he said. "We were surrounded by buildings last year." More news there. The pool report that day noted that security agents of the National Football League had found four young men taking pictures of the practice from a building on the college campus, 500 yards from the field. With the cooperation of the local police, the NFL security men confiscated the film.

One detail that was omitted from this report appeared on the front page of the *Orlando Sentinel* the next day: One of these young men was a photographer for that newspaper. In an interview, he said he was merely trying to take some feature photographs of students looking at the practice through binoculars. David Burgin, the editor of the paper, was indignant, seeing ominous First Amendment implications in the actions of the National Football League. "It's an absolute outrage, a Gestapo tactic," he said. "My best guess is that some NFL operative with the intellect of a woodpecker has figured out that what was good for news photographers in Grenada is good for news photographers at the battle of Tampa Bay." After his complaint, the NFL returned the film to the newspaper. Having won on the principle, the photographer quickly exposed the film to the light. (History has a way of repeating itself. In 1985, a few days before the Super Bowl, *The* [Oakland] *Tribune* ran a page-one story under the headline "Tribune spy sees Dolphins at work." An Oakland reporter had briefly penetrated a secret practice session of the Miami team before he was hustled away by an NFL security man.)

After the Orlando incident, the feelings of the league were bruised. "We provide all sorts of services for the press," said Jim Steeg, the special events director of the NFL. "We provide an open bar for sportswriters. We get accommodations, cars and meals for them. We don't ask much."

In return the NFL ordinarily gets a pliant press corps that accepts the Super Bowl on the NFL's terms. "It's like being in this fur-lined intestine," said Mark Heisler of *The Los Angeles Times*. "You're very comfortable, they're very efficient. You just follow everybody around. You're in their hotel, their buses, their press conferences. They have you totally surrounded. They take good care of you. There is no possibility of enterprise. Of course, it's an open question just how many of us are actually aching to get some real enterprise."

Reporters were wined, dined and entertained, in the open and almost brazenly. There were free passes to Tampa Bay Downs, St. Petersburg Derby Lane and Tampa Jai Alai. The St. Petersburg Beach Area Chamber of Commerce offered the visiting press a cruise, entertainment and meals. Walt Disney World, which often invites reporters as nonpaying guests, provided bus transportation and tickets to its theme parks seventy miles away.

One afternoon, 175 sports figures, celebrities, journalists and corporate executives played in the twelfth annual NFL golf tournament, an event underwritten by the Warner-Lambert Company, the health products and pharmaceutical concern. In each fivesome, there was one "celebrity" and one journalist along with executives from Warner-Lambert or people whose business was being courted by Warner-Lambert executives.

The most lavish event honoring the visiting journalists was staged by the NFL on the Friday before the game. This annual invitation-only party has such a high reputation that tickets to it were being scalped. There were reports of people offering $100 for an invitation to enter an exposition hall that had been transformed into a colorful indoor circus complete with clowns, high-wire acts, wagons of circus animals, stilt walkers and magicians.

Most of these perquisites were accorded only to the "official" Super Bowl press. For several days, after telling Tampa and NFL functionaries who I was and that I wished to observe the press operation for a book I was working on, I was unable to obtain credentials or any party invitations. Only through the last-minute intervention of friends did I receive an invitation to one party and a precious credential—a tiny pewter pin bearing the Roman numerals XVIII and the graven image of Tampa Stadium. This pin allowed me to walk past special security guards into the press room in the Hyatt.

It was therefore with some amusement that I picked up the *Tampa Tribune* the day before the game to read a story that referred to me. Barbara Casey of the Super Bowl Task Force, whom I had spoken to twice, was discussing those who had ingeniously tried, but failed, to get credentials. The article said that one telephone call to Casey came from "a Tom Goldstein, a University of Florida student, who gave it the good ol' college try for Super Bowl Press tickets. He said he needed them because he was a journalism student."

At the party I attended, journalists rubbed shoulders with state politicians at Busch Gardens. It was paid for by Budweiser, the owner of the park, and its host was Florida's Governor Bob Graham, a politician who is quite at home with the press—he is the half-brother of the late Philip Graham, onetime publisher of *The Washington Post*. (In 1985, California Governor George Deukmejian was the dinner host to more than one thousand reporters, who were entertained by live country music and the San Francisco 49ers Gold Rush cheerleaders.) In Florida, Governor Graham chose the day after his party as one of his "workdays"—a gimmick whereby he periodically spends a day doing something that other Floridians do. That day he chose to shovel elephant manure at the theme park. His picture was carried in newspapers around the state, many of whose reporters had attended his party the night before.

At the party the master of ceremonies was Tom McEwen, the sports editor of the *Tampa Tribune*. McEwen had recently been criticized by the *Columbia Journalism Review* for having lobbied Florida legislators for an environmental study exemption that would have given the lead to Tampa in its race with St. Petersburg to build a stadium in order to attract a major league baseball team. When they left the party, the thousand guests were given booty: a sampling of Florida fruits—honey, nuts, lime juice, dried mango, seasonings, wine and a jar of strawberry jam with a label saying, "Prepared especially for the 1984 Superbowl XVIII press corps." Afterward, a Budweiser spokesman said to a newspaper reporter that the beer company had sponsored the event "as a good corporate citizen of Tampa" and was not trying to influence the media.

The impact of these activities on journalists was a concern to the *St. Petersburg Times*. In its exhaustive coverage of the pre-game activities, the paper continually pointed out that it was against its policy for staffers to attend such events "unless they have legitimate professional reasons." Then, said Mike Foley, assistant managing editor, "we find some way to pay for our share."

Many other publications have written policies forbidding their staffs from accepting gifts. Probably the most absolute position is taken by *Consumer Reports*. In its promotional literature, the magazine says: "We *don't* accept any free samples. We buy what we test at retail, just as you do."

It is generally believed by journalists that there has been a decline in the blatant freeloading habits of the press. In one survey, conducted by Ralph Izard of the Ohio University School of Journalism in 1983, nine of ten managing editors at newspapers and eight of ten news directors at television and radio stations said they would rule out the acceptance of all but token gifts. In his study, Charles W. Bailey concluded that "the bad old days of blatant free-loading by news people are definitely a thing of the past." He noted that fewer sportwriters ride free on team planes, get paid to write for league magazines, or earn money on the side as official scorers, and fewer fashion editors get their clothes wholesale. "I haven't gotten a Christmas present of a bottle of booze in twenty years," says Benjamin Bradlee of *The Washington Post*.

Even with this new ethical sensitivity, there still are many occasions like Super Bowl week when journalists accept free items and services from sources. While many publications forbid press junkets—trips by journalists whose travel and other expenses are paid for by the news source, rather than the newspaper or television station—they, too, are still durable fixtures. As late as 1984 some large newspapers, including the *New York Daily News*, accepted free or subsidized trips for travel stories. In response to a survey, editors of the *Daily News* said they could not meet their budget if they did not accept such trips. "Collectively," said Charles Novak, corporate communications manager for United Airlines, in an essay on junkets, "the airlines get more requests than we could ever wish to honor."

Some smaller publications accept junkets on the grounds of poverty—if they did not accept the free trip, they could not cover the story. It would seem that most, if not all these stories, could safely be left uncovered. In November 1983, for example, Filenes department store of Boston arranged and paid for a trip for twenty-seven reporters in the New England area to spend a day in New York, where they ate at an expensive restaurant and went to the theater. The junket was designed to promote the store's Christmas catalogue, and there was a fashion show on the train trip down.

"You'd never guess these lithe delicately stepping models

were on a train . . . as they showed off the glamorous costumes from the amazing catalog" is how the story began in *The Enterprise*, a newspaper in Brockton, Massachusetts, with a circulation of just under 60,000.

A more serious matter is the propaganda trip. In August 1982, when public opinion was shifting against Israel, Michael Kinsley, then editor of *Harper's Magazine*, was invited along with several other journalists on an Israeli-government-sponsored trip to inspect conditions in Israel and Lebanon. Donald Petrie, then chairman of the board of *Harper's*, did not find out that Kinsley was going until the morning of his departure, and Petrie tried to stop it. He even had Kinsley paged several times at Kennedy Airport, trying to get him to change his plans. Kinsley did not speak to his boss and went on the trip. He was fired when he returned. Kinsley protested. Petrie later relented, and instead temporarily suspended the editor. Petrie's position was that Kinsley had needlessly compromised his and the magazine's objectivity by accepting a gift from the Israeli government. *Harper's* ended the year with unspent money in the budget allocated for travel.

"There are two rules that apply to *Harper's*," said Petrie, a lawyer and a partner in the investment banking firm Lazard Frères & Company. "First, *Harper's* does not solicit or accept money from people it plans to write about. And second, *Harper's* does not write about people whom it has accepted money from."

Uriel Savir, the press secretary in the Israeli Consulate in New York in 1984, said it was part of his job to "encourage journalists to go to Israel," and although tours are government-sponsored, journalists "will not only see government people." The preference of the consulate is for the publications to pay, although this frequently does not happen.

Writing about his junket nearly two years later, Kinsley said: "It's reasonable, for example, to hold newspaper reporters to a more fastidious standard than writers who are presenting opinion labeled as such. It's not that reporters can actually achieve the pristine blankness of mind (called 'objectivity') that is the conceit of their calling. Rather, it's that reporters must obscure their biases, whereas opinion writers are paid to display them for public assessment. . . . Of all the things that made it difficult for me to be clear-minded about the war in Lebanon, who was paying for my airline ticket loomed very small." Furthermore, and quite properly, Kinsley, who by that time had left *Harper's* of his own accord for the *The New Republic*, said: "Anyone who goes on a propaganda junket like mine to Israel should reveal the nature of the trip when writing about it."

Yet he obscures the central issue. The journalistic presumption should be against free trips. That presumption may be rebutted in certain situations. For example, there are some countries where journalists can travel only as guests of the government. Or a free-lance writer may have little or no money and may be able to get abroad only through the largesse of a foreign government, in which case this should be mentioned in an article. Neither applied to Kinsley's trip. He simply should have paid before he left.

In the past decade, when concern among journalists about freeloading and junkets has intensified, another less salutary phenomenon has also been apparent: The number of prizes available to journalists has grown substantially. While the intention of at least some of the givers of these awards is to encourage excellence in journalism, the awards also have a corrupting effect on news gathering. Somehow, the description of the author as "award-winning" is magically supposed to transform ordinary prose into something transcendent. But "award-winning" has become a debased description. In return for a plaque or a certificate or money, many respected journalists allow themselves to be manipulated. Too many public and private organizations use contests to stimulate coverage of their products or special interests.

At a time of heightened ethical sensitivity, journalists have become increasingly prize-happy. Each year, *Editor & Publisher* issues a directory of journalism awards. At the end of 1984 it was more than fifty pages long, listing several hundred contests, compared with 150 contests listed a decade earlier. During this period, some of the more dubious contests have disappeared. For example, no longer can a photographer win money for taking pictures of people smoking cigars. The advertisement of the Cigar Institute of America that solicited entries used to say, "Put a cigar in your photograph, and you might win $1,500." In 1969 the winning entry showed a professional football player smoking a cigar while warming the bench; the runner-up entry depicted a bathing beauty puffing away.

But more than enough awards have been added to take up the slack. Prizes are given by associations of doctors, lawyers and truckers, by travel associations, insurance agencies, shoe firms, dog-food manufacturers, religious groups and science organizations. There are Golden Hammers from the National Association of Home Builders and Golden Carnation awards for articles on nutrition presented by the Carnation Company. Those who write about the virtues of Las Vegas as a place to visit are eligible for the Frank Johnson Memorial Travel Writer Award. The American Osteopathic Society Award provides cash for articles about osteopathic services.

The richest individual awards, of $10,000 each, are the World Hunger Media Awards, established in 1982 to "encourage, honor, and reward those members of the media who have made significant contributions in bringing public attention to the critical issues of world hunger." They are underwritten by Kenny Rogers, the singer, who has reaped great personal publicity from his generosity. (The prizes have been presented at a ceremony at the United Nations.) In addition to the cash, the winner, in a grotesque gesture, receives a sterling silver spoon specially designed by Cartier.

With all these awards floating around, some news organizations are unsure about what to do. Some refuse to enter contests in which the judges are not journalists. Some will not enter contests where the name of the sponsoring organization or interest group appears in the title of the competition. For example, *The Philadelphia Inquirer* did not enter the Champion Media Awards for Economic Understanding, a popular contest with business writers with a total of $105,000 in prize money underwritten by the Champion International Corporation, a large paper and building products company. (Late in 1984, the name of the awards was changed to the Champion-Tuck Awards—the awards are administered by the Amos Tuck School of Business Administration at Dartmouth College.)

The problems with many of these awards are clear. Journalists have no business accepting cash prizes from groups whose activities they report on; this approaches bribery. In addition, some contests distort the news process. Interest groups do not generally give awards to critical stories. A writer saying nasty things about Las Vegas is not going to win the travel-writing award.

Even highly respected prizes subtly affect journalists' behavior. The rationale of the American Bar Association's Gavel Awards, a contest judged by lawyers, is to lead to an improved understanding of the law. Reporters who cover legal affairs generally covet them. In 1983 there were seventeen winners, and they were given a cocktail party the night before the award ceremony in Atlanta. At a special luncheon, each winner was introduced to the audience. Had they not won the awards, some of these reporters would not have gone to Atlanta. Once there, they covered some of the proceedings.

Some prizes, like the Pulitzer and George Polk awards for print journalism, the National Magazine Awards for periodicals and the Alfred I. du Pont/Columbia Awards for broadcasters, have panels of journalists as judges. The point of these awards is to recognize superior achievement, which in turn is supposed to stimulate better reporting. But even these awards can distort the news-gathering process because the emphasis on prizes inordinately focuses attention on blockbuster stories. Steady, mature coverage of city hall or the state house rarely wins an award. In the fall of 1984, the Pulitzer Prize board adopted a series of changes in the Pulitzer award structure. This was done, in part, said Robert Christopher, the administrator of the prizes, to reinforce the board's interest in beat coverage, such as reporting on local government.

Too many prizes preoccupy too many journalists. In their book about the Mirage tavern, Zay Smith and Pamela Zekman of the *Chicago Sun-Times* told how a rival editor discovered in advance the broad outline of their upcoming exclusive, but chose not to run a story. That is contrary to what most editors would have done, especially in Chicago, a highly competitive media city. The rival editor, Bernard Judge of the *Chicago Tribune*, did not act out of chivalry. He behaved the way he did out of self-interest. The Mirage was scheduled to run in the beginning of 1978, and if he broke the story in December 1977 and forced the *Chicago Sun-Times* to move up their series to 1977, that might have harmed *his* newspaper. The *Tribune* had just completed a major investigative series on child pornography. According to Smith and Zekman, Judge held off because he "worried that a Sun-Times tavern might prove formidable in awards competition." Therefore, he figured it was best to let the Mirage series be published during the next calendar year.

Neither story won a Pulitzer, the most prestigious award in journalism. The Pulitzers, judged by journalists and administered by Columbia University, come in for their annual share of criticism. In 1984, in *The Wall Street Journal*, press critic

Alexander Cockburn called the Pulitzer Prize process "a self-validated ritual whereby journalists give each other prizes and then boast to the public about them." (A few months before he wrote the column, Cockburn had been suspended indefinitely from the *Village Voice* for accepting a $10,000 grant from an Arab studies organization to write a book.) For months after the Pulitzers are announced, winning newspapers take out full-page advertisements trumpeting their triumphs.

In 1981, after *The Washington Post* had to return its Pulitzer because the winning story, "Jimmy's World," had been fabricated, Bill Green, the newspaper's ombudsman concluded: "The scramble for journalistic prizes is poisonous. The obligation is to inform readers, not to collect frameable certificates, however prestigious. Maybe the *Post* should consider not entering contests."

Three years later I asked Green if he knew if the *Post* or any other newspaper followed his advice. "I don't know of any newspaper that has considered not entering contests since I suggested it. Prizes proliferate. To be fair, I have little argument with contests whose entries are judged by journalistic peers and by others with neutral points of view, although there are too many contests."

Benjamin Bradlee says: "If I had my druthers, I'd get out of the prize business altogether. I know too much about the prize selection process. But you can't do that to reporters. A Pulitzer Prize is a badge they wear."

As insidious as some of them may be, journalistic awards and freebies are not about to disappear. They are ingrained in the larger fabric of society where a premium is placed on perquisites and on receiving tangible recognition and publicity for accomplishment.

The free gifts or services sometimes offered to journalists are clearly distinguishable from the privileges that accompany a journalist's job. These privileges are rooted in the notion that journalists enjoy the protection of the First Amendment. Journalists are considered surrogates of the public, and, in line with this theory, they are entitled to preferential seating in courts of legislative bodies, are allowed to park their automobiles in restricted areas, and often have use of a press room in a public building. Some of these privileges—such as preferential parking spaces—need to be limited. Others—such as exemption from jury service—are being limited.

Until quite recently, many if not most states automatically exempted from jury duty journalists and others considered essential to the daily running of a community. The premise is that their time is too valuable, that they are so indispensable they must be excused from a normal duty of citizenship.

In recent years, though, the movement has been to reduce the categories of exempt occupations. Nonetheless, the latest survey on jury service, conducted by the Conference of State Court Administrators and the National Center for State Courts in 1982, showed that in several states journalists still could be exempt. Across the country, at least forty different occupations have been recognized by legislatures as those that should be exempt from jury service. Journalists keep some odd company. Other exempt occupations include airline pilots, bus drivers, chiropractors, clergy, ferryboat operators, firemen, lawyers, nurses, persons participating in the harvest, pharmacists, police, postal employees, prison guards, school bus drivers, sole proprietors of businesses, teachers, telegraph operators, veterinarians, game wardens and cloistered members of religious orders.

Even in states where they are no longer automatically exempt, journalists can still seek to be excused from jury service after they have been summoned. In the fall of 1983, Arthur Gelb, the deputy managing editor of *The New York Times*, was called for jury duty in Manhattan. Gelb is one of the busiest and most energetic editors at the paper, and he asked to be excused. He told the judge he was a close friend of Robert Morgenthau, the Manhattan district attorney; that, as a matter of fact, he had been a dinner guest in Morgenthau's home the night before and had discussed criminal justice matters; that he was a criminal justice buff and therefore might be biased. "I thought I would never be accepted," Gelb recalled.

Benjamin Altman, then an acting Supreme Court Justice, was presiding. This is what he remembers saying to Gelb: "Newspaper people are supposed to be objective, I was sure he was, and I refused to excuse him. I concluded by telling Gelb that he was the very person all participants were anxious to have on a jury and that he would be ideal." Gelb served, and, he said, found it "fascinating."

Besides exemption from jury duty, other privileges accorded journalists are undergoing scrutiny. Shortly after taking office in 1983, Governor Mario Cuomo of New York ordered that journalists pay for transportation aboard the executive aircraft. His directive was viewed as a courageous act by his aides but received barely any mention in the press. The directive said simply: "Non-state workers not on state business (e.g. members of the press) using the executive aircraft will be required to pay commercial rates for transportation via state aircraft."

Not all privileges accorded journalists have been reexamined, and, as with many practices that start out with a perfectly legitimate rationale, certain journalists' privileges tend to be abused. A blatant example has evolved in New York City with the use of special license plates that allow journalists to park free in certain designated zones. The original purpose was to permit reporters to leave their offices quickly to dash to a scene of a crime or accident or other fast-breaking stories. But this was subverted long ago. So common are NYP (New York press) license plates in New York City that the police department now issues special cards to photographers and broadcasters to display on their windshields while at the scene of a news event.

New York City streets are crowded and congested, and traffic crawls along stretches of Sixth Avenue in Manhattan at less than ten miles per hour. Nevertheless, at six locations on the upper part of the avenue, a lane has been set aside for cars owned by journalists and media executives. The three major television networks have executive offices in this area; so do Time Inc. and the Associated Press. Very few journalists in these buildings are ever called upon to use a car to rush to the scene of a news event.

Yet in 1984 nearly fifteen hundred NYP plates were issued by the state of New York to journalists, most of whom work in New York City. Many on the list are executives, editors who stay inside, or reporters who do most of their work by telephone. (Dozens more NYP plates have been issued to journalists with automobiles registered in New Jersey, Connecticut, Vermont and other states, allowing those journalists to park in the specially designated zones as well.)

Parking is very expensive in midtown New York—a monthly parking spot can cost $300, an amount that in other cities could pay for housing. In Manhattan, at least, most reporters, editors and executives who use their cars do so to get to and from work or perhaps to go to the theater at night, thus converting a well-intentioned press privilege to a blatant perquisite.

When I worked as press secretary to Mayor Koch and had

the opportunity to change the system, I gave up in despair after a few attempts. I was advised that I would make too many enemies. Virtually my only contact with one particular editor, who held an important job but was nearly always desk-bound, was to listen to his periodic requests for more NYP spaces in the vicinity of his publication. It turned out that another news outlet had opened an office nearby, and it had become harder for him to find a convenient NYP parking space in the morning. Ultimately, he was successful in lobbying for more spots, even though his area was already unusually congested. City officials felt that it was not worth alienating an important editor.

At one time NYP plates were hard to come by. There was also a time when some reporters did not want such plates because they invited vandalism (cars bearing NYP plates were often mistaken for cars owned by New York policemen, who were far less popular a decade or so ago than they are today).

In theory, according to regulations issued by New York State, NYP license plates are denied to journalists belonging to certain categories—for example, those who work on a "publication which is devoted to a particular type of business or industry only and which would be read by a certain class of people interested in such a topic only." In practice, just about any journalist—or even ex-journalist—who asks will receive these plates.

According to the New York State Department of Motor Vehicles, in 1984, the gray Mercedes Benz belonging to Percy Sutton, a former New York politician who now runs Inner City Broadcasting, a cable television operation, bore a NYP plate. So did the Rolls Royce owned by Earl A. Graves Publishing Inc., a concern whose principal magazine is *Black Enterprise*, a monthly business publication. The 1982 brown Maserati owned by Forbes Inc., which publishes the business magazine, had an NYP plate. The black 1983 Jaguar, that belongs to (in computer print-out talk) "Straight; Arrow" bore an NYP plate. Its address was listed as 745 Fifth Avenue. That is the address of *Rolling Stone* magazine, which once had a book division named Straight Arrow Press.

In the television world, Cadillacs belonging to Walter Cronkite and Geraldo Rivera had NYP plates. Network executives also took advantage of the opportunity to have these plates. The Volkswagen belonging to Ed Joyce of CBS News, and the Jaguar owned by Roone Arledge, president of ABC

News and Sports, had NYP plates. Less well-known holders of such plates included William Federici, Gary Lewi, George Douris and Mark Lieberman. In 1984 none was a reporter. Federici, Lewi and Douris were all in the public relations business, and Lieberman worked for a state senator.

Misusing NYP plates is hardly the worst sin a journalist—or former journalist—can commit. But in a time of ethical sensitivity, the continued use of these plates suggests an attitude that journalists could well do without. If newspapers and radio and television stations wish their workers to have cars available at work, the companies should reimburse their employees for off-street parking. Otherwise, journalists should pay, just as most other people do.

9. INSIDE STORIES: WHAT THE PUBLIC ISN'T TOLD

. . . It would be a good thing if all of us who read the newspapers—and that means pretty nearly everybody—knew enough about newspaper organization and methods to be better judges of the credibility of the news. I should like to see lectures on "How to Read the Newspapers" given in colleges and schools and elsewhere. It is as essential for the citizen of this day to be able to read the morning paper with a discriminating eye—to be able to distinguish the A.P. dispatch from the special correspondent's forecast of conditions, and the fact story from the rumor story, and to be able to take into account the probable bias of the paper and make allowance for it—as it is for a lawyer to learn to assess the value of evidence.
— Frederick Lewis Allen, "Newspapers and the Truth," *Atlantic Monthly*, 1922

The press prides itself—as it should—on the vigor with which it excoriates malefactors in government, unions and business, but its own inadequacies escape both its censure and its notice. . . . The real long-range menace to America's daily newspapers lies in the unshatterable smugness of their publishers and editors, myself included.
— A. H. Raskin, *The New York Times Magazine*, 1967

For the most part [Raskin's] complaint is as true today as it was in 1967. By and large, the press is still a powerful institution dedicated to the critical examination of every powerful institution but itself.
— David Shaw of the *Los Angeles Times* in a speech to the Citizen's Choice National Commission on Free and Responsible Media, 1984

J ournalists are quite aware of how poorly they explain themselves. In a survey of publishers, editors and reporters,
Philip Meyer, of the school of journalism at the University of
North Carolina at Chapel Hill, concluded that many journalists
believe their current image problems could be overcome if only
the public understood the underlying need for journalists to
behave the way they do. The survey, which was published in
1983 and received scant media attention, found that two-thirds
of the reading public is served by journalists who agree with
this statement: "Public concern over newspaper ethics is
caused less by the things newspapers do than by their failure
to explain what they do."

How well the media explains itself goes to the root of its
credibility: If the press does so poorly at explaining itself, how
is one to judge how well it does in explaining others?

In fact, there is very little formal analysis and criticism of the
media, and what there is has come relatively recently. In the
early 1970s, a few years after Gay Talese's book about *The New
York Times*, *The Kingdom and the Power*, became a great success, the author recalled that few publishers showed any interest when he first broached the subject of the book, and one
publisher turned down his request for an $11,000 advance, a
modest sum even then. In those years, press criticism was
confined largely to *Time* and *Newsweek* and a few journalism
reviews aimed at insiders.

More recently, "Inside Story," a critique of the media, enjoyed a few seasons on Public Television. Periodically, network
television, as in ABC's "Viewpoint," will turn its eye inward,
but not on a sustained basis. A handful of major newspapers,
including *The New York Times*, *The Washington Post*, *The Los
Angeles Times*, *The Wall Street Journal* and *Newsday*, have
staff members assigned full-time to cover the media. There are
only thirty or so newspapers with ombudsmen, but not all of
them comment in print about press issues.

The amount of press criticism is small; more importantly, the
quality is spotty. There are no A. J. Lieblings writing now.

■

News organizations are in a sense semipublic, similar in
many ways to utilities or to lawyers. They have a public responsibility, and like utilities and lawyers, they tend not to explain
fully how they make decisions. They do not explain why stories

are placed where they are, why some stories are emphasized and others are not. The "news" is imprecise. It is made more mysterious by traditions of which the public is only dimly aware.

The internal dynamics of the news business sometimes has little to do with informing the public. For example, a story that is an "exclusive" may receive more attention than one that several news organizations shared, even if the underlying event is of neither more nor less interest.

On a Sunday late in January 1984, in some editions of *The New York Times*, a story with no immediate news peg appeared in the top right-hand column, making it the most important story of the day. (In other editions, it appeared in the top left-hand column of the paper—that is called the "off-lead" of the paper and is considered to be the second most important story of the day.) The story told how a federal appeals court earlier in the month had stopped the publication of an opinion by another court. This prior restraint was an interesting issue, to be sure, but it seemed a bit stale and the court, in the Midwest, was not a court that the *Times* usually pays much attention to.

The story was given the prominence it received in the *Times* for several reasons. It was a slow news week and not much had happened Saturday. The story dealt with an issue—the First Amendment—that is a preoccupation of the *Times*. And although the story was almost a month old and had been alluded to briefly in at least one Colorado paper, it was still an exclusive for the *Times*.

The newspaper got the story through no initiative of its own. The information was scheduled to appear the following day in a story in *The National Law Journal*, a weekly trade publication. The *Journal* touted its exclusive to the *Times*. "We wanted it out because it is good for the magazine, of course, but my feelings for the First Amendment were such that I knew we had to get this out in a way that would have an impact," said Timothy Robinson, editor in chief of the *Law Journal*. For that reason, the story was given by Robinson to two reporters, Stuart Taylor, Jr., a legal reporter for the *Times*, and Aric Press of *Newsweek*—which comes out on Monday, the same day as the *Law Journal*. "I knew if we released it over the wires, it would have gotten 12 inches all over and that would be it," said Robinson, who had reported on legal affairs for *The Washington Post*. "I knew if *The New York Times* realized how important it was, they would give it a good ride. It's something the *Times* is going to be keen on." He knew a front-page story in the *Times* on Sunday, when its circulation is highest, could not be ignored by other papers, and it was not. It was widely picked up and repeated.

■

On matters as seemingly straightforward as nomenclature, news organizations speak in confusing codes, failing to clarify who does what. In television, for example, audiences are misled about how news programs are put together. Mike Wallace, who appeared as the correspondent on the 1982 CBS documentary about Vietnam, was not integrally involved in its production. He spent less than three weeks on a show that took more than a year to make. The documentary was chiefly reported, written and edited by George Crile, who was called simply its "producer." "I've felt for a long time that titles like 'producer' and 'executive producer' are misnomers," Don Hewitt, executive producer of "60 Minutes," told *The New York Times*. "I'm really more an executive editor than an executive producer. The man we call a producer is really a reporter." But ordinarily producers do not appear on camera.

Similarly, at newspapers, the question of accountability is clouded because terminology varies from paper to paper. At many papers, including *The Orlando Sentinel*, *The Buffalo News* and *Newsday*, the editor is the highest-ranking person with full-time responsibility for the news operation at the paper. Many papers have no one with that title. At some papers, including *The Wall Street Journal*, *The Philadelphia Inquirer* and *The Miami Herald*, the editor is the individual who runs the editorial page. At the *Minneapolis Star* and *Tribune*, *The Washington Post* and *The New York Times*, it is the executive editor who is the highest-ranking news official. At some papers the executive editor plays a subordinate role. At *The Detroit News*, the editor is the top person in the news department, and he supervises an executive editor. Across the street, at the *Detroit Free Press*, the highest-ranking position is executive editor. Beneath him is the editor. Of course, one can read a newspaper in ignorance of who holds these positions, but just as a byline lets the reader know who is responsible for an individual story, the masthead should let the reader know who is responsible for putting out the paper.

More significant is a failure to explain terminology that the press takes for granted. An example is "off the record." This phrase has often become part of the news itself because the reporter and the source have disagreed over the meaning of the ground rules.

At a breakfast in January 1984, Jesse Jackson let down his guard with Milton Coleman of *The Washington Post* and a black reporter for *The New York Times*, and referred to Jews as "Hymie" and to New York as "Hymietown." Jackson prefaced his remarks by saying: "Let's talk black talk." Writing later in the *Post*, Coleman explained:

"That is a phrase that Jackson often uses to talk on what reporters call 'background,' one of several mechanisms used when sources want or are willing to tell something to a reporter but don't want to be identified. In print, those comments come out as information from an unnamed source, the pronouncements of a 'senior official' or as 'private conversation.' But the assumption on both sides, unless some other arrangement is made explicitly clear, is that the substance of the conversation will someday find its way into print.

"I don't know what Jackson says to white reporters when he wants to talk on background. But with me and other blacks, he has placed it in a racial context: 'Let's talk black talk.' I understood that to mean background, and I assumed that Jackson, an experienced national newsmaker now running for the presidency, knew that no amnesia rule would apply."

Coleman, who had been metropolitan editor at the *Post* when it ran "Jimmy's World," did not write about Jackson's remarks himself. He related the incident to another *Washington Post* reporter, who included it in the thirty-seventh paragraph of a fifty-two paragraph story on Jackson's relations with the Jewish community: "In private conversations with reporters, Jackson has referred to Jews as 'Hymie' and to New York as 'Hymietown.' "

For two weeks, as the remark ballooned into a major campaign issue, Jackson denied having said it, and then when he finally apologized, he gave a dishonest explanation of what had happened: "At first I was shocked by the press interest in private conversations apparently overheard by a reporter."

Jackson had ignored a cardinal reality of public life: If you do not want something repeated, do not say it to anyone, especially a reporter, in the first place.

"Government officials who genuinely wish to keep a secret will begin by not discussing it with any reporter, regardless of the ground rules," said William Greider, Washington editor of *Rolling Stone*, who became the center of an earlier highly publicized Washington controversy over sources and ground rules.

While assistant managing editor for national news at *The Washington Post* in 1980 and 1981, Greider had interviewed David Stockman, director of the Office of Management and Budget, for nine months "off the record," just before he took office and during his first months there. Greider's understanding of their agreement was that the particulars of the conversations would be reported later. In the long article Greider wrote for *The Atlantic* late in 1981, Stockman's candor was remarkable in that he suggested that some of the Reagan economic policies he was publicly backing were unworkable. "None of us really understands what's going on with all these numbers," he said at one point. The article embarrassed the Reagan administration and delighted its political opponents.

Greider was castigated by some of his colleagues for betraying his own newspaper and not reporting Stockman's comments there. (In fact, much of what he wrote in his magazine article had already appeared piecemeal in the *Post* and other newspapers. Also, it is doubtful that Stockman would have been as forthcoming had he been talking for immediate publication.) In an interview with Laurence Barrett of *Time* magazine more than a year after *The Atlantic* article appeared, Stockman said, "We never did have a clear understanding on the ground rules. . . ." Coleman and Greider both stuck to what they thought the ground rules were. Jackson and Stockman both felt victimized by these rules.

The extensive use of background briefings and interviews is taken for granted by journalists and officials. The justification is that it serves as an antidote to a system by which information is supposed to be released only through official channels. It protects middle-level bureaucrats, and it gives officials the ability to test reaction to an idea or plan. If the reaction is harsh, they can back off and deny what has not been attributed directly to them. To those not on the inside, the Washington code resembles a charade.

In the accepted Washington code, "off the record" means that the public official cannot be quoted either directly or indirectly, and the information may not be used. The "off the record" interview, writes Greider, is still valuable "because it usually provides an unvarnished and relaxed glimpse of what a public official really thinks." The interview educates the journalist and makes him a more perceptive and knowledgeable reporter.

"On background," on the other hand, is taken to mean that the information can be used only if attributed to an unnamed source. When Henry Kissinger engaged in shuttle diplomacy, he insisted on being quoted as "a senior official on the Secretary of State's plane"—a true but intentionally misleading characterization. Background briefings, when properly used, help reporters understand the nuances of a complicated issue and allow them to explain more fully the issue to the public.

In a poll of newspaper editors conducted three years after the "Jimmy's World" episode, many of those who responded felt that anonymous sources were abused in Washington. Sourcing certainly is *confused*, both in Washington and outside it. The code words mean quite different things to different journalists and newsmakers:

• "Backgrounders and off the record are just about the same," Phillip Record told a group of Southern journalists at a convention in 1984. "You can talk about something so long as you don't quote them." Record is associate executive editor of the *Fort Worth Star-Telegram* and president in 1984 of the Society of Professional Journalists, Sigma Delta Chi.

• "If you say, 'Keep this off the record,' that means I don't put it on the news," Chere Avery, the Fort Myers, Florida, anchorwoman, testified at the trial at which her role as government informant was brought out. "That doesn't mean I don't tell someone."

• Don Kowet no longer felt bound by any ground rules once CBS officials criticized his book on the network's Vietnam documentary. He turned over to lawyers for General Westmoreland off-the-record conversations he had secretly taped with a CBS executive. Because of the CBS attacks, said Kowet, the "gentlemen's agreement" that the conversation was off-the-record was voided.

• In its report on leaks relating to the Abscam investigation in 1981, the Department of Justice said: "Interviews with agents and attorneys have indicated, for example, widely divergent views as to the meaning of 'off the record.' The meaning of the term to some is that particular information disclosed to reporters may not be used at all. To others, it is that the information must be confirmed by other sources, without attribution to them. To still others, it means that the information may be used on a background basis without direct attribution. A number have lamented the ambiguity after seeing in print sentiments or information they believed they were conveying in confidence."

The lesson in all this is obvious: Journalists and sources, before they start talking, should make clear in uncoded language exactly what the rules of the conversation are.

■

Not only do journalists fail to explain fully the special rules of their craft; they too often fail to disclose subtle but fundamental conflicts of interest. The press seems unequipped to be forthright about itself even on many simple issues.

In January 1984 a book by Frye Gaillard, Dot Jackson and Don Sturkey was reviewed in the *Charlotte Observer*, which called it "gentle, insightful and important." Gaillard is an editorial writer for the paper. Jackson used to work there as a columnist, and Sturkey was its chief photographer. None of this was mentioned.

Lapses of disclosure spill over into self-promotion. Early in 1984, in the fast-growing national edition of *The New York Times* (the two-section paper that is distributed outside the Northeast), an article appeared about how eight editors, reporters and columnists of the *Times* would speak before public affairs groups in Cleveland and San Francisco as part of a lecture series called "Keeping up with the Times." There was no further explanation. A careful reader might wonder: Why Cleveland and San Francisco? Why a story at all? That same week, a short article in *Editor & Publisher* supplied at least a fragmentary answer. That article began: "The New York Times began a promotional campaign in Cleveland and San Francisco offering reduced subscription rates for its national edition. . . ."

Some of the most egregious examples of self-promotion have appeared in *USA Today*, a national newspaper begun in 1982. The paper has at times been quite lively, but it has also been embarrassingly self-conscious.

To celebrate its first birthday, *USA Today* ran an interview in its regular "Inquiry" feature on the op-ed page with Allen H. Neuharth, chairman of the Gannett Company, the paper's parent company. (I spent the 1983–84 academic year as the Gannett Visiting Professor at the College of Journalism and Communications at the University of Florida. The Gannett Foundation supplied money for an endowment directly to the university. I am grateful that Gannett did so, but beyond being called Gannett Professor, I had no dealing at all with anyone from Gannett, and I am grateful for that, too.) Neuharth was interviewed by a *USA Today* staff member, Peter Prichard. There were no curveballs. Prichard tossed lobs and Neuharth slammed them out of the ballpark.

Prichard: "Since the beginning, some critics have said *USA Today* is not a substantial newspaper, that it has too many short articles—they called it 'McPaper.' Has that criticism changed?"

Neuharth: "I hope and expect we'll always have critics. But in the last six months, the professional criticism of *USA Today* has diminished a great deal. There is more recognition now, by the critics, that *USA Today* was designed to be a different form of daily print journalism. Some of the things for which we were initially criticized are really some of the more popular features with our particular audience. Even journalistic critics are becoming aware that this is a reader's newspaper."

Far too often, in order to get full benefit of a newspaper or television news show, the public needs a scorecard to identify the players and the ground rules. That should not be necessary. Insiders have such "scorecards." They know the nomenclature, such as the subtle difference in meaning between "off the record" and "on background." They know what the code phrases mean. They know which reporter is well disposed to which politicians, and they know which are the pet peeves and pet projects of a particular editor. They know when deals are struck.

There are other, more significant, relationships that shape the news. Most news organizations have a point of view on any number of topics, though most of the time this viewpoint is left unstated. For example, most media in Florida are boosters of a state that is booming. This is fairly obvious from a cursory reading of just about any Florida paper or by watching any of the state's television stations. Whenever they can, they mention the citrus industry favorably (or at least uncritically) and they cloyingly emphasize the weather, especially in winter, when it is cold and wet in the North.

A more subtle and significant example is coverage of First

Amendment issues by *The New York Times*. If a press-law historian a century from now tried to figure out what happened in the 1970s by referring to *The New York Times* (a likely assumption, because the *Times* has been the country's only true "paper of record"—it is indexed and widely available on microfilm), that scholar might receive a distorted notion of the condition of the First Amendment. It was not emasculated. It survived that decade basically intact, and of twenty or so cases involving freedom of the press that were decided by the Supreme Court, nearly half were decided in favor of the media. That would not have been the impression one got from reading the *Times*.

The First Amendment is a motherhood and apple pie issue to the media; and *The New York Times*, as the country's premier paper, has taken the lead in its defense. The *Times* litigated important cases, such as *The New York Times* v. *Sullivan*, which in 1964 restricted the circumstances in which a public official could recover for libel, and the Pentagon Papers case in 1971. The paper also devotes a large number of news stories to First Amendment issues.

The attitude of the paper was summed up by A. M. Rosenthal in a speech to a group of lawyers in 1976: "The latest and perhaps most dangerous threat to the existence of the free press comes from . . . court rulings, high courts and low courts, decisions rippling across the country." In its earnest desire to protect the First Amendment, the *Times* often has overreacted and overplayed stories involving press-law issues. That, I think, has unintentionally been harmful in the long run to the First Amendment. What the *Times* has done smacks of special pleading. It and other major papers are in danger of crying wolf too often—a phenomenon that has been recognized and decried by Floyd Abrams, a prominent First Amendment lawyer who has long represented the *Times*. In a speech in 1984 at the University of Michigan, Abrams said that "so long as the press focuses intently on only one word out of one Amendment of the Constitution—even the First Amendment—it focuses too narrowly. And unpersuasively. And ultimately self-defeatingly."

The *Times* has viewed just about every decision that has gone against the press as a fresh menace to freedom, no matter how inconsequential. In 1978 the Supreme Court, in a case involving the student newspaper at Stanford, permitted surprise police searches of newspaper offices in limited circumstances.

That decision was met with typical alarm by the press, including the *Times*. Yet after the decision, few, if any, newsrooms were subjected to searches.

In its news stories, the paper adopted the same posture it took in litigation. The *Times* felt that it needed to protect the First Amendment, often to the exclusion of other compelling Constitutional interests. For example, a reader rarely got a clear idea of why a defendant's Sixth Amendment right to a fair trial might arguably be a limitation on the First Amendment freedom of the press. A notable example of this fuzzy coverage were the articles written about *Gannett* v. *DePasquale*, a 5-to-4 opinion by the Supreme Court holding that the public, including the press, had no right to attend pretrial hearings—hearings that are held to determine if confessions and evidence were properly obtained and therefore are admissible at trial. The court (in an opinion that was far from a model of clarity) held that the rights of an individual defendant were paramount.

No news story began: "In a victory for the presumption of innocence . . ." The emphasis was on the loser—the press. A summary of the Gannett decision in a news article in the "News of the Week in Review" section of the *Times* began: "It has to be small consolation to the news gatherers of the land that the United States Supreme Court will rule no more until this fall . . ." Allen Neuharth called the decision "another chilling demonstration that the majority of the Burger court is determined to unmake the Constitution."

Amid this hyperbole, a cautionary note was sounded by Harry Wellington, dean of the Yale Law School: "It seems to me that we ought to be slow about drawing the broadest of conclusions, which seems to be the way it has been interpreted by journalists." In fact, over the next several years, the Supreme Court changed its mind in subsequent court decisions and virtually nullified the Gannett ruling.

Cases that have not promoted First Amendment values have sometimes not been covered in the *Times*. For example, the lawsuit brought by Clarence Arrington, whose picture appeared on the front page of the *Times* magazine, was barely mentioned in the paper. More recently, the *Times* failed to cover an arbitration proceeding involving Richard Severo, a difficult but talented staff reporter, who claimed he had been punitively transferred after he chose to have a book that he was writing published by Harper & Row, the highest bidder, rather than by the book publishing company then owned by the newspaper. The Severo case was more than an internal squabble—*Newsweek* called it "a highly publicized controversy." It caught the attention of the national media in the summer of 1984 after a lawyer for the *Times* demanded that Severo turn over copies of his notes used in preparation of stories originally appearing in the newspaper which became the basis of the book, *Lisa H.* This offensive demand by a newspaper on one of its own reporters was not mentioned in the *Times.* Indeed, the first mention of the book in the newspaper came on February 6, 1985, when it was reviewed—negatively.

Judges who are antagonistic to First Amendment interests have found themselves ignored, or at risk of being criticized, in both the news and editorial columns of the *Times.* After Myron Farber, the *Times* reporter, was jailed in 1978 for failing to disclose the identity of a source, I was told by one senior editor to "get" judges for what they had done to Farber; after that, I had the unmistakable feeling that stories I wrote critical of judges received better play in the newspaper than they deserved.

Judges friendly to the First Amendment have generally been treated with deference. One First Amendment champion in particular, Irving Kaufman of the federal appeals court based in Manhattan, has received exceptionally favorable coverage. (In a letter to me, Judge Kaufman bristled at the suggestion that the *Times* "has been protective of me or vice versa." As evidence that this was not so, he referred to a column that I had written in 1979 which he said was "damaging" to him.)

■

On May 4, 1983, the off-lead of *The New York Times* was an exclusive: President Reagan was going to name a commission to study the impact of organized crime in America, and Judge Irving R. Kaufman of the United States Court of Appeals for the Second Circuit had agreed to serve as the commission's chairman. (Close readers of the *Times* should not have been terribly surprised by this. Seven months earlier, the paper carried a five-paragraph item on an inside page saying that Kaufman had been "approached by Administration officials" about this job.)

The article examined Kaufman's background in order to supply the reader with his credentials for the position: "In 1957 the judge, who is known for liberal rulings in such areas as free speech and civil rights, presided at the trial of 20 men who attended an Apalachin, N.Y. conclave of organized crime figures." The article left something out. The Apalachin case was appealed, the convictions of the twenty men were reversed, and Kaufman was criticized for having failed to analyze carefully enough whether the government had made a sufficient case against each defendant. In the carefully coded language of appeals courts, Kaufman's lapse of caution was a serious error.

The omission of what finally happened in this case was perhaps inadvertent, but those who were knowledgeable in the legal community thought it consistent with the way the *Times* has treated Kaufman—gingerly and lovingly, playing up his strengths while overlooking his failings. Over the years Kaufman has received special treatment from the *Times*—treatment accorded to few other public figures. The judge has many friends among those who own and run the *Times*. But his special treatment has less to do with these friendships than with his friendly approach to the First Amendment.

Of course, there is no way of proving this in an evidentiary sense, but it is hard not to conclude that Kaufman's extraordinary access to the pages of the newspaper and the uncritical coverage given his activities are directly related to his court decisions dealing with press issues and his numerous public statements supporting the press. (In his letter to me, the judge wrote: "To say that I have been uncritical of the media is simply an error of those who wrap themselves in First Amendment protection.") The judge is now in his mid-seventies and too old to be considered for a seat on the Supreme Court. But until a few years ago, that was one of his great ambitions. It was a plausible ambition, and the exposure in *The New York Times* did him no harm.

When Kaufman was formally appointed by President Reagan to be chairman of the crime commission in July 1983, a "Man in the News" was written about him. It was a generally flattering profile, but it did contain two negative notes. It mentioned that there were critics of the death sentence he imposed in the Rosenberg espionage trial. It also noted that while many of his "law clerks are intensely loyal to him," others chafed at his sternness and did not complete their year-long clerkships. This was mild—and factual—criticism indeed, but as an indication of how glowingly he was accustomed to being treated, many people at the *Times* felt that even these mild critical notes were a breakthrough in the paper's coverage of the judge. The profile had been sanitized by editors. It carried no byline, a sign to insiders that the author was unhappy with the way it had been edited.

The court on which Judge Kaufman sits is considered the second or third most important appellate court in the country. From 1973 to 1980, he was chief judge of the court, and thus, after the nine United States Supreme Court justices, one of the country's two or three most influential judges. The court is arguably the most important one to deal with communications and First Amendment issues, given the concentration of book publishers, broadcasters, magazines and newspapers in New York. There are usually a dozen judges on the court, and they ordinarily hear cases in three-member panels. Judges are chosen by lot to these panels. But in just about every First Amendment case, Kaufman was a member of the panel. It was never clear whether he somehow sought these cases out or whether statistical odds were defied. In any event, he has consistently emerged as a champion of the free press.

The New York Times was directly involved in only one of these cases, it filed friend-of-the-court briefs in two more, but it benefited from them all in the sense that a victory for the First Amendment helps everyone in the press. In the past decade, Kaufman was involved in several media cases, including:

• *Edwards* v. *The National Audubon Society and The New York Times*, 1977: Kaufman staked out a new area in libel law by ruling that when a newspaper accurately reports defamatory charges made by a responsible organization against a public figure, the publication may not be held liable for its accurate reporting.

• *Herbert* v. *Lando*, 1977: Kaufman ruled that in attempting to prove actual malice (defined in libel cases as knowledge that a statement was false or "with reckless disregard of whether it was false or not"), the person bringing a libel suit was not entitled to inquire into the journalist's "state of mind" during the editorial process. The *Times* filed a friend-of-the-court brief in this case. (After his opinion was overturned by the United States Supreme Court, Kaufman in a speech warned that "the courts are wielding the cutting edge against the press.")

• *Harper & Row* v. *The Nation*, 1983: Kaufman wrote an

opinion upholding *The Nation* magazine's constitutional right to print an article quoting from the memoirs of Gerald Ford before their publication. The *Times* submitted a friend-of-the-court brief in this case on the side of *The Nation*.

During the time that Kaufman was writing these opinions, the *Times* served as his platform. At a time when the newspaper began to cover fewer speeches, it carried articles about his speeches, and it ran news stories on law review articles he had written. He was a prolific writer of nontechnical articles as well, and the *Times* became his chief outlet for these. He became one of the most frequent outside contributors to the paper.

In each of the six years from 1979 to 1984 he had at least one article published in *The New York Times Magazine*, which is a remarkable output, considering that it is difficult for someone who makes his living exclusively by writing to complete one of those articles in less than a month. It made Kaufman the most consistent and frequent nonjournalist contributor to the magazine. Indeed, aside from staff members of the *Times*, there are only a handful of free-lance journalists who sold as many articles to the *Times Magazine* in that period.

In the five-year period from 1981 to 1985, he had another nine articles published on the Op-Ed page—an extraordinarily high output for that page as well. Kaufman has a lot to say, but so do a lot of other judges and public officials and professors. His articles dealt with the insanity defense, juries, juvenile justice, jurisdiction of the Supreme Court. And, of course, the press.

For all this, Kaufman is still best known to many people for his role in the Rosenberg case. In 1951, he presided over the espionage trial of Julius and Ethel Rosenberg, who were charged with conspiring to steal and deliver atomic secrets to the Soviet Union. A jury convicted the couple, Judge Kaufman pronounced the death sentence, and the Rosenbergs were executed in 1953. It is one of the most famous trials of the century, and it is a case that continues to arouse strong emotions.

On June 19, 1983, the thirtieth anniversary of their execution, a long story about the Rosenbergs appeared in the *New York Daily News*. There was no story about the anniversary in the *Times*. (A few years earlier, when Kaufman celebrated his thirtieth anniversary on the bench, there were over the course of several weeks four separate stories or items in the *Times* about Kaufman.)

From 1973 to 1979, the years that I worked at the *Times*,

Kaufman seemed obsessed with his image, as he seemingly sought to erase the negative impression that had formed around his role as the judge who had condemned the Rosenbergs to death. He would call *Times* executives, editors, editorial writers and reporters, to complain about stories dealing with the Rosenbergs and to cajole them to write about his activities on behalf of the First Amendment.

Although I did not cover Kaufman's courthouse, I was assigned many articles about the judge's activities, speeches and administrative accomplishments. No other judge enjoyed such coverage. When Kaufman was involved in an event, normal news judgments were suspended. Often the judge would send several copies of a speech to the *Times* office before he delivered it. That is standard procedure for politicians. But he sometimes asked, and the *Times* often obliged, to have the speech appear in the paper *before* he gave it.

I once wrote a story that appeared on page one that began: "Such is the state of justice in America that, when a Federal appellate court operates on schedule, some of the country's leading lawyers feel that there is cause for a celebration." The special ceremony at the courthouse was arranged by Judge Kaufman. He called me the morning after the story appeared and accused me of nasty sarcasm.

He reacted most bitterly in 1977 when more than one hundred law professors joined in a letter to the House and Senate Judiciary Committees, asking for an investigation of whether Kaufman had had improper out-of-court conversations with the prosecution while the Rosenberg trial was in progress. Kaufman and his most visible defender, Simon Rifkind, a former federal judge and prominent New York lawyer, called the metropolitan desk repeatedly in attempts to kill any story dealing with this. For a while, they succeeded. The story, because it dealt with a legal issue, fell within my beat. I began writing a story. The editors kept on coming back to me with new questions. "One hundred law professors, that's not so many. How many law professors are there in the country?" I pointed out it was extremely unusual for 100 law professors to agree on anything. And so it went. That story never ran, but the letter was finally mentioned as part of another story.

In 1977, before the judge became a frequent contributor to the *Times Magazine*, Dorothy Rabinowitz, a free-lance writer, was assigned to write about Kaufman for the magazine. She later talked about this assignment in several interviews: "The element of the personally ridiculous in Kaufman is very large. He called me 40 times a day. He would read me commendatory letters he had received, and his voice would change and take on a Lionel Barrymore tone." Rabinowitz said that before she wrote the profile, she was unaware of Kaufman's friendship with Arthur Sulzberger, publisher of the *Times*, "but Irving would be the first to tell you as soon as you sat down with him. It was every five minutes." The article was not rejected, but the author said: "I came to understand that there were some things one could not say. I withdrew the article before they [the editors] were put in the position of not behaving well."

The judge could also be interesting, kind and charming. Rabinowitz was struck by his "large-sized humanity." In her opinion, "everyone had outlived the stigma of McCarthyism. Only Judge Kaufman bore this stigma." Despite his occasional criticism of me, I think he liked me, and on three occasions I was approached to work for his organized crime commission. I declined.

The *Times* has been too close to a judge, just as the judge has been too close to the newspaper. This set of relationships suggests how newspapers make decisions about some stories. A newspaper should be writing about special interest politicking like this, not engaging in it. It would make a terrific story. But readers have never been given a chance to read it in the *Times*.

10. NONE OF THIS IS MADE UP: FAKING AND PLAGIARISM

Moralists who do not understand precisely what "faking" in newspaper parlance means will be gratified to know that it is not exactly lying. Between ordinary "faking" and ordinary lying there is a difference that most newspaper correspondents fully understand. The reading public may not be so quick to see the distinction, but the correspondents appreciate it, news editors and managing editors recognize it, and the reading public, maybe, would think itself the loser if the distinction were not made. . . .

What then, is "faking"? the uninitiated moralist asks. If he wants a practical example of it, he has only to look in the news columns of the first paper that comes to hand. Hardly a news story is telegraphed today from one city in the country to another that is not "faked" in some degree. If the story is an ordinary one, the "faking" may be in-considerable. If it is a romance, or a sensation, the chances are that the correspondent has yielded to temptation and the tendency of the time, and that a good part of the charm of his narrative is due to the brilliancy of his imagination and to his skill in making the most of the facts which he may possess.
— William Hills, "Advice to Newspaper Correspondents," *The Writer*, 1887

Few outsiders who have watched news reporting over any extended period of time doubt that anonymous quotes are occasionally cooked up or rewritten. But it is one of the most difficult offenses to prove since it involves the logical impossibility of proving a nonevent.
— Jody Powell, *The Other Side of the Story*, 1984

When Truman Capote died, the kindly ones of the world press

asked me to comment. But I made no comment of any kind to press or television. Now, in the absence of any public statement from me, *New York* claims that I said that Capote's death was "a wise career choice." Is this the new New Journalism? If it wasn't said, make it up; then it will be "fact."
— Gore Vidal in letter to *New York*, November 1984

In the fall of 1982 I wrote an article for *The New York Times Magazine* on New York Senator Alfonse D'Amato, and in it I described in detail something I had never seen. I did so with the full knowledge and encouragement of my editor. In an earlier draft, my lead referred to a reception D'Amato had given at the Senate Caucus Room to celebrate New York Farm Harvest Day. I was there and I described what I saw. Legislators stuffed their faces and their pockets with free food from New York. My editor at first liked this lead.

But the article sat around for a while, it was already winter, and no matter how apt the image of overstuffed lawmakers, I was told that an article that would appear in February 1983 just could not refer to a harvest in the lead. I needed a fresh angle fast. But D'Amato was not available to see me, and Congress was in recess. So after some introductory material, I came up with this passage showing the Senator's perseverance in watching over the preservation of operating subsidies for public transportation:

"D'Amato seldom left the Capitol. Late one night, he pulled off his trousers to preserve the crease, put on sweat pants and managed to get 25 minutes sleep on a couch in his office before he was awakened for a vote on the Senate floor. During another all-night session, aides wheeled in an upright piano they had discovered in the hallway, and for nearly an hour the Senator broke the tension by playing three songs—'Heart and Soul,' 'It's a Sin to Tell a Lie' and 'Blue Moon'—over and over again.

"D'Amato was signing papers in his office one afternoon when the debate on the floor, which he was monitoring on a squawk box, unexpectedly turned to mass transit. It sounded like trouble, and D'Amato grabbed an aide and a jacket and dashed down the long hallway to an elevator, a balding 45-year-old echo of the high-school hurdler he had once been. Minutes later, breathing hard, he rose on the floor to defend mass transit funds. . . ."

I interviewed several people to reconstruct these scenes, and after I talked to them, I spoke briefly with D'Amato. I was confident that something roughly equivalent to what I described had taken place. But I included lots of details—the Senator's folding his trousers, his twenty-five-minute catnap, his playing the songs, his racing down the corridor gasping for breath—that are meant to suggest I was a witness. I was not, and it made me a bit uneasy to leave that lingering impression.

Another problem in writing the D'Amato piece was deciding how accurately to quote him. Like most of us, he does not speak in perfect sentences. Indeed, if politicians were to be quoted directly all the time, it would seem this nation is governed by a group of inarticulate mumblers. One of the nastiest things a print reporter can do to a politician is to quote him verbatim and at length. Not cleaning up a politician's quote by leaving in the "uh's," "y'knows," "I means" and sentence fragments, for example, can be terribly harmful and unfair to him.

This does not mean that language has to be totally sanitized. When I interviewed him, D'Amato repeatedly confused "incredulous" with "incredible," as in: "People find it incredulous that I come from such a poor place." That lapse probably is not as important for readers to know about as his voting record, but I felt it was significant to convey his imperfect command of the language, and I quoted him directly in the article.

■

Admonitions to quote precisely were fixtures in written codes of journalists in the early part of the twentieth century. The rules of *The Christian Science Monitor* warned reporters to "verify all quotations, especially from the Bible, whenever time will permit." The code of ethics of the Kansas Editorial Association condemned "the publication of interviews in quotation unless the exact, approved language of the interviewed be used." The code of the *Springfield* (Massachusetts) *Republican* said: "When people are quoted, the paper is placed in the position of assuring its readers that the quoted passages were literally spoken; consequently, inaccuracy in quotation is unpardonable."

Few of the current written codes express these warnings so explicitly. One that does is ABC's, and the emphasis is on judicious editing: "We need not be a slave to original sequence, but when questions and answers are presented out of actual sequence, the sense of the interview must not be changed. In editing interviews, answers must always follow questions to which they are actual responses"

The New York Times maintains a strict policy on the use of quotations. On February 26, 1984, Ariel Sharon was quoted in the *Times* as having said of southern Lebanon: "That was a center of world terror that doesn't exist anymore." What he actually said—and what the reporter filed—was a bit longer: "That was a center of world terror; that center of world terror doesn't exist anymore."

"Scant difference in meaning," noted *Winners & Sinners,* the in-house critique of the newspaper, a couple of months later, "but a large difference ethically: Quotation marks guarantee the reader that we're transmitting the subject's words, *literally.* If the speaker isn't terse enough to suit us, we can tidy up the prose—but only after removing the quotation marks."

In practice, though, many journalists veer from these proscriptions. It is their general view that they can edit quotations so long as they are faithful to the content, tone and intention of the quote. That seems reasonable enough, especially for those writing longer pieces of journalism or books, and if they disclose what they are doing.

In the afterword to *Indecent Exposure,* the author, David McClintick, said that he "of course does not claim that the dialogue represents the exact words used by the characters." McClintick used several direct quotations in the book, which was a meticulous dissection of the embezzlement of more than $60,000 from Columbia Pictures by David Begelman. In the afterword, McClintick, who was trained at *The Wall Street Journal,* said the dialogue captures "the essence or spirit of the conversation." He says this reconstruction is better than paraphrase: "Human beings do not speak in paraphrase."

In a note appended to *Eleni,* Nicholas Gage's account of how he tracked down his mother's killer, the author wrote that in some instances, where he was given only the "rudiments" of a conversation, he "followed the example of Thucydides: I put into the mouth of the speaker the sentiments proper to the occasion, expressed as I thought he would be likely to express them."

One problem with using quotation marks for something other than an absolutely accurate quote is that it allows the subject of an interview to say afterward: "I did not say that or I was misquoted or I was quoted out of context." Misquoting happens often enough to lend credibility to the disclaimer. Often, words have been changed, even if the interview has been taped. A lot of the mistrust between journalists and those whom they interview could be reduced if journalists were more willing to clear quotations or articles with the subjects of interviews before publication.

In an effort to "rethink accuracy," Loren Ghiglione, editor and publisher of the *News* in Southbridge, Massachusetts, has recommended that reporters sometimes read articles back to their sources. It is not a new idea. In *The Brass Check*, a book that sold 100,000 copies in its first six months of publication in 1920, Upton Sinclair proposed that a law be enacted forbidding a newspaper from publishing an interview without first having received approval from the person who was interviewed.

At a conference of investigative journalists in 1984, Bruce Selcraig, a former investigative reporter in Dallas now working as a Senate investigator, said: "The real reason we don't show stories to sources is that we don't like to be confronted with our own mistakes, we don't like to negotiate about unflattering prose or quotes, and in short, are tired of the story and don't want to do more work. The plusses—you may actually be wrong. Your attempt at fairness looks great in court."

Similarly, in the D'Amato article, I should have been more open about my absence from the scene. I should have signaled that I was writing about something I had not witnessed. Without employing lots of footnotes, attributions and qualifiers, I should have written something like: "Stitched together from interviews with participants, this is what happened."

This approach was spelled out by Anthony Insolia, editor of *Newsday*, in a memorandum to his staff in January 1981, shortly after the release of the American hostages in Iran: "We sometimes take too much literary license in stories by recreating situations and conversations without giving some clue to the source of our information. In one of the hostage stories we reported on a meeting between a hostage wife and Alexander Haig. The report contained dialogue and description. We obviously were not present at that meeting, but nowhere did we indicate who or what our sources were. . . . Since we were not witnesses to the events we were writing about, we should let readers know how the pieces were put together. I'm not suggesting that every paragraph contain 'he said she said' attribution. It is possible to describe sources in an unobtrusive way, in a single sentence so as not to interfere with the writer's pace and style. . . . "

■

There is, of course, a major distinction between a journalist's failure to disclose that he has described a situation he has not witnessed but has good reason to believe actually took place and his describing a situation that he knows never took place.

Nearly a quarter of a century ago, Alastair Reid, a *New Yorker* writer, fabricated a scene. In a "Letter from Barcelona," he described Spaniards sitting in "a small, flyblown bar," openly jeering a television speech by Francisco Franco. In fact, the bar no longer existed. Reid had watched Franco's address in the home of the tavern's onetime bartender. This rearranged scene, and several other instances in which Reid acknowledged that he may have modified facts, were disclosed in June 1984 in a page one story of *The Wall Street Journal*. It was followed the next day by a front-page story in *The New York Times* and by major stories in other publications across the country.

In his own mind, Reid had done nothing wrong, and he felt the controversy was much ado about very little. "In reporting with some accuracy, at times we have to go much further than the strictly factual," Reid said. "Facts are part of the perceived whole." The article that attracted the greatest attention had been published in December 1961, and *New Yorker* readers lived quite comfortably in ignorance of the fact that the bar had been closed for years before then. No one was harmed. No one would have remembered anyhow after a few days whether such jeering even took place. (At *The New Yorker*, quotations are generally not subjected to the magazine's rigorous fact-checking requirements. The rationale for this, according to Martin Baron, the magazine's chief fact-checker, is that a source cannot be expected to remember weeks or months later his precise words. Further, said Baron, a source might subsequently deny having said something because the statement placed him in an unflattering light.)

Initially, Reid was supported by *The New Yorker* editor, William Shawn. Subsequently, in a memorandum, Shawn wrote Reid had made a "journalistic mistake." Shawn wrote:

"We do not permit composites.

"We do not rearrange events.

"We do not create conversations."

Even though Reid's intent was honorable—he said he wanted to make "the larger truth clear," he did not wish to subject those he interviewed to possible repercussions in Franco's Spain—he nonetheless deceived readers and abused journalistic license.

In an essay published in 1980 in the *Yale Review*, another *New Yorker* writer, the novelist John Hersey, argued forcefully that the one "sacred rule" of journalism is: "The writer must not invent. The legend on the license must read: *NONE* OF THIS IS MADE UP. The ethics of journalism, if we can be allowed such a boon, must be based on the simple truth that every journalist knows the difference between the distortion that comes from subtracting observed data and the distortion that comes from adding invented data."

Reid's mistake could have been resolved easily. All he needed to do here—as he, in fact, had done elsewhere—was to tell the reader that he was inventing or disguising characters, rearranging events and composing conversations.

Reid's fabrications were unfortunate misdeeds. They became front-page news because of *The New Yorker*'s vaunted reputation for accuracy and because they were thought to be unusual. But in fact they were aberrations only in that the author got caught. Faking and manufacturing stories—like posing—have roots deep in the history of journalism.

For several years in the middle of the eighteenth century, before embarking on his *Dictionary of the English Language*, Samuel Johnson wrote reports of what went on in Parliament for a publication called *The Gentleman's Magazine*, without ever having attended the sessions himself. In his *Life of Samuel Johnson*, James Boswell recalls: "Johnson told me that as soon as he found that the speeches were thought genuine, he determined that he would write no more of them; for 'he would not be accessary to the propagation of falsehood.' And such was the tenderness of his conscience, that a short time before his death he expressed a regret for having been the author of fictions that had passed for realities."

It may be a matter of self-mockery, self-flagellation, or self-pity that journalists have reveled in portraits of their jobs that show them in the least-flattering light. There are exceptions—

the films *All the President's Men* and *Superman,* and the Lou Grant show on television. But probably the favorite work of fiction among journalists is *Scoop,* the malicious and hilarious 1937 novel by Evelyn Waugh about British reporters in East Africa in the 1930s who file dispatches out of thin air. (There are no concordances for such things, but *Scoop* most likely ranks as the most quoted book by journalists who are trying to make one point or another.)

In *Scoop,* the revolution in the African country of Ishmaelia has just begun, but on Fleet Street, the publisher of the daily *Beast* is already instructing his impressionable correspondent, William Boot, who had been a garden columnist, on precisely what coverage is expected: "A few sharp victories, some conspicuous acts of personal bravery on the Patriot side, and a colourful entry into the capital. That is the *Beast* Policy for the war." The editor reassures Boot: "You'll be surprised to find how far the war correspondents keep from the fighting. Why, Hitchcock reported the whole Abyssinia campaign from Asmara and gave us some of the most colourful eye-witness stuff we ever printed." A colleague tells Boot of the legendary Wenlock Jakes, who went out to cover a revolution in one of the Balkan capitals: "He overslept in his carriage, woke up at the wrong station, didn't know any different, got out, went straight to a hotel, and cabled off a thousand-word story about barricades in the streets, flaming churches, machine guns answering the rattle of his typewriter as he wrote, a dead child, like a broken doll, spreadeagled in the deserted roadway below his window. . . ."

Passages like this are quoted with gleeful regularity by journalists, often comparing what happened in Boot's day to what is going on in contemporary Africa and other far-off places. *Scoop* is not pure invention; part of it is anchored in reality. *When the Going Was Good,* a recently reissued record of Waugh's travels between 1929 and 1935, contains descriptions of how in Ethiopia in 1930, Haile Selassie was about to be crowned emperor. Most of the buildings planned for the event were barely half-finished. Verifiable information was hard to come by, and the reporters were faced with inadequate communication facilities. Therefore, many reporters filed their stories before the event had taken place. "With little disguised irritation, they set to work making the best of their meager material," Waugh writes. A cathedral was cordoned off. That did not discourage the journalists. "Some described the actual coronation as taking place there; others used it as the scene of a state reception and drew fanciful pictures of the ceremony in the interior of the cathedral, 'murky, almost suffocating with incense and the thick, stifling smoke of tallow candles . . . authorities on Coptic ritual remarked that as the coronation proper must take place in the inner sanctuary, which no layman might glimpse, much less enter, there was small hope of anyone seeing anything at all.' " In fact, the ceremony was held in a light and airy tent.

The portrayal of journalists in *The Front Page*—still the most beloved piece of film and theater among journalists—is similarly harsh. First staged in 1928 and filmed for the first time three years later, it includes raucous scenes where journalists invent the news and ignore what happens before their eyes.

When the latest movie version was released in 1974, Nora Sayre wrote: "For all the yuks, the parent script is truly scornful of the profession. Here (as in most newspaper movies) 'news' is equated with gossip and scandal, and 'color' merely means lying. You say that the arrested man 'put up a desperate struggle' when he actually surrendered meekly."

Sayre interviewed Billy Wilder, the director of the latest movie version of the classic. (He was also the director of another newspaper movie, *The Big Carnival* [originally titled *Ace in the Hole*], a cynical 1951 film in which Skeets Miller, the heroic real-life reporter who actually tried to save a man's life in a Kentucky cave, was transformed into an ambitious fictional reporter—Chuck Tatum, whom Bosley Crowther of *The New York Times* called a "double-dyed, unregenerate heel of the sort that offends all decent instinct and would put the teeth of a snake on edge.")

Wilder, an ex-reporter himself, told Sayre that he viewed the reporter of the past as a "warrior, a soldier of fortune. There was something slightly illicit about it. And half the time, he got thrown down the stairs." Wilder recalled the days when a reporter was "a mixture of a private eye and a poet. If you were any good, you could improve the story. You felt that you were an inventor, a discoverer, an explorer, a dramatist. You let yourself go: The story started as something rather simple, and you blew it up into 'The Three Musketeers.' "

It is hardly surprising then that, as Wilder suggests, some of the journalists who have embellished their stories have also been some of the country's very best writers. Late in 1917 H. L. Mencken wrote a newspaper column in the *New York Evening Mail* celebrating the seventy-fifth anniversary of the introduction of the bathtub into the United States. He made it all up. The editor's note began: "Here's a series of inspiring bath hour thoughts." Mencken told how the first tub was installed in Cincinnati and how most Americans fought against its introduction. In the 1840s, he wrote, the price for installing one was $500. He related how Millard Fillmore, when he was vice president, became the champion of the tubs. This imaginary history had an unintended effect. Readers, Mencken wrote later, "took my idle jocosities with complete seriousness." Soon, Mencken said he began to encounter his "preposterous 'facts' in the writings of other men." Finally, he began to find them in standard works of reference.

Fabrication was a fixture of yellow journalism in the 1890s. (Papers owned by William Randolph Hearst and Joseph Pulitzer had similar cartoons, both called "The Yellow Kid," printed in yellow, and the Hearst-Pulitzer circulation war, which featured a mix of scandal, gossip, adventure and stories of outlandish scientific discoveries gave birth to "yellow journalism.") Even after yellow journalism receded at the turn of the century, the faking of stories and events was still used to boost circulation. The *New York Graphic* was the most sensationalist tabloid of the twenties. It ran a "picture" showing Rudolph Valentino entering Heaven, where he was greeted by Enrico Caruso. "Pictures" of Valentino's funeral procession were shown in the issue of the *Graphic* that was sold to mourners waiting for it to happen. Its editors posed models to duplicate events that its photographers had missed—and then superimposed the heads of actual participants. Editors coined the word "composograph" for this. It faked a photo of Charles Lindbergh parading past the Arc de Triomphe in 1927. That same year Bartolomeo Vanzetti was executed, and he appeared in a "composograph" as he was led to the electric chair.

The feeling among many journalists was that much of this fakery amounted to wry, innocent pranks, not ethical lapses. The always shrewd, cynical and wise cabdriver in New York papers and the cheery elevator operator in the Chicago press were journalistic staples. Often, they existed only in the imagination of reporters. The chestnut vendor in Paris who often graced the pages of *Time* magazine never existed either. "The assumption was always, among those in the business, that he was fictional, or that the wisecrack was thought up by the writer himself or was an improvement on something he had heard," a former *Time* editor recalls. "No one would have faked anything in his mouth on a subject of serious moment." Paris in the fifties "with all those old newspapermen camping out and living well, was full of feature stories which counted on none of the participants being able to read English; the sources would never see the story and rarely were they named."

Most of the time pranksters got away with their inside jokes. Occasionally, they did not. Before using his considerable talents at *The New Yorker* to skewer the press, A. J. Liebling edited sports copy at *The New York Times*. There, he had to deal with reporters who left out names of referees in basketball games. Liebling wrote in his autobiography that rather than research this mundane detail on his own, he would insert "Mr. Ignoto," the Italian for "unknown." When this bit of mischief was exposed, the twenty-one-year-old deskman was fired.

But in the retelling, Liebling seems to have fudged some of his facts as well. In *Wayward Reporter: The Life of A. J. Liebling*, Raymond Sokolov relates how Liebling probably embroidered upon the reason for his being fired. Liebling had used "Ignoto" on occasion; but according to Sokolov, the real reason Liebling was dismissed resulted from a little joke he played on the *Times* boxing writer, James Patrick Dawson. Liebling altered the name of the writer, who he thought was becoming somewhat too self-inflated. In the paper it came out as James Parnell Dawson (after Charles Stewart Parnell, the nineteenth-century Irish nationalist). The *Times* had no place for an editor who would change the name of a writer, and Liebling was fired.

Four decades later, in 1966, a young *Times* stringer from City College, Clyde Haberman, was also fired for a prank. In a list of awards given at the school's graduation, he inserted the "Brett Award to the student who has worked hardest under a great handicap." The fictional winner was Jake Barnes, a friend of Lady Brett Ashley in Hemingway's *The Sun Also Rises*, who was impotent. This appeared in the paper and when the prank was discovered, Haberman was told by A. M. Rosenthal, then the metropolitan editor: "You will never be able to write for this newspaper again." (More than ten years after, Rosenthal relented, and Haberman did rejoin the *Times*. He performed with such distinction that in 1983 he was named chief of the paper's Tokyo bureau.)

The mid-1960s brought New Journalism, or at least a new label and newfound popularity to an old technique: intermingling fact with fiction. In an advertisement, *Harper's Magazine* tried defining New Journalism metaphorically as "somewhere west of journalism and this side of history," the "place where reporting becomes literature." In this uncharted territory, writers embellished quotes, burrowed into characters' interior thoughts, created scenes that may have happened but did not, and made up characters who were collages of real people. Among the leading practitioners were Tom Wolfe, Gay Talese, Norman Mailer and Truman Capote.

For the past twenty years, dozens of books and magazine articles have been shaped from a mixture of fact and fiction, and the technique has generally been accepted in the book publishing world. Several recent best sellers rely on reconstructed dialogue. In some of these books the authors have attributed feelings and quotations to individuals who said they had never been interviewed by them.

In 1968, when the influence of the New Journalists first began to spread, Joseph Eszterhas, who later worked for *Rolling Stone*, wrote a long article for the Sunday magazine of the *Cleveland Plain Dealer* about the family left behind by Melvin Cantrell, one of forty-four people killed when the Silver Bridge across the Ohio River collapsed in December 1967. Eszterhas covered the original disaster and wrote a feature on Cantrell's funeral at Point Pleasant, West Virginia, and the impact of his death on the survivors in the Cantrell family.

Five months later, he returned to Point Pleasant and went to the Cantrell home. Mrs. Cantrell was not there, but he talked to the children. In the article, he stressed the family's poverty, their ill-fitting clothes and the deteriorating condition of their home. Eszterhas also wrote: "Margaret Cantrell will talk neither about what happened nor about how they are doing. She wears the same mask of non-expression she wore at the funeral. She is a proud woman. She says that after it happened, the people in town offered to help them out with money and they refused to take it."

Mrs. Cantrell and her children sued the newspaper for invasion of privacy, claiming that the article placed her and her family in a false light. Eszterhas never testified at the trial about whom he interviewed to justify his writing that she wore a "mask of non-expression." He did not interview her, and by using the present tense—"she wears"—he gave the unmistakable impression that he was with her, observing her. In 1974 the United States Supreme Court said that descriptions in the article were "calculated falsehoods" and ruled that the Cantrell family should be allowed to collect the $60,000 that was awarded by a jury.

John Hersey's *Hiroshima*, written after World War II, is often credited as being the forerunner of New Journalism, but in his 1980 essay in the *Yale Review*, Hersey tried to dissociate himself from this overlapping of fiction and journalism. Hersey said: "As to journalism, we may as well grant right away that there is no such thing as absolute objectivity. It is impossible to present in words *'the* truth' or 'the whole story.' The minute a writer offers nine hundred ninety-nine out of one thousand facts, the worm of bias has begun to wriggle. The vision of each witness is particular. Tolstoy pointed out that immediately after a battle there are as many remembered versions of it as there have been participants."

Hersey later asks: "Can we always rely on what others tell us about what is 'really' going on? A suspicion that we cannot has led to the great fallacy, as I see it, of the New Journalism, and indirectly to the blurring in recent years of fiction and nonfiction.

"That fallacy can be crudely stated as follows: Since perfect objectivity in reporting what the eyes have seen and the ears have heard is impossible, there is no choice but to go all the way over to absolute subjectivity. The trouble with this is that it soon makes the reporter the center of interest rather than the real world he is supposed to be picturing or interpreting."

Such is the condition of contemporary journalism that in a report in 1983 that sought in part to answer the question: "How do I know this news account is true when I don't even know where it comes from?" A. H. Raskin, a former reporter and editorial writer for *The New York Times*, asks rhetorically:

"Does the proliferation of new journalistic forms, ranging from straight news reporting through a sometimes bewildering assortment of analytic, entertainment and gossip columns, require notice to the public that varying gradations of credence ought to be applied to the varying types of news treatment?" In other words, are different standards of accuracy applied for news reporters and, say, columnists?

Hyperbole and exaggeration have generally and unfortunately been tolerated in gossip items and in certain other columns. In May 1983, Irving Berlin celebrated his ninety-fifth birthday. An item on the *New York Daily News* People Page elaborately described how his daughters and their families "gathered to sing 'Happy Birthday' after dinner at his Beekman Place apartment." No such family gathering took place. This is not harmless error, and it is ill-becoming to a major newspaper that values its credibility. That same column, and columns like it, contain news of politics and business, and there are people who make decisions on the basis of what they read there, as if the column were warrantied by the *Daily News* as being accurate.

This double journalistic standard—one for gossip, the other for news—creates problems that are often inexcusable. An example occurred in an article in 1980 in the *Columbia Journalism Review*, the most highly regarded journal that deals with the press. An article about the manipulation of the New York press by Roy Cohn, the lawyer, mentioned that several journalists, including me, A. M. Rosenthal and William Safire of the *Times*, joined him in celebrating his fifty-second birthday. The article said I had attended his birthday party at Studio 54. That was true; it did not mention that I was on assignment for the *Times*. It also said that Rosenthal "declined to attend the evening bash but joined Cohn for lunch at The 21 Club." Rosenthal was in fact having lunch that day at "21"—but at a different table.

The erroneous assumption that Rosenthal was lunching with Cohn originated with an item on Page Six of the *New York Post* —a well-read gossip page. The item, in fact, said that Cohn and his guests "ogled such other diners" as Rosenthal. The *Village Voice*, in an article critical of Cohn, picked up on this, and said that several journalists, who were identified, paid "homage" to Cohn by attending his party that night and that earlier in the day Rosenthal had lunched with him. Then Liz Smith, in her column in the *New York Daily News*, repeated the error in an item defending journalists, including herself, me Rosenthal and many others, for having dealings with Cohn. "I don't think people like Abe Rosenthal . . . can be bought or influenced by a mere party invitation," she wrote. "But it surely was in their paper's or network's interests for them to be on hand at such an occasion."

The *Columbia Journalism Review* further legitimized the error without checking with any of the principals. The *Review*,

in a subsequent apology, said it had relied on "previously published materials," without specifying what these "materials"
were. (The error was never brought to Smith's attention. Had
it been, she said later, she would have acknowledged her mistake in her column. "Most gossip columnists would rather die
than say they're wrong," she says. "The chances of being
wrong are overwhelming. I naturally make mistakes. When I
find out about them, I correct them in the column.")

At the *Daily News*, where Smith is published, feature columnists are given leeway to express their personal opinions and to
report their own impressions and feelings. Jimmy Breslin, for
instance, signals his readers when he is dealing with hypothetical characters who do outlandish things. He creates people
like Marvin the Torch, Klein the Lawyer, Fat Thomas (who
weighed 475 pounds) and Un Occhio, the mythical boss of all
bosses. Sometimes his signals are not clear. His spoof on the
Sicilian don was so true to life that many readers never caught
on, and the Arizona state police wrote for more details so they
could put out an all-points bulletin.

Late in 1984, two of Breslin's former editors, Michael O'Neill
and William Brink, collected dozens of Breslin's columns in a
book, *The World According to Breslin*. "His nonconformist reporting," writes O'Neill, "has brought his readers closer to the
truths about their society than much of the conventional journalism which his critics so righteously espouse."

Similarly, at *The New Yorker* some license is granted to writers to make up characters. In the memorandum in which he
criticized Alastair Reid for inventing characters, editor William
Shawn said: "The only exceptions are characters invented in
the spirit of fun for The Talk of the Town (Mr. Stanley, Mr.
Frimbo, the Long-Winded Lady, various 'friends'), and when
this is done it is well understood by our readers."

Calvin Trillin, another *New Yorker* writer, collected 50 hu-
morous columns that he wrote for *The Nation* in a book called
Uncivil Liberties. In the introduction, Trillin, tongue-in-cheek,
admits that he has not "made a fetish of the old traditions of
journalism—the tradition, for instance, of covering events only
when they actually occur"—and he explains that he was paid
"in the high two figures" for each of these columns. "At those
rates," he says he told to Victor Navasky, the magazine's editor, "you can't always expect real quotes." Trillin's humor is
unmistakable: "As Frank Boyden, the legendary headmaster of

the Deerfield School, said upon his retirement after eighty-nine years at the helm, 'I know from preppies already.' "

In just about all contexts other than humor columns or pieces of the "Talk of the Town" type, fabricated quotes and fictional characters are not acceptable. In 1975 Robert Darnton, a former reporter at the *Newark Star Ledger* and *The New York Times* and now professor of history at Princeton University, wrote in *Daedalus* how he never got over his "amazement" at the ease with which reporters got "reaction" stories by informing parents of their children's death:

" 'He was always such a good boy,' exclaimed Mrs. Mac-Naughton, her body heaving with sobs. When I needed such quotes, I used to make them up, as did some of the others—a tendency that also contributed toward standardization, for we knew what 'the bereaved mother' and 'the mourning father' should have said and possibly even heard them speak what was in our minds rather than what was on theirs."

Journalists who make up quotes and scenes are known by their colleagues as "pipe artists."

Janet Cooke was a pipe artist.

■

"Jimmy is 8 years old and a third-generation heroin addict, a precocious little boy with sandy hair, velvety brown eyes and needle marks freckling the baby-smooth skin of his thin brown arms.

"He nestles in a large, beige reclining chair in the living room of his comfortably furnished home in Southeast Washington. There is an almost cherubic expression on his small, round face as he talks about life—clothes, money, the Baltimore Orioles and heroin. He has been an addict since the age of five.

"His hands are clasped behind his head, fancy running shoes adorn his feet and a striped Izod T-shirt hangs over his thin frame. 'Bad, ain't it,' he boasts to a reporter visiting recently. 'I got me six of these.' "

So began an article by Janet Cooke on the front page of *The Washington Post* on Sunday, September 28, 1980. In a particularly vivid simile near the close of the 2,400-word piece, Ron, the lover of Jimmy's mother, grabs the boy's left arm, and "the needle slides into the boy's soft skin like a straw pushed into the center of a freshly baked cake."

The reaction to the article was immediate and intense:

- Admiring editors promoted Cooke from a weekly suburban section to the far more prestigious metropolitan section.
- Some readers were outraged. There was a flood of calls and letters complaining about the insensitivity of the newspaper. The readers' concern was for Jimmy.
- Washington Mayor Marion S. Barry, Jr., ordered police and social service agencies to find the boy. At one point, Barry announced—prematurely, it turned out—that city officials knew who Jimmy and his family were and that he was under medical treatment. At another point, police threatened to sub-poena Cooke in an effort to force her to reveal the names and addresses of her sources. The *Post* supported Cooke in resisting the issuance of the subpoena. In the middle of October, with the search for Jimmy going nowhere, Barry denounced the article: "I've been told the story is part myth, part reality. We all have agreed that we don't believe that the mother or the pusher would allow a reporter to see them shoot up."
- Milton Coleman, the *Post*'s city editor, established an eleven-member reporting team to follow up on the story and to find more children like Jimmy. A colleague was sent to do a follow-up with Cooke, and he reported back that she seemed to him to be unacquainted with the neighborhood where Jimmy was supposed to live.

Red flags were hoisted, and they were largely ignored. The editors stuck by the reporter; even after serious doubts were raised about the story in early January 1981, they submitted it for the Pulitzer Prize. In April, after the prize had been won and then returned, Benjamin Bradlee, the executive editor of the *Post*, explained why the *Post* had entered "Jimmy's World" in the competition: "Not to submit it would have meant something that you didn't want to say, that you didn't believe the story." Bob Woodward, the editor in charge of metropolitan news, used an aphorism: "In for a dime, in for a dollar." That reasoning seems brittle. Hundreds of compelling stories are written each year, and most are not entered for prizes. That alone does not mean the editors did not "believe" them.

On April 13, the day Cooke's prize was announced publicly, Vivan Aplin-Brownlee, Cooke's first editor at the *Post*, said to Coleman, according to an article by the *Post*'s ombudsman: "I hope she has committed the perfect crime." She had not. A profile done on Cooke in *The Toledo Blade*, her hometown paper where she had worked before joining the *Post*, did not mesh with the biography that was carried by the Associated Press. The wire service got its information from the Pulitzer Prize office, which in turn had used a biography Cooke had submitted. She had embellished her credentials on her resumé. Cooke said the was an honors graduate of Vassar. In fact, she had dropped out after a year and finished up college at the University of Toledo.

In an 18,000-word report, Bill Green, the *Post*'s ombudsman, noted that when Cooke first applied to the paper it was her Vassar credentials that had caught Bradlee's attention. Bradlee had underlined Phi Beta Kappa graduate of Vassar and sent her clippings and resumé along to Bob Woodward. On her letter he told his secretary that he would see Cooke personally.

After Cooke confessed that she had lied about her background, she was interrogated by *Post* editors for several hours, and finally she admitted that she had fabricated the story as well as her resumé. She was allowed to resign, and her resignation letter read: "Jimmy's World was in essence a fabrication. I never encountered or interviewed an 8-year-old heroin addict. The September 28, 1980, article in *The Washington Post* was a serious misrepresentation which I deeply regret. I apologize to my newspaper, my profession, the Pulitzer board and all seekers of the truth. Today, in facing up to the truth, I have submitted my resignation."

The initial reaction among news executives was to isolate Cooke. "She was a one-in-a-million liar," said Bradlee. The acute embarrassment of the *Post* reverberated throughout the world of journalism. "Unfortunately and unfairly, it will hurt all newspapers and help our critics because of the wide publicity one instance of fraud in one newspaper has received," wrote Jim Ottaway, Jr., president of the Ottaway chain, a Dow-Jones subsidiary that includes small- to medium-circulation papers. "This tragedy for truth should lead all of us to review and tighten, if necessary, our procedures and policies for checking an unnamed source when a reporter insists that confidentiality is essential to publishing an important story," said Ottaway in a memorandum to publishers and editors under his supervision. Sober warnings like this were repeated across the country: Let a lesson be learned from the misdeeds of one misguided individual.

At the *New York Daily News*, after the hoax was exposed, editor Michael J. O'Neill summoned his top editors together to remind them of the paper's policies: Editors had the obligation to ask for the source on sensitive stories and to run cross-checks. He made known his concern that tighter enforcement of editing standards was "urgently needed." Within a month of the Cooke episode, an anguished O'Neill accepted the resignation of Michael Daly, the young columnist who in 1979 had written about Sylvester Peacock.

In a column filed from Belfast, Daly wrote as if he had been an eyewitness: "Peering over the hood of an armored car, gunner Christopher Spell of the British Army watched a child not yet in his teens fling a gasoline bomb." He quoted another soldier who fired a shot as saying: "If I'm lucky, the little Fenian will die." When confronted by *Daily News* editors, Daly maintained that he had spoken to the soldier in a British unit involved in the shooting of an Irish teenager. But he admitted that he was not on the patrol himself, that "Spell" was a pseudonym, and that he had re-created scenes he had not witnessed. In resigning, Daly said the column was not materially different from three hundred others he had written. "The question of reconstruction and using a pseudonym—I've done it a lot. No one has ever said anything." A few days before he left the paper, Daly had been named the recipient of the Columbia University's Meyer Berger Award for distinguished reporting.

Shortly after the resignations of Cooke and Daly, A. M. Rosenthal of *The New York Times*, said: "What happened in both cases is the writers wrote fiction, and we don't write fiction." The *Times* had reviewed its fact-checking procedures—scrutiny by editors (and by researchers in the case of magazine articles) and checking back with the reporters; but, said Rosenthal, "we haven't changed them. We think they are very good." His confidence was misplaced, for within a year, Rosenthal faced a similar embarrassment.

A free-lance writer fabricated an article that appeared in the *Times Magazine* in December 1981. Without ever leaving Spain, the author, Christopher Jones, wrote an article that created the illusion that he had visited remote regions of Cambodia. "It was a gamble—that was it," said Jones after he was caught. "Unfortunately the gamble was too big, and wasn't sufficiently researched or tied down." The *Times*'s checking procedures, explained Rosenthal, "failed to uncover the clues in the text that would have led us to doubt the veracity of the piece. We do not feel that the fact the writer was a liar and hoaxer removes our responsibility. It is our job to uncover any falsehoods or errors."

Like A. J. Liebling and Clyde Haberman when they were fired from the *Times*, like Joe Eszterhas at the *Cleveland Plain Dealer*, like Janet Cooke and like Michael Daly, Christopher Jones was young and relatively inexperienced.

Journalism is a field for young people; they have energy and enthusiasm and are willing to work for relatively poor pay. One survey showed that the typical American journalist is thirty-two years old. Even while in their twenties, journalists can reach the top of their field—something that is possible in professional sports or the performing arts, but certainly not in law, medicine or academia. But there are dangers. Those with little experience can be careless. They can overlook rules requiring proper checking and sourcing. They can react badly to pressure to perform. After "Jimmy's World" was exposed, Janet Cooke said one reason she had faked the story was that she had spent so much time unsuccessfully looking for a young drug addict that she felt she could not return empty-handed to her desk. "If I did not produce a story, then how was I to justify my time?" she told Phil Donahue of NBC in an interview in 1982.

■

Janet Cooke was able to hide behind confidentiality. What made it possible for her to fabricate was that she was allowed to keep the identity of the boy and the adults secret. She did not tell the names to her city editor, Milton Coleman. Nor did Bob Woodward, Coleman's supervisor, insist on knowing the names. (Woodward, along with Carl Bernstein, built a reputation on painstaking research, making sure that every detail of their Watergate stories was verified by a second source.) In a survey done three years after the Janet Cooke scandal, the ethics committee of the American Society of Newspaper Editors found it had become a general rule among newspapers that a reporter must share with an editor the identity of a confidential source.

The survey found that many newspapers had adopted written policies regarding sources. A memorandum of November 1982, from William Thomas, editor of *The Los Angeles Times*, reads:

"1. Unnamed sources should not be used unless there is no other way to get needed information into the story. And, unless it's obvious, tell us why we can't name them.

"2. When we do use them, we should give the reader all the information we can—short of indirectly identifying the source —that establishes his or her credibility. . . .

"3. Editors should know the identity of unnamed sources whose information is the slightest bit sensitive or which is central to the story's thesis."

Implicit in this memorandum is the notion that some important stories are impossible to do without anonymous sources. The amount of useful information available to the public would be less were all reporters forced to write only what they could attribute by name and title. Some anonymous sources, for example, are whistle-blowers, and they use anonymity as protection against reprisals from superiors. But the problem with the anonymous quote is that it holds no one accountable, and there is great potential for someone with an axe to grind—including a reporter—to malign or ridicule from the safety of anonymity.

At *The New York Times,* writers are forbidden from using anonymous pejorative remarks. Rosenthal has issued several memoranda on this topic. His latest, issued in September 1984, says that "there is hardly ever a reason to give somebody who attacks another person or an institution the cloak of anonymity." He concedes that "this does make reporting more difficult. This means that sometimes nice juicy quotes cannot be used, or that we have to work harder to get at reality."

In an earlier memorandum, he noted, "A direct quote has little meaning unless the reader knows the name and personality of the person being quoted. To put a direct quote around the words of an anonymous source is jarring in a literary way and journalistically makes life too easy for reporters and editors. If we can't name the source, we have to forego the luxury of having the source comment directly."

This policy is probably as fair a one as can be devised, but it builds restraints into journalism which make it especially difficult for reporters to assess a public figure currently in a powerful position. In the minuet that passes for political discourse, few public people say on the record what they really think of people with whom they must deal regularly.

A natural limitation of the *Times* policy is that there are occasions when a public official really is monstrous or close to it, and those in a position to criticize him intelligently are unwilling to do so on the record. In writing profiles of judges, for example, I found myself constantly hamstrung. Few colleagues wished to incur the wrath of a judge they privately felt wanting, and the lawyers who knew the judge best—those who appeared in court—were not going to say something derogatory about a judge before whom they had active cases. Therefore, because of the restriction on anonymous quotes, some judges who were regarded as sons of bitches came out looking like they were closer to saints.

Once I had to do a profile of a judge who had recently joined an appeals court. I wished to find out what his colleagues thought of him. Quite understandably, they would discuss him only on the condition that they be granted anonymity. I agreed, and they unanimously criticized their new colleague. That was a good story, but its impact was diluted since their anonymity would have been illusory had I written: "All the judges' colleagues—none of whom spoke for attribution—thought poorly of him." I partially salvaged the story by expanding the universe of those whom I interviewed. I talked to judges on other courts and law professors. Some thought highly of the new judge. So I was able to say, "Most of a group of lawyers and judges, including colleagues of the judge, feel he is doing poorly. . . . Others disagree."

■

If she had not been permitted to use unidentified sources, Janet Cooke most likely would have been unable to write "Jimmy's World" in the first place. Once a faked story is published, it is almost impossible to detect as a fabrication. When a wrongdoer is caught, it is almost always by accident. Had Janet Cooke not won the Pulitzer Prize, her hoax might still be undetected. That Alastair Reid of the *The New Yorker* rearranged facts was exposed on the front page of *The Wall Street Journal*. He was the victim of a chance encounter. How did a reporter uncover out of the blue a bit of minor fakery nearly a quarter of century earlier? The idea for the story originated in the spring of 1983, when its author, Joanne Lipman, was still a student at Yale. Reid spoke at a seminar there on literary law and ethics, and he illustrated, from examples of his own writing, how a reporter might take liberties with factual circumstances to arrive at a "larger" truth. She got the tip from that class, and followed up once she became a reporter.

Editors ordinarily are not on the lookout for hoaxes. They spend their days inside the home office, and they can be deceived by reporters out in the field. It is a general rule among journalists, following the dictates of *Scoop*, that the farther away one is from the home office the easier it is to take liberties. The prescription did not hold for Michael Daly, whose column from Belfast was challenged by the *London Daily Mail*. It almost succeeded for Christopher Jones, the free-lancer for the *Times Magazine*. Before commissioning the article about remote areas of Cambodia, *Times* editors had checked Jones's credentials with editors at *Time* magazine, where he had worked briefly as a stringer. When Jones submitted the article, it went through normal editing procedures, but was not shown to a specialist on Southeast Asia on the *Times* staff.

Jones's elaborate fabrication began to unravel only after Alexander Cockburn, then a columnist for the *Village Voice*, pointed out that the lines about a blind guitar player chanting in the moonlight, which Jones used to end his article, were almost identical to language in André Malraux's *The Royal Way*, a novel published in 1930 about his Cambodian travels some years earlier. "I needed a piece of color" was Jones's explanation for his act of plagiarism.

■

Plagiarism stands at the opposite extreme from faking. But just as journalists who invent or fake stories often escape detection, so too do plagiarists. There is no doubt that plagiarism in journalism happens far more often than is discussed. It is a dirty little secret, what Roy Peter Clark, associate director of the Poynter Institute in St. Petersburg, Florida—an organization devoted to the continuing education of journalists—calls "the skeleton in journalism's closet."

While using someone else's descriptions is plagiarism, it is not clear where journalistic "rewriting" ends and plagiarism begins. The rewriteman is a time-honored, sometimes mythologized fixture in the newspaper firmament. The rewriteman is rumpled, but resourceful, and on deadline he writes effortlessly —or so it seems—with several editors hunched over his shoulder, alternately encouraging him and trying to second-guess him. He also literally rewrites the stories of other reporters, either from his newspaper or from other publications.

How much borrowing is too much? Three words, four words, a paragraph? What about lifting quotes from another article and not sourcing them? Writers do this all the time. Newspapers are stubbornly and notoriously ungenerous about giving credit to others, even though the lack of credit can easily mislead readers. If the rule were, as it should be, that any published quote that is republished must identify the publication or at least the context where the quote first appeared, then the practice of journalism would change dramatically.

For example, in August 1984 readers of the business section of *The New York Times* were seriously misled. The following sentence appeared in an article on multimillion-dollar bonuses for corporate executives: "When a reporter asked Betsey Caldwell, the wife of Ford chairman Philip Caldwell, whether he deserved a bonus of $7 million, she said, 'How can I answer that without sounding like Marie Antoinette?' " This statement was made to "a reporter." But the reporter worked for *The Washington Post*, not the *Times*, and the statement had been made three months earlier. And the speaker was not Mrs. Caldwell, but Barbara Smith, wife of the chairman of General Motors, who was talking about her own husband's $1.4 million salary.

In this case—an extreme one, to be sure, because the quote was misattributed as well as stolen—one particular reader, Philip Caldwell of the Ford Motor Company, knew which editors at the *Times* to call, and a correction was printed. It is not known, of course, how many times readers fail to complain about being misquoted or how often writers are unaware that their material has been improperly borrowed by someone else.

Most editors mistakenly feel that plagiarism is a cut-and-dried issue. In the questionnaire I sent to fifty of the country's largest papers, I asked if they had a written policy regarding plagiarism. Few newspapers did. James Greenfield, assistant managing editor of *The New York Times*, said, "Why would anyone want" a written policy—"it's so obvious." Charles Stabler, assistant managing editor of *The Wall Street Journal*, concurred: "If it happened, it would be grounds for firing, not just for ethics but for terminal stupidity."

The Washington Post is one of the few major papers that specifically addressed plagiarism. In its *Deskbook on Style*, Benjamin Bradlee says: "Attribution of material from other newspapers and other media must be total. Plagiarism is one of journalism's unforgivable sins." At its seventy-fifth anniversary convention in 1984, the Society of Professional Journalists adopted an amendment to its code of ethics that said: "Plagiarism is dishonest and is unacceptable."

The most thorough definition I have come across appeared

in the stylebook of *The National Observer*, a Washington-based weekly newspaper published by Dow-Jones until its demise in 1977. Reporters were warned: "Do not at any time steal paragraphs, sentences, phrases or even distinctive terms from other publications or research sources. A descriptive phrase or an explanation found in research may very aptly express what you want, but the facts are all you are permitted to use; the language must be entirely your own. Loose paraphrasing or substitution of synonyms for some of the key words is not sufficient; an entire reworking of the idea in your own language is required. Violation of this rule is considered a grave offense." (In 1972, an *Observer* reporter left the paper after it was discovered that the reporter's profile of a congressman had appeared almost verbatim just a week earlier in *The Washington Post*. A former *Observer* staff member gave this explanation of how this transgression slipped by *Observer* editors: On the Sunday that the original profile appeared in the *Post*, the Washington Redskins played the Dallas Cowboys in the National Football Conference championship game, and the attention of the editors, who ordinarily were quite diligent about reading the *Post*, was on the game instead of the news.)

Naturally, newspaper editors say they take a hard line on plagiarism. "It is, of course, understood that no writer uses another's work without attribution," said James Minter, editor of *The Atlanta Journal & Constitution:* "We consider it a firing offense." At *The Christian Science Monitor*, Katherine Fanning, the editor, said, "It's understood plagiarism is cause for instant dismissal."

Occasionally punishment is sure and swift. In December 1982 *The New York Times* published a profile of Richard Dreyfuss, who talked about his identification with the paralyzed sculptor who was the hero of the film *Whose Life Is It Anyway?* "I became dependent, physically ill, sluggish and lethargic," Dreyfuss told the interviewer. Two weeks later, *Newsday* carried a profile of Dreyfuss, who is quoted saying, "I became dependent, physically ill, sluggish and lethargic." Other quotes —and chunks of narrative—were identical to the *Times* piece. The reporter left *Newsday*.

In fact, though, punishment often falls far short of dismissal in what typically seem to be extenuating circumstances. This may demonstrate that editors are kind souls and are slightly soft on crime, but it is also at wide variance with their strict pronouncements. In late 1983, the *Cleveland Plain Dealer* ran a piece on its forum page by George Jordan, a young staff reporter, who, it turned out, had pirated his commentary from a column written a couple of years earlier by Carl Rowan. Jordan began his column: "At times I wish the Lord would deliver me back to the days of Stepin Fetchit, Aunt Jemima, and Uncle Tom. The old-style black, illiterate 'handkerchief heads' were an embarrassment, but they were harmless in comparison to 'educated' blacks. . . ." The changes from Rowan's column were slight. That column began: "There are times when I want to ask the Lord to deliver us back to the days of Stepin Fetchit, Aunt Jemima, and Uncle Tom. The old-style black, illiterate, obsequious 'handkerchief heads' were an embarrassment, but they were harmless compared with the 'educated' blacks. . . ."

Jordan offered to resign. Instead, he was suspended for three days. "I thought it was a punishment consistent with the crime," said David Hopcraft, who was then the *Plain Dealer*'s executive editor. (Hopcraft himself left the paper in the spring of 1984, after a second incident that was embarrassing to the paper: He had shown questionable judgment in trying to influence a disciplinary proceeding brought by state authorities against his personal lawyer.) In explaining why Jordan was permitted to stay on, Hopcraft said, "It wasn't a case where he had made up stories or facts, but a case where he could learn and grow to become a productive journalist."

In crime statistics, there is what is known as the "dark figure"—the number of crimes that are never brought to the attention of the police. While the precise dimensions of this figure are obviously not known, these unreported crimes are thought to outnumber those that are reported by a factor of two or three. Similarly, the reported cases of plagiarism are relatively few, and one can assume that the dark figure is much larger. Ordinarily, as with fabrications, plagiarism is detected only by accident. The plagiarism by Christopher Jones, the free-lancer for the *Times* who also fabricated in his long article, was discovered by a well-read columnist. George Jordan's plagiarism was exposed publicly in a column by William Buckley, Jr., who was less concerned with the plagiarism than he was with the use of what he referred to as "assembly-line techniques" by liberal blacks to attack conservative blacks.

And in Miami, Tom Archdeacon, a sports columnist at the

Miami News, was caught because, like Janet Cooke, he had won a prize. He was accused of lifting material from a book written many years before his column appeared. But that book had enjoyed only a limited success and was no longer available in bookstores. It was Archdeacon's misfortune that his prize-winning column was reprinted in a collection that caught the eye of one of the few people in the world who could have spotted the plagiarism—the original author.

Roy Peter Clark of the Poynter Institute edits an annual collection, *Best Newspaper Writing*, taken from the winners of the writing competition sponsored by the American Society of Newspaper Editors. On September 1, 1982, Clark got a call from Jerry Bledsoe, a columnist for the *Greensboro* (North Carolina) *Daily News and Record*. Bledsoe had just read the 1982 edition of *Best Newspaper Writing*. In 1975, Bledsoe had written a book called *The World's Number One, Flat-Out, All-Time-Great Stock Car Racing Book*, and one chapter was devoted to Linda Vaughn, the "queen" of the racing car circuit. One of the winning submissions in the contest was a collection of columns written by Tom Archdeacon. One column dealt with Linda Vaughn, and Bledsoe recognized several passages. They were suspiciously similar to ones he had written. Bledsoe sent Clark a copy of his chapter, underlining ten examples in which he felt Archdeacon had failed to attribute phrases and sentences to Bledsoe.

For Clark, who wrote about this incident in detail in *The Washington Journalism Review*, the "most damning passage" was one in which Archdeacon used Bledsoe's language to describe the reaction of the mechanics to Vaughn. Bledsoe wrote that the sight of the buxom woman made them "stand in awe, made them punch one another in the ribs and giggle like little boys. . . ." In Archdeacon's version, they "stand in awe, bashful, punching each other in the ribs, giggling like schoolboys."

Confronted with the charges, Archdeacon, an amiable former high school English teacher in his early thirties, told his editors he had used Bledsoe's book for background on Vaughn and had inadvertently mixed up Bledsoe's words with his own.

Archdeacon explained that before he wrote the story, he had reread Bledsoe's chapter, and "wrote down notes on a few things he had mentioned, taking some points down word for word and partially paraphrasing others." In a written apology, Archdeacon said: "I wanted to be sure and check out his observations, many of which I had already experienced myself." When it came to writing the story, it was late at night, and he found he had "more than a hundred note pages, napkins, scraps of paper, a few things on a matchbook cover and even a few ideas written on the palm of my hand." He was writing slowly, and soon "was in a bit of panic." What happened then in the "heat of writing" was that "without thinking" he used "some of the notes" he had made when he had read Bledsoe's piece. "It was sloppiness on deadline in assimilating information into my story."

Archdeacon flew to Greensboro to apologize to Bledsoe. He apologized again, in writing, in the newsletter of the American Society of Newspaper Editors: "I swear to God there was no deviousness intended."

He was chastised by the ASNE board: "While what happened is a journalistic misdemeanor and not a felony—and appears to be a mistake rather than plagiarism—the board deplores that such gross carelessness and sloppiness could be part of the working procedure of such a talented writer. We hope full public airing of what took place will discourage such casual practices in the future, both for the individual involved and for all those who might take shortcuts under deadline pressure."

Archdeacon was very lucky. He was permitted to keep the award and his job.

11. LOST CREDIBILITY: MISTAKES AND CORRECTIONS

One of the principal marks of an educated man, indeed, is the fact that he does *not* take his opinions from newspapers. . . . He knows that they are constantly falling into false reasoning about the things within his personal knowledge,—that is, within the narrow circle of his special education—and so he assumes that they make the same, or even worse errors about other things, whether intellectual or moral. This assumption, it may be said at once, is quite justified by the facts. I know of no subject, in truth, save perhaps baseball, on which the average American newspaper, even in the larger cities, discourses with unfailing sense and understanding.
— H. L. Mencken, "Newspaper Morals," *The Atlantic*, 1914

Every American knows that when there is an article or a story on television about something he was personally involved with, it is always wrong.
— Frank Mankiewicz, a public relations adviser and political consultant who also was president of National Public Radio, 1984

It's hell when you know the facts and see how they are mishandled. We all should have that experience and then we would better understand how our readers must feel sometimes.
— Gregory Favre, who left the *Chicago Sun-Times* after it was purchased by Rupert Murdoch, 1984

People make honest mistakes, and reporters are people.
— Judge Abraham D. Sofaer during the trial of libel action brought by Ariel Sharon, 1984

In a six-week period in the fall of 1981, the following items appeared in *The Washington Post* concerning reports that President Carter had bugged Blair House a year earlier to spy on the incoming President, Ronald Reagan:

• October 5, p. D1: One paragraph item in "The Ear" column—"Word's around among Rosalynn's close pals," the column says, that Blair House was *"bugged*. And at least one tattler in the Carter tribe has described listening in to the Tape Itself. . . .Ear is absolutely appalled. Stay tuned, uh, whoever's listening." "The Ear," written by Diana McClellan, was only in its second week at the *Post* after shifting from the *Washington Star*, which had shut down.

• October 6, p. C1: A nine-paragraph news story—A White House spokesman says there is no evidence the Reagans were bugged by the Carter administration. Jody Powell, the former president's spokesman, is quoted as saying it was "just preposterous" and "if *The Washington Post* believed it to be true, it should be on the front page."

• October 9, p. A3: An eighteen-paragraph news story— Former President Carter plans to sue *The Washington Post*. Carter's lawyer demands a retraction and a full apology. Benjamin Bradlee, executive editor of the *Post*, is quoted in the article as saying: "It will be perfectly obvious that there is no retraction in the paper tomorrow."

• October 12, p. D2: A two-paragraph item—Edwin Meese, counselor to President Reagan, says that "to the best" of his knowledge it was "highly unlikely" Blair House was ever bugged.

• October 14, p. A3: A six-paragraph story—Jimmy Carter says Meese was "accurate" in his Blair House statement. Rosalynn Carter says: "We did not bug Blair House."

• October 14, p. A24: An editorial defends publication of the rumor but notes that "we find that rumor utterly impossible to believe." The editorial explains that "the point was that *a story was circulating* (various unnamed bearers of it were alluded to) that Blair House had been 'bugged' while the Reagans were staying there during their pre-inaugural/post-election visit to Washington. . . . It is one thing, however, to read that item to say that such a tale is circulating and being given currency by estimable public figures who repeat it—and quite another to conclude from this that the place was in fact bugged and that the Carters did in fact perpetrate such a scheme." A week later, *Time* magazine comments that this editorial "may have set a new standard for journalistic sophistry."

• October 15, p. A2: A nine-paragraph news item—Carter criticizes the *Post* for its failure to apologize. "The *Post* is taking the position that there was nothing wrong with printing a rumor it believed to be false," says Jody Powell. "The editorial speaks for itself," says Donald E. Graham, publisher of the *Post.*

• October 22, p. A30: Twelve letters to the editor are printed. All attack the *Post*'s editorial of October 14.

• October 23, Front Page: A fifteen-paragraph story is accompanied by the text of a letter by Donald Graham apologizing to the Carters. "When we published the item we had a source whom we believed to be credible and reliable, and he identified his sources as two members of your family," Graham says. "We now believe the story he told us to have been wrong and that there was no 'bugging' of Blair House during your administration. Nor do we now believe that members of your family said Blair House was 'bugged.' " Although the *Post* obviously is aware of the identity of the "credible and reliable" source of the initial gossip item, his identity is not disclosed.

• October 25, p. A7: A twelve-paragraph story—Carter says he is dropping his plans to sue the *Post* after receiving the letter of apology and retraction from Donald Graham.

• November 12, p. A4: Instead of carrying its own story identifying by name the source of the initial gossip item, the *Post* carries a twenty-seven-paragraph story by David Shaw, of *The Los Angeles Times*, who identifies Dotson Rader, a freelance magazine writer, as the source whose confirmation persuaded the *Post* to publish the Blair House item in the first place. Rader is not available for comment, but his literary agent says that he had told her he was under the impression he was "one of several people being called to verify a story that originated elsewhere."

Bradlee is interviewed in Shaw's article, and he recounts an interview he instituted and conducted with Rader after the controversy began. (Bradlee said later he himself could not have initiated a story in the *Post* because he was bound by the columnist's pledge of confidentiality to Rader—a pledge that he felt was moot once Shaw questioned him.) Rader informed Bradlee that Rosalynn Carter and the ex-President's sister, Ruth Carter Stapleton, had told him in separate conversations that Blair House was "bugged." Rader alluded to a rumor that a UPI reporter possessed a tape recording of Mrs. Reagan in which she said she wanted the Carters to move out of the White House early. Rader told Bradlee he had not meant that Blair House actually was bugged but only that a tape existed of Mrs. Reagan's comments.

Terrence Adamson, Carter's lawyer, is reported in the Shaw article as having said that Mrs. Stapleton had no recollection of having heard the bugging rumor and that Mrs. Carter had heard the rumor but had no recollection of telling Rader about it.

• November 13, p. A22: Letter to the editor of the *Post* from Adamson. He says he told David Shaw that Mrs. Carter had not heard the Blair House rumor.

• November 13, P. A2: A one-paragraph correction, reprinted here in its entirety: "A Los Angeles Times story yesterday on the source of a controversial gossip item about former President and Mrs. Carter said that Mrs. Carter told their attorney that she had heard a rumor that the Blair House was bugged. What Mrs. Carter said was that she had heard a rumor that a reporter had a tape of Mrs. Reagan saying she wanted the Carters to move out of Blair House (*sic*) early during the transition between the two Administrations." The reference in the correction should have been to the White House, not Blair House.

During the controversy, after the Carters challenged the *Post*, Bradlee was quoted as asking: "How do you make a public apology—run up and down Pennsylvania Avenue barebottom, shouting 'I'm sorry'?"

In a study on news sources prepared for the National News Council, A. H. Raskin quotes Bradlee as saying: ". . . Nobody is quicker to admit error than the press. Where else do you see the equivalent of a first-page story admitting error? Do the auto companies or anyone in any other industry do anything to match that?"

Getting things right is not easy.

■

Before I met Donald D. Jones, the ombudsman for both Kansas City newspapers, I wrote to him, telling him a bit about myself and why I wanted to interview him. One afternoon soon after, Jon Roosenraad, the chairman of the journalism department at the University of Florida, where I was teaching, called me into his office and asked me, with an uncharacteristic edge in his voice, if I had written to Jones. It sounded like a reproof, which confused me, because I was certain I had already informed Roosenraad of my plans to visit the Middle West. I replied that I had written, and he then asked to see a copy of the letter. I gave it to Roosenraad, without looking at it first myself. Roosenraad read it and began to laugh.

I had misspelled the name of my previous boss, Edward Koch, in a most unfortunate way. Jones, who had just given a well-received speech on how journalism schools fail to inculcate in students the value of accuracy, spotted this misspelling right away, of course. Even though I had written on official stationery of the College of Journalism and Communications at Florida, Jones was suspicious. So he had called Roosenraad to see if, in fact, I existed. Jones is a careful man.

He told me a story about Calvin Trillin, the *New Yorker* writer who grew up in Kansas City. In a 20,000-word article on Kansas City, Jones said Trillin had made two minor mistakes that escaped the attention of the magazine's esteemed fact-checkers. (The checking process at the magazine is so thorough that it has been emulated, but probably not equaled, by other magazines.) One mistake Jones found was that Trillin had someone living in Shawnee Mission, Kansas. There is no such town as Shawnee Mission; it is a post office designation for a group of small suburbs. Trivial indeed, and so trivial as to be excusable in the eyes of Jones, who had read the article twice, the second time to see what mistakes he could come up with. "Insignificant errors," he said. "Damned good reporting and checking."

Jones was twenty-two when he became a full-time staff member of *The Kansas City Times* in 1950. There already was a reporter named Don Jones, so an editor gave him the name Casey, which is still his newsroom name. In his long career at Kansas City, he has held a number of responsible jobs, but he never quite made it to the top. "I had my day," said Jones, who was a reporter and copy editor at the *Times*, and later city editor, assistant managing editor and, briefly, national editor. As a significant shareholder in the company, Jones became wealthy when the papers were sold to Capital Cities Communications Inc. in 1977. Since then, the stock of Capital Cities has doubled many times.

Now Jones is a paid nitpicker for the two papers, the *Times* and the *Star*. He says that he is "too old, too rich, too fat" to do much else. He writes daily memos that run two or three pages and are posted on bulletin boards throughout the spacious second-floor newsroom that the papers share. Some memos contain starchy language, singling out reporters and editors who have performed poorly. It is peer humiliation.

The week before I visited, the lead of a story in *The Kansas City Times* said that a prominent local man had decided not to be a candidate for Missouri secretary of state. The man called up, and said that he was, in fact, intending to be a candidate. Jones interrogated the young reporter. Her notes of the conversation, Jones told me, were "pitiful." In his memo that day, he scolded the reporter by name for not having "complete notes." In addition, he said, "there were three minor errors which didn't help in trying to establish the authority of your reporting."

A correction was published the next day. In the two newspapers, as in many others across the country, corrections appear in the same place every day. In the past decade, many newspapers have become more inclined to acknowledge errors and correct them publicly. Before the arrival of the ombudsman in January 1982, corrections at the Kansas City papers were ordinarily made under duress or threat of legal action, or else they said little. For example, Jones showed me a 1968 correction that appeared under a small headline that did not even indicate a mistake had been made. It said: "Helped with gorilla." The corrective article noted that a veterinarian at the Kansas City zoo who had assisted in removing a newborn baby gorilla from the arms of its mother had been misidentified.

In addition to the reporters and editors at the two papers, and to the readers who take note of the daily corrections, Jones tries to reach a broader audience. Wherever and whenever he can, he gives a standardized speech, preaching the gospel of accuracy, and damning the two sins he finds the worst—errors and arrogance.

In a speech in the fall of 1983 to a group of journalists in St. Louis, he said: "There are plain old errors of fact. We get names wrong, we get addresses wrong, we get locations wrong for public buildings, we get sports scores wrong. And every error of fact erodes our credibility." Then choosing a rather curious comparison, he continued: "More than any other thing, the tide of errors of fact is the cause of newspapers' ranking below banks in the eyes of the American people as an institution that can be trusted."

Having an ombudsman is one way that some newspapers are trying to emphasize accuracy. Jones calls this willingness to criticize the profession "a sort of self-flagellation." While he says that many of his colleagues now view him as an apostate, he has managed to bring a touch of honor and grace to a vocation that has about as much glamour as a coroner's.

Although some major papers have ombudsmen, it is not an idea that has caught on. Most editors believe that the person who should handle complaints is the editor himself. "It's a cop-out, a P.R. stunt," says A. M. Rosenthal. In the mid-1980s, nearly two decades after the first newspaper ombudsmen went to work in Louisville, there were no more than thirty or so newspaper ombudsmen in the country. As Jones wryly noted, the representatives of more than 100 million newspaper readers were easily able to fit into one small bus at a recent convention.

No two ombudsmen do their jobs exactly alike. Jones has a nuts-and-bolts approach. He does not write a regular column commenting on the press, as do some ombudsmen, such as the one at *The Washington Post*. He feels it is his job to represent the readers exclusively. (Nearly 300,000 copies of the *Times* are sold each morning, and 250,000 copies of the *Star* are sold each afternoon. Combined circulation on Sunday approaches 400,000.)

Jones sits in a corner together with secretaries, news executives and the newspapers' lawyer. Every day in both newspapers his phone number is published underneath his picture, where his face appears owlish and his manner slightly affected —his chin is perched between his thumb and forefinger. In fact, he is tall and relatively lean, and his movements are sharp and decisive.

Typically, he receives two dozen telephone calls a day, and either he or a secretary answers the telephone. He is gracious and sounds sincere and polite. Sometimes his job is almost an incarnation of Nathanael West's Miss Lonelyhearts. Some of his callers are rejects from late night call-in shows. His technique with them, he says, is to "listen to them politely for a while, then say, 'My calls are stacked up. I have to get going.' "

One reason the new correction policy at Kansas City seems to have worked is that the burden for making corrections no longer rests with reporters, as it does at most newspapers.

Reporters naturally guard their reputations and stiffen their resolve when a caller complains. At the Kansas City papers, the complainant is directed to call Jones. If he calls the reporter directly, the reporter is instructed to notify Jones. "The person who made an error is not the person to complain to," Jones says.

For this and other reasons, Jones is not the most popular person in the newsroom. The staff is young and has no union to protect its interests. Many view his bulletin-board memos as gratuitously insulting. Jones says his notes are not meant to "keep score" of poor performance, but inevitably some reporters and editors read them that way.

Jones insists he does not have an old war-horse feeling, but he is openly unhappy with the quality of the staff of the two papers, and a sense of nostalgia creeps into his conversation. "Twenty years ago we had people from Harvard and Yale. That's not so today." He sees other problems with young reporters, many of whom use the Kansas City newspapers as a stopping off point, usually as their second newspaper job, gathering clippings and experience before moving up the career ladder to Denver, Dallas or Chicago. "They have no allegiance to the city," Jones says. "They come in. They have nothing to do after work. They do not get into community affairs. Afterward, they go and drink and re-live the work day with others like themselves."

The staff is inexperienced, and some of his written comments deal with some rather fundamental situations. One reader complained that there was not enough coverage of local news and, specifically, that the papers did not fully cover an accident in which there was a fatality. "The Times story on the fatal accident was obviously sloppy," Jones said in his daily memo. "It said the accident occurred on I-435 and that's all. Now I-435 is a pretty long road. The story never says when the accident occurred. The 'when and where' of the story were missing. But maybe that's new journalism."

In his memos, like the one on the accident, Jones can be snide or stinging. At other times, he can impart a folksy, homespun wisdom, giving useful tips to young reporters. "Don't ever say anybody was the first anything," he said in referring to an erroneous report in the *Times* which misidentified someone as the first farm bureau president in Kansas history to hold office without being elected to it.

Given his position of independence, Jones can second-guess high-ranking editors. He answers only to Mike Waller, the editor of the papers. Waller is a protégé of Norman Isaacs, who as editor of the *Louisville Courier-Journal* appointed the first ombudsman on an American paper, in late 1967.

Usually those with serious complaints will come in to the newspaper office. Jones thinks the building, a fortresslike structure, with its papers' "100-year reputation of economic influence" in the Kansas City area, can be intimidating. So, he is willing to travel to a complainant's home or office. More often than not, though, the person with a serious complaint will come to Jones to talk.

One meeting with a civic leader making a complaint lasted half a snowy afternoon. The atmosphere was formal and tense. Jones was joined by David Zeeck, the managing editor of the *Star*. They listened to William Poindexter, a prominent local lawyer, complain that two young reporters had consistently misinterpreted a situation he was involved in. Poindexter requested that they be removed from covering him.

Several months earlier the reporters had written a story whose lead may not have been warranted: "Vague policies of the Land Trust of Jackson County and the agency's bargain-basement sales of public lands have helped speculators buy scores of properties in Midtown Kansas City neighborhoods, the agency's records show." Jones was more sympathetic to the complaint than was Zeeck, who at times appeared to be irritated with Jones. Ultimately, Jones said that Poindexter's request could not be granted, in large part because he had not complained vigorously when the story first appeared.

After the two-hour meeting, the two reporters happened by chance to walk past Jones's desk. "They look young," he said. "Don't they look young to you?"

■

Although most papers now run correction boxes, many papers are still reluctant to admit they are wrong. "We'd sooner drown our children," Michael Gartner, then of the Des Moines Register and Tribune Company, told a group of Florida lawyers and journalists in the winter of 1984. "What do many papers and editors—and their lawyers, I should add—do when a paper errs? We equivocate. We bluster. We alibi. We hide behind technicalities. We hide behind secretaries. We hide behind lawyers. Sure, we run corrections—Joe Smith lives at 732 40th Street, we trumpet to our readers, not 734 20th Street, as we reported. And we'll make a big deal out of that."

Letters to the editor are another mechanism that publications use to correct errors. But just as corrections too often deal with relatively unimportant matters, so too letters to the editor are often a flawed and unsatisfactory means of rectifying mistakes. Publications use the letters-to-the-editor page as a catch-all to clarify the news, but as often as not letters lead to greater confusion. Publications often offer readers little help when competing versions of the truth exist. This letter by a Polish diplomat was published in *The New York Times* in 1983. Without doubt, the diplomat is partisan, but also without doubt, he is someone who bears listening to:

To the Editor:
I would like to raise our strong objections to the extreme inaccuracies contained in John Kifner's Aug. 9 report 'Polish Primate Halts Farm Aid Talks,' alleging a recent conflict between the Government and the church, a refusal by the Polish primate to meet with the Prime Minister.

As Mr. Kifner should know very well, this allegation is totally groundless—'completely false,' as put by the Polish Episcopate press spokesman, the Reverend Orszulik, when he was asked by Warsaw correspondents of A.P., Reuters and A.F.P. The Reverend Orszulik has also authorized the embassy to issue a denial. The New York Times has never corrected this misinformation.

We are sorry to say that this example of inaccurate reporting by The New York Times correspondent in Warsaw is no exception. Mr. Kifner's reports very often are misleading and generally biased. The question is whether this is his purposeful activity or just a case of poor journalism.

In the long run, the picture of Poland gets more and more distorted, hindering the understanding of our affairs, while perhaps pleasing those who still harbor most ridiculous illusions about Poland.
Andrzej Dobrzynski
First Secretary, Embassy of the Polish People's Republic
Washington, Aug. 25, 1983

Who is right, Kifner or the diplomat? I know Kifner, respect his reporting, and take his word, but this is not an easy case since I (and I am sure most readers) have no independent knowledge of what is going on in Poland. It is the Olympian policy of the *Times not* to have the last word, not to comment on letters. "The tendency is to let the letter writer have his or her say," says A. M. Rosenthal. "We've already had ours." As in the diplomat's letter, that disserves the reader. (Another problem is that the diplomat's letter does not reach the dozens of papers that subscribe to *The New York Times* news service— papers that published the Kifner article.)

Even more irritating than no response to a letter is the terse "We stand by our story" that some publications append to a letter with no further explanation. This letter to *Newsweek* was written by someone whom I know and whose credibility I rely on:

> You quote an anonymous aide at the International Monetary Fund (BUSINESS, March 7, 1983) concerning a conversation between IMF head Jacques de Larosiere and Citibank chairman Walter Wriston. Your reporter was kind enough to query the parties involved prior to the printing of the story. One wonders why, since the story ignores the fact that both de Larosiere and Wriston emphatically deny that such conversation took place. NEWSWEEK readers have both the right and the ability to decide whether to believe the two participants in the alleged exchange or the anonymous aide cited in your article. They cannot make that decision, however, if NEWSWEEK fails to inform them of the denial which was in your possession.
>
> Will R. Sparks
> Vice President, Citibank
> New York, New York

The magazine's unsatisfactory response was: "NEWSWEEK stands by its story."

■

In recent years, there have been attempts to go beyond the traditional methods of correcting errors. The National News Council, a promising approach to holding the media accountable, died with barely a mourner in 1984 after a decade of ineffectual service. The council, a voluntary body consisting of journalists and members of the general public, reviewed complaints that were submitted by viewers and readers and competitors about unfair or inaccurate reporting. Its findings were not binding. Few newspapers or broadcasters reported on its decisions.

The News Council, which was based in New York, had problems from the start when it was boycotted by major news organizations. When the council was formed in 1973, Arthur Ochs Sulzberger, publisher of *The New York Times*, said: "As we view it, we are being asked to accept what we regard as a form of voluntary regulation in the name of enhancing press freedom."

The announcement that the council voted itself out of existence in March 1984 was greeted with glee by many of the nation's editors. James B. Squires, editor of the *Chicago Tribune*, said, "Terrific. That makes my day." Creed Black, president of the American Society of Newspaper Editors and chairman of *The Lexington* (Kentucky) *Herald-Leader*, said: "An editor is accountable to his readers, and not to some self-appointed group."

The News Council believed that higher standards were possible by creating a channel through which the public could complain about irresponsible reporting. But the council could never overcome its lack of acceptance by the media. Many journalists retained their unproved—and unprovable—fear that a voluntary council would be the first step toward government regulation.

Some of the organization's work, such as its report on Florida media that lobbied against casino gambling, was first rate. However, much of the time it dealt with relatively minor and local issues. It took far too long to render its judgments, which came too late to do much good. Toward the end, the council also became a sounding board for special-interest groups—often to the right of center—that complained about stories that did not fit their political viewpoint. Too few people were aware of what the council did.

■

The New York Times never supported the National News Council, nor does it have an ombudsman. But on its own the *Times* has done much to strive for accuracy. It was one of the first papers to introduce a correction box that always appears in the same place. In 1983 it introduced an additional device to handle inaccuracies. Under the heading of "Editors' Note," the *Times* amplifies articles or rectifies what the editors consider significant lapses of fairness, balance or perspective. These notes are uneven and sometimes seem to be carried for the benefit of insiders. But they do make a start in demystifying the news process and in holding journalists accountable. In three years, *The Times* printed more than one hundred "Editors' Notes," including the following:

• a rebuke of one set of editors for running an article that was "too long and too prominently displayed";

• a criticism of editors of the *Times Book Review* for distorting, in the editing process, a reviewer's judgment;

• the calling to task of a well-known free-lance author for failing to check directly with a person a reference that he had suffered "a mild stroke";

• the singling out of a reporter for, first, failing to meet the *Times*'s "standard of fairness" in a story about conflicts of interest in certain activities of Navy officials and then, compounding his lapse by failing to make explicit his error in a corrective article;

• in probably the most cryptic of the notes, the pointing out, five days *before* an article was scheduled to appear in the *Times Magazine* (it had already gone to press), that the term "activist left" was an "incorrect generalization" to characterize the organizations that participated in a march in Washington.

There are other ways that newspapers have demonstrated a willingness to listen to readers. Newspapers like the *Detroit Free Press*, the *Grand Forks* (North Dakota) *Herald*, *The Miami Herald* and the *Charlotte News and Observer* have sought out, from time to time, the reactions of subjects of news stories to determine if they feel they were treated fairly. Predictably, the reactions have been mixed.

But generally the media resist introducing methods that might lead to greater accuracy and accountability. There seems to be a collective unwillingness to test time-worn assumptions that no longer necessarily make sense. For example, the general wisdom is that newspapers cannot afford to have "fact checking," a mechanism, whereby facts in each story are independently verified. This clearly would not be possible on late-breaking stories, but there is no reason it could not be tried with longer stories that are prepared well in advance of publication.

The need for such checking is great. With technology improving and newspapers and magazines going on computer data bases, past issues of newspapers are becoming more accessible than many books, which may go out of print in less than two years. (Despite the notion of permanence that hard-cover books suggest, they are not necessarily more accurate than newspapers and periodicals. Book publishers contend that accuracy is the author's responsibility, and little fact-checking is done.)

■

Many mistakes are unavoidable. The elegant formulation of Philip Graham, the publisher of *The Washington Post* from 1946 to 1963, that journalism is but "the first rough draft of history," presupposes that there will be mistakes. The pressure of time makes mistakes inevitable. Mistakes are made by editors in deciding what is news, and by reporters in the interpretation of news. Mistakes are made because people lie, or because people misunderstand each other. Mistakes are made because the world is complex.

In *Times Talk*, an in-house publication of *The New York Times*, Linda Greenhouse, the newspaper's Supreme Court reporter, wrote about one court decision in the summer of 1983 "that was such a total botch that one wire service moved a lead calling the decision a great victory for civil rights and the other wire service simultaneously sent out a story calling it a great defeat for civil rights. Depending on how you counted up the votes, each was a reasonable conclusion, though they obviously couldn't both be right. Dave Jones, the national editor, called me to tell me, encouragingly, that he had never been more confused. I assured him that it was the Court, not him; while my story, I fear, left readers scratching their heads, I hope it also induced them to blame the Court and not the *Times* for their befuddlement."

But the press is sloppy often enough that public officials can sometimes muffle or escape their own shortcomings and mistakes merely by dismissing newspaper or television accounts as inaccurate. Their claims are plausible since the media are wrong at least some of the time.

Several months after he was elected governor of New York, Mario Cuomo expressed his distrust of reporters and their use of unattributed sources. "I have this abiding reservation about 'aides close to the Governor said.' Sometimes I think that's made up."

In the fall of 1983, Cuomo, who had already become an influential figure in the national Democratic party, spoke at a gathering of important Democratic patrons in the Washington home of W. Averell Harriman. It was reported in *The New York Times* that Cuomo told the group that, with a proper approach, voters could be persuaded that "even though Mr. Reagan has a nice face, he lies." A few weeks later, early on a Sunday morning, Cuomo appeared on an interview show on Cable News Network and denied that he had ever said that Reagan lied. He said he had spoken to the reporter about this and had written a letter to the President assuring him that he had not called him a liar. (The reporter was not an eyewitness but did interview those who were at the get-together.)

Cuomo implied that the reporter and the *Times* had erred. But few people are able to follow up his statement for verification. In fact, in this case there was no correction in the *Times*, apparently because none was requested. The reporter denied ever being contacted by Cuomo, and after several months of inquiring, I never heard from Cuomo's office as to whether he actually wrote to the White House.

This anecdote—and the Blair House fiasco in *The Washington Post*—make clear why accuracy is more than just a concern for nitpickers. In order to do its job of monitoring government, the press must be accurate and must be perceived to be accurate. Ultimately, the damaging cliché—that no article accurately reports something an individual was personally involved in—can never be successfully contradicted. People will always tend to believe what they want to. But the press must be sufficiently respected so that politicians like Cuomo will have a very hard time wiggling out of their own mistakes by claiming error by the press.

12. THIN SKINS: WHEN JOURNALISTS BECOME THE STORY

The more potent is a man, the less accustomed to endure injustice, and the more his power to inflict it, —the greater is the sting and the greater the astonishment when he himself is made to suffer. Newspaper editors sport daily with the names of men of whom they do not hesitate to publish almost the severest words that can be uttered; —but let an editor be himself attacked, even without his name, and he thinks the thunderbolts of heaven should fall upon the offender. Let his manners, his truth, his judgment, his honesty, or even his consistency be questioned, and thunderbolts are forthcoming, though they may not be from heaven.
— Anthony Trollope, *Phineas Redux*, 1874

The press does not have a thick skin, it has no skin.
— A favorite saying of Edward R. Murrow

Some of the old newspaper traditions, of course, we maintain. Our self-righteousness, I can assure you, is undiminished. Our capacity to criticize everybody and our imperviousness to criticism ourselves, are still, I believe, unmatched by novelists, poets or anybody else.
— James Reston, *Columbia Journalism Review*, 1966

One of the worst jobs a reporter can draw is to interview a newspaper person. Neither one trusts the other.
— D. R. Segal, president of Freedom Newspapers, Inc., *Editor & Publisher*, 1980

If journalists do a poor job of correcting themselves, they are even worse at reporting about themselves. For example, in February 1984, sports fans in Jacksonville, Florida, had good reason to be puzzled. On a Friday night, a sportscaster on the local CBS affiliate reported an exclusive: David Lamm, a popular sports columnist for the local paper, was *about* to be fired for violating the paper's code of ethics. Apparently he had accepted a free football and discount hotel rooms for his family, and he had resold tickets to the Super Bowl.

No word of this appeared on Saturday in the local newspaper, the *Florida Times-Union*, where Lamm worked. There was no mention on Sunday or Monday either. On Tuesday, Lamm's resignation was announced in a rambling, unsigned article. The story referred to Lamm's letter of resignation, in which he said he was forced to leave the paper "under duress" because he had been accused of violating the paper's code of ethics. The article quoted Lamm's letter as saying that the newspaper's code was not well understood and that other staff members were violating it, too. The *Times-Union* then stonewalled the issue: "Neither Lamm nor Frederick W. Hartmann, executive editor of the Times-Union and Jacksonville Journal, would discuss details of the code violations that Lamm refers to in his letter." That was the end of it.

Such high-handed behavior by a politician involved in a newsworthy event would—or should—be greeted with indignant editorials. But when journalists are the story, they operate under a double standard.

Many journalists cannot imagine how they or their colleagues can possibly be part of a story—or the subject of a story itself. They cling, sometimes mindlessly, to the textbook definition of themselves as observers. (The pronoun "I" almost never appears in the daily press.) That is an attitude essentially unshaken by the liberalizing winds of New Journalism that encouraged reporters to express their feelings. Aggressive journalism, many reporters feel, should be pointed outward at the world, not at themselves.

"Whose side are we on?" asked Geraldo Rivera at the 1984 convention of Investigative Reporters and Editors. "We should lower the intramural criticism. It is self-destructive. It is a lot easier to attack a colleague than to do the real business of getting where it's at."

Rivera, who helped popularize the ambush interview, counseled other journalists to "kill" their targets with fairness. In the past several years, journalists have become much better at finding the subjects of their stories and giving them an opportunity to comment. I can remember watching reporters not too many years ago hold back in trying to get comments from someone who was being attacked in a story. If a reporter wanted to appear to be fair, but really did not wish the subject of a story to comment substantively, a call would be placed, say at 6:30 P.M.—after normal business hours, but still in time for deadline. Then a "so-and-so was unavailable for comment" would appear. Such halfhearted and often deceptive efforts seem on the wane. Today, if a person is unavailable for comment, the reporter will often, and quite appropriately, say why. If a reporter is unable to reach that person, frequently an explanation will be given.

But journalists who are so dogged in their pursuit of reaction from others are sometimes the most reluctant to comment about themselves or their colleagues.

For example, a short item appeared in *New York* magazine in June 1983 that Clay Felker might become editor of a new business magazine. Felker, the founder of *New York* magazine, left a message for the reporter from *New York* that he "doesn't comment on his personal or professional life." Felker never started that business magazine. Instead, he began a slick weekly newspaper in Manhattan called *East Side Express*. It was unexpectedly short-lived. When it folded four months after it began, early in 1984, Felker refused to discuss it.

At *The New York Times*, many reporters and editors have ambivalent feelings toward A. M. Rosenthal. They respect his abilities but are uneasy with what they regard as his unpredictability and authoritarian style. The ambivalence of the staff was described in a profile of Rosenthal in the *Washington Journalism Review* in 1983. Probably the most revealing part of the profile was the difficulty the coauthors had in getting journalists to talk to them, even off-the-record. Gerald Lanson and Mitchell Stephens, teachers of journalism at New York University, described their problems: "Twenty-four present and former Times men and women, including the paper's publisher and almost every one of the top editors who work directly under Rosenthal, either refused to be interviewed or did not return calls. Of the 44 people who have worked at the Times and were willing to be interviewed, more than half spoke only on the condition that their names not be used."

Yet when journalists get into serious trouble in their personal or professional lives, they may be treated more harshly by their colleagues than if they were in some other occupation.

On these occasions newspapers have left no detail unexamined in investigating the private life of a staff member or ex-staff member. This often has less to do with the inherent newsworthiness of the incident than with the defensiveness of editors; they either want to exonerate themselves or avoid being beaten by a competitor in telling the story. Therefore, they tell too much. This public airing of dirty linen invariably unfairly victimizes the errant journalists.

Shortly after Laura Foreman was forced to resign from *The New York Times* in September, 1977, her old paper, *The Philadelphia Inquirer*, published "The Full Story of Cianfrani and the Reporter." The story, by Donald Barlett and James Steele, a Pulitzer Prize–winning team, went on for seventeen thousand words, covering nearly six full pages of a Sunday paper. The story discussed rivalries at the paper, and it went into Foreman's private life, including details of her love affairs, including two with *Inquirer* staff members, neither of whom was named. A great deal of space was devoted to determining how much top editors of the paper knew about her private life; the results were inconclusive. The story said that while Gene Roberts, the executive editor, "maintains that Ms. Foreman always denied the existence of an affair with any politician in conversations with him, several persons say Ms. Foreman told them that she had informed Roberts of her relationship with Cianfrani."

After the *Inquirer* article appeared, A. M. Rosenthal said that he was "appalled" that the *Inquirer* would delve so deeply into her life. "The only reason was to whitewash the editors of the *Inquirer*," he said. "That was the whole thing. It was so sanctimonious, so sadistic. That woman had suffered enough and paid an enormous price for her errors."

The *Inquirer* would not have treated a public official the way it treated Foreman. It is standard practice in journalism to delve into the private life of a public official only if there is some relevance to a public act. Thus, the dating habits of a congressman would not be mentioned unless it somehow could be demonstrated that his performance as a public officeholder was impaired. Under this formula, the Foreman-Cianfrani relationship was a story; but it certainly did not merit the microscopic inspection it received.

Similarly, in the fall of 1983 the *Kansas City Times* gave excessive coverage to the personal life of a journalist who had been killed. A long story in the *Kansas City Times* probed the gruesome triple murder in Fort Wayne, Indiana, of Dan Osborne, his wife and their young son. Until a few months before his death, Osborne had worked for the *Kansas City Star*, the sister publication of the *Times*. His family had been pictured as an All-American family. They were not, but that in itself is not the material for a long feature.

The article gave details of the couple's marital problems and portrayed Osborne as a troubled man beset by unhappiness at work and at home. It spoke of his difficulty at the Kansas City paper and how he had expressed his dislike for David Zeeck, who, upon becoming managing editor in the middle of 1982, had sought to remove Osborne from his job as assistant business editor. The article euphemistically said Zeeck felt that Osborne "did not rise to the challenge."

After this article appeared, in his daily memorandum to the staff, Casey Jones, the ombudsman, said: "More in sorrow than in anger, I join many readers and staff members in deploring the article in the *Times* Saturday on the Osborne tragedy. It was uncalled for." C. W. Gusewelle, a columnist for the *Star*, wrote in the paper that the investigative piece "savaged" the Osbornes "a second time in a manner almost as inexplicable" as the murders. Gusewelle wrote that the personal details contained in the story did not "clarify their final misfortune or suggest who might have done the murderous act."

On first reading I thought the original article was well done. On rereading it, I thought the article skillfully intended to leave with the reader the impression that somehow the slayings were an outgrowth of a family quarrel—a possibility the police had already dismissed as irrelevant to the crime. Nor was the impression left by the article borne out by subsequent events. A neighborhood youth, arrested for another crime, confessed to the murders, and shortly after confessing, killed himself in his jail cell. The case was then officially closed.

In his column, Gusewelle wrote: "In this office, the resentment, the anger, at the newspaper's treatment of a former colleague is very general and very deep. . . . there is a devout prayer among us that, when we have the bad luck to die, no one will be found who knew us well or remembered that we ever worked here." The columnist received a note from Mike

Waller, the editor of the *Kansas City Times* and the *Star*, and the person who had decided to run the damaging story in the first place: "Damn good column."

Probably the most extensive coverage by a paper of a rogue reporter was the treatment by *The Wall Street Journal* of R. Foster Winans, one of the writers of the *Journal*'s "Heard on the Street" column. The *Journal* was generally praised in the journalistic community for its forthrightness in covering the Winans matter, but in its desire to protect its own reputation, it, too, appeared blind to how unfairly it dealt with a recently departed staff member.

Early in 1984 *Fortune* magazine ranked Dow-Jones, the publisher of *The Wall Street Journal*, as a company with one of the best reputations in the country. Warren H. Phillips, publisher of Dow-Jones, reflected on the success of his company: "I think reputations are built very slowly over many years—on consistency of service to the consumer, high ethical standards, and in the case of journalism, accuracy, reliability and trustworthiness. And those are not built overnight. Once the public judges you well, that's great. But if you trip and do a number of things that are unreliable, untrustworthy, what you've built up can collapse overnight . . . a bad reputation you can get overnight." That March the paper's reputation began to wobble.

"Heard on the Street" is a collection of gossip, tips and analyses of the stock market; although it is buried deep in the paper—it regularly appears on the penultimate page of the second section—it is one of the best-read features in the paper. A positive story in the column can push a company's stock up, and a negative one can depress it. Someone with advance knowledge of a column could make a great deal of money. Despite the obvious temptations, since the column began in its present format in 1967, no infraction had ever been detected.

The first hint that a *Journal* reporter was in trouble appeared on March 2, 1984, in a brief reference in the middle of a long *Wall Street Journal* article that had long been in the works: "It was learned yesterday . . . that the SEC is informally investigating allegations that a stock trader had advance knowledge of certain articles that have appeared in The Wall Street Journal." In fact, this was "learned" in an extraordinary way—from a phone call from John Fedders, director of enforcement of the Securities and Exchange Commission, who notified the Dow-Jones's in-house counsel on March 1 that an informal investigation was under way. Later that month, a lawyer for the *Journal* was told that the informal investigation had become a formal one. This was not a general press release from the SEC. Rather, the paper was notified because one of its reporters was a target and the SEC was conducting an investigation that would involve editors of the paper.

The SEC gave the paper this information for one reason—to let it know it was under investigation—but the *Journal* used it for quite another as well. The paper was in a unique situation. It had exclusive knowledge of an investigation involving itself, and what it knew was newsworthy. The *Journal* therefore did what journalists do—treated it as a news story. The *Journal* cooperated with the investigators, and wrote exclusive stories about it, managing to stay a day ahead of competition.

On March 29, on page 3, the *Journal* reported that Winans had been fired and that he was understood to have told the SEC that he leaked sensitive information on articles he wrote. The day the article appeared, Norman Pearlstine, managing editor of the *Journal*, declined to say how the *Journal* had concluded that Winans admitted passing information improperly. The SEC refused even to acknowledge publicly that an investigation was under way.

On April 2 a dozen reporters and editors collaborated on a 5,000-word article presenting the story behind the story. This was the lead article in the paper, and it recounted how Winans, who earned $610 a week, complained often about being underpaid. It mentioned that Winans had been reprimanded for errors on the paper, and told how he was helping to support his homosexual lover, David J. Carpenter, who was described as ill and a free spender.

The article was extremely blunt about the homosexual aspect. It reported that Winans confided to friends that he felt he was being treated unfairly because he was homosexual. "Journal editors deny this assertion," the article said in what came across as a self-serving rebuttal. In language that certainly would not appear in most other newspapers or, ordinarily, in the *Journal* itself, the article said of Winans and Carpenter: "The two were lovers. . . . They live together, and Mr. Winans wears a gold ring given to him by Mr. Carpenter."

Two weeks later, in an editors' note responding to several letters the paper had published about the incident and the article, news executives of the paper went into detail why the

Winans-Carpenter relationship was "potentially of central relevance." To make its case, the editors said, "the SEC must demonstrate that Mr. Winans received some financial benefit, directly or indirectly. We have seen no evidence that Mr. Winans took money for his tips or traded securities on the information. Mr. Carpenter, however, made profits of about $4,000 on shares of two companies that he bought before Mr. Winans wrote favorable articles on them, and it seems that Mr. Winans provided Mr. Carpenter with financial support. Thus, it can be argued that Mr. Carpenter's profits were an indirect benefit to Mr. Winans."

Journal editors were sufficiently worried about the homosexual reference in the April 2 article that during the editing process, they substituted a female name for one of the partners to see if the relationship had been stressed too much. They concluded that "the language of the story seems perfectly ordinary and straightforward." Of course it does. But I doubt that the *Journal*, having established that Dick and Jane were roommates, would bother to say that Dick wore a gold ring Jane had given him.

Thomas Griffith, the former editor who now comments on the press for *Time* magazine, observed: "The editors concluded that the homosexuality had to be printed. Besides, how would the Journal have looked later had another paper come out with the 'real, untold story'?"

With all its precautions, the *Journal* was still too hasty in its speculation, and the homosexual affair was not the "real, untold story" at all. The *Journal* was covering the investigative phase of an SEC inquiry, always a precarious assignment since the investigators control most of the information. Indeed, additional information about Winans did come out later. He had indeed benefited financially from the scheme, thus diluting the significance of the Carpenter connection, relegating it to secondary legal importance.

In the middle of May, when Winans, Carpenter and three others were charged by the SEC with acting illegally by profiting from advance knowledge about *Journal* columns, the *Journal* noted, only in passing, that "the agency's lawsuit provides the first explanation of the reporter's motive for sharing advance information on stories." In the article reporting the SEC action, the *Journal* described Carpenter as "a former news clerk at the Journal who lived with Mr. Winans and shares his income and expenses." No reference to homosexuality was made. By the time Winans and Carpenter were indicted in late August for conspiring to profit from advance knowledge of *Journal* articles, Carpenter was identified merely as "a former news clerk at the Journal and Mr. Winans's roommate"—a description that would have been adequate from the beginning of the *Journal*'s coverage. When they came to trial in January 1985, a similar description was used.

In the April 2 story, the *Journal* had published information from Winans's personnel records, an apparent breach of his privacy. The editors defended this action by saying "this information was routine, and it was relevant in allowing readers to assess our management and supervisory practices." But these supervisory practices are not addressed. In their attempt to brand Winans as the bad apple and exonerate others on the paper, his supervisors—many of whom wrote and edited the stories about the incident—did not explain why Winans was entrusted with the column when he was relatively inexperienced in business reporting. Nor did they wish to explain why he was paid so modestly given the importance of his assignment and compared to salaries received by reporters working on other New York City papers.

While these stories were running, Winans had the bad luck of being under formal investigation, and, on the advice of his lawyer, he quite properly kept his mouth shut. This worked to his severe detriment. The editors said that "we have made strenuous efforts to get more of his side of the story in our coverage," but they were "rebuffed," as the editors knew they certainly would be, given Winans's precarious legal situation.

In early May, Norman Pearlstine, the *Journal*'s managing editor, spoke to the annual convention of the American Society of Newspaper Editors. "We felt that we owed our readers as much information as we possibly could to explain what happened, why it happened and what the significance was," he said. That is a fine and proper sentiment for a paper that has a long tradition of exposing insider trading and of exposing journalistic lapses. But this same sentiment led to the exoneration of the editors and unfair treatment of Winans. At the time of the April 2 story, he was only a target of an investigation, nothing more, but the *Journal* treated him as if he were a convicted freak.

Cases of journalistic misconduct such as Winans's are, of

course, rare. When routine conduct of journalists—especially celebrity journalists—comes under scrutiny by journalists themselves, a double standard is again at work.

In September 1981, "60 Minutes" took an unusual step and opened its season with a show called "60 Minutes Looks at Itself." On it, newspaper reporters, editors and Don Hewitt and Mike Wallace of "60 Minutes" watched and then commented on a series of segments in which controversial reportorial methods were employed. In these snippets, CBS journalists used false identification to get a story, posed as patients at a cancer clinic, filmed a story behind a one-way mirror, kept a camera focused on a man who refused to be interviewed, and watched a man squirm on camera as he was surprised and confronted with incriminating information. These techniques did not meet with immediate approval from the guests on the show, and even Wallace and Hewitt acknowledged they had cut back on some of these methods, including the ambush interview.

Jeff Greenfield, whom "60 Minutes" had drafted as moderator for this show, asked at one point: "If I, as a sometime media critic, hired a camera crew to infiltrate and put a camera in the offices of '60 Minutes' to show how you guys got a story and you found out, I really don't think you would accept this as an investigative, entrepreneurial report. I think you guys would hit the ceiling. . . . I guess the question is: How would you like it done to you? How would you like somebody to point a camera at you that you didn't know was there, to confront you with embarrassing material, perhaps about a life you once led or something you once did?"

"I wouldn't like it," said Wallace, "which is why I lead a life beyond reproach."

That remark got a big laugh. But soon after, Wallace was the subject of two embarrassing stories. In 1981 he asked his colleague Morley Safer not to do a story about Haiti because he feared there would be reprisals against his wife's family, who still lived there. A few months later, Wallace made a derogatory racial reference. Under the impression that no cameras were rolling, he suggested that lien contracts were especially hard to read "if you're reading them over the watermelon or the tacos."

In his book, *Close Encounters*, Wallace says he was "justly reproached" for his behavior in both incidents and that "there was no doubt a certain poetic justic at work." But in both instances he describes himself as a victim. In the stories that resulted from his conversation with Safer, he said he was "the victim of internal leaks" at CBS. As for the second incident, he said the remark was "wrenched out of context." He said he was the victim "of a camera crew that had been instructed to record my comments without my knowledge." Actually, the camera crew had been hired by a bank officer whom he was interviewing. During the interview, the CBS cameraman ran out of film and was changing film, but the camera crew hired by the banker continued to film—in violation of the ground rules, according to Wallace. It was during this period that he made his ill-advised remark about watermelon and tacos. Once he realized that this had been taped, Wallace called officials at the bank and suggested they erase the portions of the tape "that, ethically never should have been recorded in the first place." (A half-hour later, he called back and told them to forget about that extraordinary request.)

Wallace had fallen victim to a candid camera, just as his CBS colleague Dan Rather had in 1983. In the trial of a slander suit brought by a doctor in California, CBS was forced to make public its outtakes—footage that had been edited out and had not appeared on television.

The network won the lawsuit, but its reputation was damaged by questions about the way Rather and his producer gathered information for a segment on "60 Minutes" in which they charged collusion among doctors and lawyers to bilk insurance companies through phony medical claims. On the witness stand, Rather was confronted with some factual errors, and he acknowledged that his effort to reach the plaintiff, Dr. Carl A. Galloway, for comment had been minimal. He had left two messages for Dr. Galloway, but the doctor never responded. The jury and audience heard Rather's view, which he had expressed in a deposition: "My experience with guilty people is that they don't call back. They usually get a lawyer."

Several months after the verdict, Rather, in a speech to lawyers specializing in media litigation, acknowledged the damage done to CBS: "A boxing ring is small. There is nowhere to run, nowhere to hide. Once inside the ropes, you will receive no mercy. At the Galloway trial, we did not realize soon enough and emphatically enough that there is one arena inside the courtroom and another outside the courtroom. We lost in the outside arena. That is a lament."

A footnote to the Galloway trial may have embarrassed Dan

Rather most of all. Several weeks after the trial ended, a reporter from a new syndicated television program called "Breakaway" caught Rather by surprise outside CBS headquarters and began asking questions about his involvement in the slander suit brought by Dr. Galloway. According to the reporter, Steve Wilson, Rather had not answered his phone calls or responded to a registered letter, and so Wilson and the camera crew confronted him, camera rolling, in front of CBS. Rather put his hand on Wilson's shoulder and calmly said, "Get that microphone right up, will you?" Then, Rather said: "Fuck you," adding, "You got it clearly?" The expletive was bleeped out when the show was broadcast.

Rather apologized in a letter to Wilson: "That was inexcusable, rude and un-Christian behavior for which I am remorseful." In an interview with *Playboy*, Rather commented on his behavior: "I mistook who he was. I thought I was being harassed again by people connected with the 60 Minutes Galloway case. . . . As soon as I realized he was legitimate, I apologized to him and offered to do the interview with him. What I feel worst about is having mistreated a fellow reporter."

Rather said the incident became overblown when producers of "Breakaway" tried to generate some publicity. "Fair enough. At first, nobody bit—not even the gossip columnists. Then *The New York Times* ran it, and once that happened, the other media picked it up. It's funny. The *Times* gave more space to a story about Dan Rather's using profanity than it did to a story about CBS's announcing a new prime-time news broadcast a few days earlier. It makes you think, Aha, is somebody trying to do us in?"

A short article on Rather's use of an obscenity did appear in the *Times* on September 20, 1983, the day after the segment had been shown on more than sixty stations across the country and the very day one would expect to read about it.

Rather wishes to be thought of as victimized by other journalists. That is a role that Roone Arledge, the president of ABC News and Sports, also seems comfortable with. Like Rather, Arledge has a skewed recollection of stories written about him. At ABC Arledge has tried to cultivate the image of an innovator. He also has shown insecurity about not being accepted as a "serious" journalist and has been quick to jump on those who question his soberness of purpose. He has gone so far as to mount unseemly and unwarranted attacks on other journalists.

In the summer of 1983 Arledge granted a long interview to Nancy Collins of *New York* magazine. Arledge came across as shrewd and diplomatic. A letter to the editor, however, questioned the accuracy of one of Arledge's recollections, and after I checked some of his statements, it became clear to me that either he has a memory more selective than most or that he was trying to buy his reputation at the expense of other journalists. At a critical point in the interview, Arledge talked about the impression people had of him when, in addition to being head of ABC Sports, he also took over the ABC News operation:

"I remember US magazine—which, to my amazement, is still being published—wanted to do a bio on me, but I refused. So US just made it up. They made it look like they had interviewed me, took some old pictures and quotes and made it sound like I was some sort of hippie, wearing shirts open to the waist with gold chains."

Q: "Were you, in fact, wearing gold chains and open shirts?"

A: "Only if I popped a button. But I did want people to know I was a hands-on executive. So I used to go down to the editing room a lot, where you naturally wear different clothes than when you are speaking to affiliates. Sally Bedell came to interview me one day when I was editing and had a sport shirt on. By the time she got done describing it, it had turned into a polka-dot shirt, and from that time on, any time people did a caricature, there I'd be in the polka-dot shirt. . . ." (He skirts the issue of gold chains and leaves aside the rather anomalous suggestion that those who wear them are "hippies.")

In that one passage, Arledge made some insulting charges, questioning the integrity of a national magazine and the reportorial abilities of Sally Bedell (now Sally Bedell Smith of *The New York Times*). Not surprisingly, Arledge recalled events in ways most favorable to the image he would like to project of himself.

The profile in *US* that Arledge complained about was written by Fred Ferretti, a *New York Times* reporter and rewriteman. There is no confusion about whether Arledge was interviewed specifically for this article. In his article, Ferretti says straight out: "Arledge refused interviews." It is hard to be confused after reading that. Ferretti used quotes from other sources and tried to add color to the profile. He hardly, as Arledge suggests, "just made it up." Indeed, with the benefit of hindsight, Ferretti wrote a rather complimentary article on how hard-working Arledge was.

Smith, for her part, wrote the following letter to *New York* magazine:

"It's hard to blame Roone Arledge for taking a stab at sartorial revisionism. In his interview with Nancy Collins (August 15: ABC News Under the Gun) he mentioned an interview with me some years back in which he had worn a sports shirt that in my subsequent article I 'had turned into a polka-dot shirt.'

"I can fully understand Roone's wanting to forget the bright green shirt with white polka dots that he wore that day in October 1977, but I could not."

A third paragraph of her letter was not published. She later sent it to me. It said: "Just to show that his taste on that occasion wasn't some teensy aberration, I have enclosed a Xerox of a photograph of Mr. Arledge from New Times on January 23, 1978—different polka dots, but you get the idea."

In her letter to me, Smith said: "Although a reference to Roone's shirt was not the most consequential piece of news, I was nevertheless put out by his charge that I had misrepresented something. The *New York* magazine fact-checking department never called before the interview appeared, by the way, which surprised me a bit."

After Smith's letter appeared in *New York* magazine, she said that Arledge called her to say that he had been misquoted in the original interview—an accusation that he did not repeat to Nancy Collins.

Like Mike Wallace and Dan Rather, Roone Arledge possesses a finely tuned double standard. In this sense, journalists are just like anyone else. They have thin skins and prefer to criticize rather than be criticized.

In 1981, after "Jimmy's World" had been exposed as a hoax, there was much blame-shifting and introspection. Amid all this, Jonathan Moore, director of Harvard's Institute of Politics, offered a very shrewd observation to a *Newsweek* reporter: "One of the most interesting things is the reaction of astonishment— as if the media were different and the people working in it didn't misbehave. . . . Presumably, the press is a community of human beings. An assumption of purity is unrealisitic for the press to assume about itself and unfair for others to assume about it."

Journalists do not live in isolation: Their values and techniques are part of their culture's larger fabric. Their imperfections are not theirs alone. More than fifty years ago, Bruce Bliven, who was to become editor of the *New Republic*, observed that "the chief frailty of the newspapers is the frailty of human kind."

Journalists do not belong on a pedestal, but it is not too much to ask that they be less hypocritical, more humble, and that they remember, when they report stories that hurt and embarrass others, the way that they feel when they are the subjects of stories.

The New York Times cut through the legalities and set forth sensible—and idealistic—standards for journalists in its editorial on the verdict in the libel case brought against *Time* by General Ariel Sharon of Israel:

"The jury found an absence of malice, but no shortage of arrogance. It went out of its way to reprimand Time for 'negligently and even carelessly' defaming the general. It seemed to give voice to widespread discontent with influential media that are quick to dish out criticism but unwilling or reluctant to present a contrary judgment or to confess error.

"Time thinks the jury misread the crucial paragraph [concerning Sharon's responsibility for a massacre of Palestinians in Beirut]. But these jurors were typical readers of Time. If they found its words more maligning than the magazine intended, it should not require a long, costly trial to resolve the ambiguity.

"If after studying the reporting, writing and editing routines at Time, jurors find some of them careless and negligent, it's time for journalists to stop muting their criticism of one another. The best protection of free speech is more free speech, not less.

"To deserve the extraordinary protections of American law, Time and all of journalism need a stronger tradition of mutual and self-correction. The more influential the medium, the greater the duty to offer a place for rebuttal, complaint, correction and reexamination. Beating the arrogance rap is even more important than escaping one for libel."

NOTES

Chapter 1

Page 10
To recover libel. *Chapadeau* v. *Utica Observer-Dispatch*, vol. 38 of second series of reports of decisions of New York Court of Appeals, p. 196.
In my testimony. From transcript of testimony. March 25, 1983.
After Daly left. *New York Times*, May 10, 1983, p. 34.

Page 11
Peacock's lawyer then. The article appeared in the *New York Daily News*, February 12, 1979, p. 9.

Page 14
When I returned. The profile of Tom Downey appeared in *Rolling Stone*, April 14, 1983, p. 38.

Page 16
The jury eventually. *New York Times*, January 26, 1985, p. 1.
With all this. *Newsweek*, February 4, 1985, p. 54.

Page 18
Fifty-three percent. *Newsweek*, October 22, 1984, p. 68.
Later in 1984. *presstime*, January 1985, p. 53.
Statistics compiled. Floyd Abrams, speech at the University of Michigan, March 22, 1984.
He had been accused. *Washington Post*, November 30, 1979, p. 1.
He wrote that. *New York Times*. May 3, 1983, p. 1.

Page 19
"We're delighted." *New York Times*, May 3, 1983, p. 1.
(In a 1983 public.) Louis Harris, "Does the public *really* hate the press?" *Columbia Journalism Review*, March/April 1984, p. 16.
In a 1980 book. Frank M. Coffin, *The Ways of a Judge: Reflections*

From the Federal Appellate Bench (Boston: Houghton Mifflin Co., 1980), p. 7.

Page 20

This practice and. Formal opinion 337 of the American Bar Association Committee on Ethics and Professional Responsibility.

"We are not." Sanford Levinson, "Under Cover: The Hidden Costs of Infiltration," reprinted in *Abscam Ethics: Moral Issues and Deception in Law Enforcement*, Gerald M. Caplan, ed. (Washington: Police Foundation, 1983), pp. 57–58.

Page 21

But a journalist. Jeff Greenfield, *Penthouse*, March 1982, p. 82.

Page 22

In a well-received. Louis Boccardi speech to publishers in Montreal, April 30, 1984.

Chapter 2

Page 27

His death, after. *New York Times*. February 17, 1925, p. 1.

In *Only Yesterday*. Frederick Lewis Allen, *Only Yesterday: An Informal History of the Nineteen Twenties* (New York: Blue Ribbon Books, 1931), p. 193.

In his review. *Sunday Observer*, March 13, 1966, *Weekend Review*, p. 1.

Page 28

Capote called the. *New York Times*, March 27, 1966, p. 85.

At one of the many postmortems. Seib's remarks were made at the convention of the American Society of Newspaper Editors, Washington, April 22, 1981.

Page 29

"Like it or." "Inside Story," April 28, 1983.

Page 30

"Quite simply, you." "Media professionals respond to burning," *News Photographer*, July 1983, p. 16.

"If you've never." Harris interview on "Inside Story," April 28, 1983.

Page 31

In 1865, after. Junius Browne, *Four Years in Secessia* (Hartford: O. D. Case & Co., 1865), p. 30.

In 1961, toward. The role of *The New York Times* in the Bay of Pigs controversy was outlined by Clifton Daniel, managing editor, in a speech in 1966 at Macalester College in St. Paul, Minnesota. Excerpts, *New York Times*, June 2, 1966, p. 14.

Page 32

"I'm proud they." Carl Bernstein, "The CIA and the Media," *Rolling Stone*, October 20, 1977, p. 55.

In contrast to World War II. *Washington Post*, December 16, 1983, p. A10.

There was agreement. *Washington Journalism Review*, December 1984, p. 16.

Page 33

"A journalist should." *East Hampton Star*, July 21, 1983, p. Il1.

In the paper's written. *Philadelphia Inquirer*'s Standards of Professional Conduct, fall, 1978, p. 6.

Page 34

He was told by a spokesman. Ruth Adler, ed., *The Working Press* (New York: G. P. Putnam's Sons, 1966), p. 187.

"When I was a reporter." A. M. Rosenthal, "The Trees of Warsaw: A Return to Poland," *New York Times Magazine*, August 7, 1983, p. 24.

In *How True*. Thomas Griffith, *How True: A Skeptic's Guide to Believing the News* (Boston: Atlantic Monthly Press Book, 1974), p. 23.

Page 35

In an interview several. Victor Navasky, *Kennedy Justice* (New York: Atheneum, 1971), p. 316.

Arthur Schlesinger, Jr. Arthur Schlesinger, Jr. *Robert Kennedy and His Times* (Boston: Houghton Mifflin Company, 1978), p. 400.

Page 37

"She committed a major." *Newsweek*, November 14, 1977, p. 48.

After Cianfrani was. Laura Foreman, "My Side of the Story," *Washington Monthly*, May 1978, pp. 51–53.

Since the fall. The *Inquirer*'s Standards of Professional Conduct, p. 6.

Page 38

For example, at *The Atlanta*. Memorandum to staff. Undated.

The *Chicago Tribune*. Ethics Policy, June 24, 1982.

At the *New York Daily*. Ethics in Journalism: Some Guidelines at the *Daily News*, October 1980.

At *The Denver*. Response to author's questionnaire, January 1984.

At the Kansas. Code of Ethics, *Kansas City Star* and *Kansas City Times*, undated.

At *The New York Times*. Conflict-of-Interest Policy, December 14, 1983.

Page 39
At *Newsday*. Memorandum to author from Anthony Marro, January 19, 1984.
ABC discourages its. ABC News Policy, March 10, 1982, p. I.4.
Jerrold Footlick. Interview with author, March 12, 1984.

Page 40
After she was fired. Jacquelyn McClary, "My firing raises a lot of questions. . . ." *ASNE Bulletin*, September 1983, p. 36.
"I see no valid." Ralph L. Millett, Jr., "I see no valid comparison," *ASNE Bulletin*, September 1983, p. 37.

Chapter 3

Page 43
Probably best. *Fort Myers News-Press*, August 28, 1983, p. 3f.
She testified: "If." *Fort Myers News-Press*, August 20, 1983, p. 1.
When Averill bragged. *Fort Myers News-Press*, August 20, 1983, p. 1.

Page 44
Several months after. Southeast Regional Meeting of the Society of Professional Journalists, Sigma Delta Chi, Miami Beach, April 7, 1984.
The report, issued. "Unauthorized Disclosures Regarding Abscam, Pendorf and Brilab, A Public Report of the U.S. Department of Justice," January 14, 1981, p. 18.

Page 45
In a "Letter." *Fort Myers News-Press*, August 28, 1983, p. 3f.
"The press and the government." Interview with author, November 8, 1983.
"We can do things." Remarks at convention of Investigative Reporters & Editors, Miami, June 9, 1984.
In the spring of 1983. Speech reprinted in *ASNE Bulletin*, September 1983, p. 26.

Page 46
In an earlier speech. Presidential address, Annual meeting of the American Society of Newspaper Editors, Chicago, May 5, 1982.
In his graduation. Text of speech of Joe Dealey at the University of Texas, April 23, 1983.
"Good reporters have." Text of speech at meeting of members of Investigative Reporters & Editors in Palm Springs, California, October 10, 1983.

"Every time I." Miami meeting of Investigative Reporters & Editors, June 10, 1984.

Jack Newfield. Jack Newfield, "Journalism Old, New and Corporate," *The Reporter as Artist: A Look at the New Journalism Controversy*, ed. Ronald Weber (New York: Hastings House, 1974), p. 65.

At the Miami. Speech at Miami meeting of Investigative Reporters & Editors, June 9, 1984.

Page 47

Gilbert Cranberg. Interview with author, November 7, 1983.

"They promised to." Interview with author, November 10, 1983.

Charles Thompson. Gilbert Cranberg, "What Price Cooperation Between the Press and Law-Enforcement Agencies?" *ASNE Bulletin*, November 1981, p. 27.

Page 48

"Reporters feel more." Interview with author, October 31, 1983.

"In essence, the tape." Interview with author, November 1, 1983.

Page 49

"The linebacker had." Interview with author, November 7, 1983.

The *Indianapolis*. Guide for Editorial Employees, August 1983, p. 22.

Page 50

When Edwin Meese. Article reprinted in *Atlanta Journal & Constitution*, February 5, 1985, p. 14D.

Page 51

A report detailing. "Unauthorized Disclosures Regarding Abscam, Pendorf and Brilab," January 14, 1981, p. 13.

One note, from. Victor Navasky, *Kennedy Justice*, p. 427.

Page 52

The prosecutors concluded. Whitney North Seymour, Jr., *United States Attorney: An Inside View of "Justice" in America Under The Nixon Administration* (New York: Morrow, 1975), pp. 219–21.

"If a reporter comes." Interview with author October 31, 1983.

Robert Fiske. Interview with author November 1, 1983.

Page 54

In the commission's report. Report of the State Commission of Investigation, November 18, 1976. In December 1975 and January 1976, the commission held four days of public hearings on the issue of grand jury leaks.

His critics frequently. Anthony Lewis, "The Zeal of Maurice Nadjari," *New York Times Magazine*, March 28, 1976, p. 80.

At a lecture at. Anthony Lewis's magazine article, p. 86.

After Nadjari left. Jack Newfield, *The Education of Jack Newfield* (New York: St. Martin's Press, 1984), p. 97.

Page 55

This was the first. My article appeared in *The New York Times*, April 9, 1974, p. 16; "The Ten Worst Judges in New York" was the cover story in *New York* magazine, October 16, 1972.

Page 56

Even though it. *New York Times*, April 9, 1974, p. 16.

Shortly after this. Jack Newfield, "The Next 10 Worst Judges," *Village Voice*, September 26, 1974, p. 5.

In the introduction. Jack Newfield, *The Education of Jack Newfield*, p. 2.

Page 57

("He has more.") Interview with author, August 1, 1984.

In a long letter. *Village Voice*, May 22, 1984, p. 5.

In an affidavit. John Scanlon's affidavit, sworn to May 17, 1983.

Page 58

In a preliminary version. Tom Goldstein, "Odd Couple: Prosecutors and the Press," *Columbia Journalism Review*, January/February, 1984, p. 23.

In his letter. *Columbia Journalism Review*, March/April 1984, p. 59.

Chapter 4

Page 60

Until the early. Robin Reisig, "The Biggest Freeloaders Around," *More Magazine*, May 1972.

Page 63

"My thanks to." Mayor Koch's monologue, March 20, 1982.

Page 64

As he notes. Edward I. Koch, *Mayor* (New York: Simon and Schuster, 1984), p. 335.

In it, Koch. Edward I. Koch, *Mayor* (New York: Warner Books, 1985) p. 369.

Page 65

Speaking early in 1983. *Editor & Publisher*, May 7, 1983, p. 36; *Los Angeles Times*, May 25, 1983, p. 1; *Los Angeles Times*, May 27, 1983, p. 1.

Sulzberger recalls. Letter to author, September 20, 1984.

Page 66
"We are advocates." *Los Angeles Times*, May 27, 1983, p. 1.
In 1980, the *Columbia*. *Columbia Journalism Review*, January/February 1980, p. 23.
"Rupert Murdoch's." "Responsibility & Freedom In the Press: Are They In Conflict?" The Report of the Citizen's Choice National Commission on Free and Responsible Media (Washington: Citizen's Choice, 1985), p. 88.
In the 1977. *New York Times*, August 28, 1977, p. 42.

Page 67
Robert Christopher, administrator. Letter to author, October 25, 1983.

Page 68
He had ample. Harold Evans, *Good Times, Bad Times* (New York: Atheneum, 1984—United States Ed.), p. 165.

Page 69
In a predictable. *New York Post*, June 21, 1984.
In reviewing Evans's. *St. Petersburg Times*, January 22, 1984.
In 1982 he was honored. Copy of invitation to dinner, April 21, 1982.
In the *Post*. April 22, 1982, p. 9.

Page 70
He was the first. Letter to author from Israel Levine, director of communications, American Jewish Congress, August 1, 1984.
(None of those.) Letter from Israel Levine, February 25, 1985.
In his speech. *New York Post*, April 22, 1982, p. 9.
In the midst. Tom O'Hanlon, "What Does This Man Want?" *Forbes*, January 30, 1984, p. 78
The *Forbes* profile. *Chicago Sun-Times*, January 22, 1984.

Page 71
Forbes magazine gushed. *Forbes* article, p. 86.
In contrast to. *Chicago Tribune*. November 13, 1983.
Martin Tolchin. Letter to author, September 4, 1984; Michael B. Grossman and Martha Joynt Kumar, *Portraying the President: The White House and the News Media* (Baltimore: Johns Hopkins Press, 1981), p. 207.

Page 72
The advice of. Letter to author from Philip Meyer, August 21, 1984.

The danger that. Quote comes from *I. F. Stone's Weekly*, a documentary reviewed in *The New York Times*, October 19, 1973, p. 52.

In 1983 Mary. Charles W. Bailey, *Conflicts of Interest: A Matter of Journalistic Ethics* (New York: A Report to The National News Council, 1984), p. 12.

("Scratch a journalist.") Leo Rosten, "The Social Composition of Washington Correspondents," *Journalism Quarterly*, June 1937, p. 128.

In a 1984. Bailey's pamphlet, p. 12.

In an acerbic. Henry Fairlie, "How Journalists Get Rich," *Washingtonian*, August 1983, p. 86.

Page 73

"I was invited." Letter to author, September 4, 1984.

The Washington Post commented. *Washington Monthly*, March 1983, p. 7.

In a column on. *Buffalo News*, June 28, 1983, p. 14.

Page 74

(But the official biographer.) Chalmers Roberts, *The Washington Post: First Hundred Years* (Boston: Houghton Mifflin Company, 1977), p. 341.

In 1956 Graham. Roberts, *The Washington Post*, p. 337.

In *A Thousand*. Arthur M. Schlesinger, Jr., *A Thousand Days: John F. Kennedy in the White House* (Boston: Houghton Mifflin Company, 1965), pp. 41–45.

Page 75

The role played. Theodore H. White, *The Making of the President 1960* (New York: Atheneum, 1961) pp. 189–93.

Graham felt that. Theodore H. White, *The Making of the President 1964* (New York: Atheneum, 1965), pp. 407–15.

Here is Chalmers. Roberts, *The Washington Post*, p. 361.

Page 76

In it Bradlee describes. Benjamin Bradlee, *Conversations With Kennedy* (New York: W. W. Norton & Company, 1984 paperback ed.), p. 21.

Bradlee wisely. Bradlee, *Conversations With Kennedy*, p. 26.

In those years. Osborn Elliott, *The World of Oz* (New York: Viking Press, 1980), p. 21.

He could, as he recounts. Bradlee, *Conversations With Kennedy*, p. 10.

It was a glimpse. Bradlee, *Conversations With Kennedy*, p. 10.

Page 77

More important than scoops. Bradlee, *Conversations With Kennedy*, p. 134.

"The *Newsweek* story." Kenneth Thompson, ed. *Ten Presidents and the Press* (Washington: University Press of America, 1983), p. 72.

In the story itself. *Newsweek*, September 24, 1962, p. 86.

In his book, Bradlee. Bradlee, *Conversations With Kennedy*, p. 116.

The chapter, which. Robert A. Webb, ed. *The Washington Post Deskbook on Style* (New York: McGraw-Hill Book Company, 1978), p. 2.

In *The Powers*. David Halberstam, *The Powers That Be* (New York: Alfred A. Knopf, 1979), p. 376.

Page 78

He wrote the book. Interview with author, October 12, 1984.

Halberstam notes that. Halberstam, *The Powers That Be*, p. 351.

He recalls that "several." Bradlee, *Conversations With Kennedy*, p. 50.

Page 79

In January 1981, just. *Newsweek*, January 19, 1981, p. 92.

Will was introduced. George Will, "Backstage at the Presidential Debate," *Washington Post*, July 10, 1983, p. B7.

Will commented. "Where There's a Will," *Columbia Journalism Review*, September/October 1983, p. 25.

Nor was it mentioned. *Wall Street Journal*, July 8, 1983, p. 13.

Will's role in the debate. Jack Germond and Jules Witcover, *Blue Smoke and Mirrors: How Reagan Won and Jimmy Carter Lost the Election of 1980* (New York: Viking, 1981), p. 277; Lou Cannon, *Reagan* (New York: Putnam, 1982), p. 95.

It was raised. Laurence Barrett, *Gambling With History: Reagan in the White House* (Garden City, N.Y.: Doubleday, 1983) p. 382.

("It was amazing.") Jody Powell, *The Other Side of the Story* (New York: William Morrow and Company, 1984), p. 277.

Page 80

David Broder. The National Ethics Committee. Society of Professional Journalists, Sigma Delta Chi, *The 1983 Journalism Ethics Report*, p. 12.

Jack Germond. *The 1983 Journalism Ethics Report*, p. 12.

Joseph Sobran. *ASNE Bulletin*, October 1983, p. 29.

Max Lerner, *New York Post*, July 13, 1983, p. 31.

In *The Washington. Washington Post*, July 10, 1983, p. B7.

Ronald Steel. Ronald Steel, *Walter Lippmann and the American Century* (Boston: Atlantic Monthly Press Book, 1980), p. 96.

Page 81

Later, in a letter. The letter was reprinted in the *ASNE Bulletin*, November 1983, p. 12.

Its editorial, citing. *New York Daily News*, July 10, 1983, p. 41.
In an interview, James. *Editor & Publisher*, April 14, 1984, p. 37.

Page 82
"It would be." Interview with author, October 12, 1984.
"When we endorse." Michael Gartner, "The First Rough Draft of History—An Interview with Benjamin Bradlee," *American Heritage*, October/November, 1982, p. 34.
Charles Perlik, Jr. *Washington Journalism Review*, December 1983, p. 9
In a letter to. Letter to Francis X. Clines, November 1, 1983.
Perlik's defense. *Editor & Publisher*, June 2, 1984, p. 6.

Page 83
In announcing to. *Baltimore Sun*, October 28, 1984, p. 6D.
In defense of this. Tom Goldstein, "The Press Has No Business Meddling in Election Process," *Buffalo News*, October 5, 1984, p. C3.

Chapter 5

Page 85
Several months before. *New York Times*, December 1, 1983, p. 1.

Page 86
The invitation read. *Village Voice*, May 8, 1984, p. 11.
"Among the tasks." *Editor & Publisher*, August 18, 1984, p. 25.
(In March 1985.) *Wall Street Journal*, March 22, 1985, p. 25.

Page 87
(In a 1984 editorial.) *New York Times*, July 9, 1984, p. A18.
It is the view of. Interview with author on October 12, 1984.
In a speech in 1983. Dealey's speech at the University of Texas, April 23, 1983.

Page 89
"Generally speaking." Interview with James Squires, January 28, 1985.
"The World is the people's." W. A. Swanberg, *Pulitzer* (New York: Charles Scribner's Sons, 1967), p. 104.
The paper carried many. *New York Daily News*, May 18, 1984, p. 6.
The *News* was. *New York Daily News*, December 12, 1984, p. 16.

Page 90
In 1978 a group of Florida. *In the Public Interest II—A Report by*

The National News Council, 1975–1978. The National News Council Inc., 1979, pp. 393–414.
"While proprietors of." Interview with author, May 8, 1984.

Page 91
A survey conducted in 1981. *Editor & Publisher*, May 1, 1982, p. 51.
In a 1911 editorial. Referred to in speech by Michael Gartner of *Des Moines Register and Tribune*, June 8, 1984, at the British-American Media Conference at Duke University.
For example, in a 1983. *Walton Reporter*, October 19, 1983.
A weekly in a neighboring. *Hancock Herald*, June 13, 1984.

Page 92
Just before he left. Letter from Lee Guittar to author on September 11, 1984.

Page 93
Richard Reeves in. Richard Reeves, *American Journey* (New York: Simon and Schuster, 1982), p. 81.
In the spring of 1984. *Gannetteer*, May/June 1984, p. 19.

Page 94
In the late 1970s. *Columbia Journalism Review*, May/June 1979, pages 19–20.

Page 95
In the early 1970s. *Wall Street Journal*, September 4, 1970, p. 1.
In 1984, Richard. The material on board memberships comes from proxy statements that are mailed to shareholders and filed with the Securities and Exchange Commission.

Page 96
Until a few years ago. Material on Jacksonville comes from the following magazines articles: William Souder, "Jacksonville Learns to Love Its New Press Lord," *Florida Trend*, October 1983, pp. 62–72; Clark Newsom, "Publisher Flies High but Keeps Low Profile," *presstime*, November 1983, p. 28; and Bill Cutler and Mitchell Shields, "Is Jacksonville Jinxed?" *Columbia Journalism Review*, March/April 1984, pp. 32–35.

Page 97
Edward King Gaylord. The material on Oklahoma City comes from a speech given by E. K. Gaylord to the Newcomen Society in North America at Oklahoma City on March 25, 1971; a letter by his son, Edward L. Gaylord, to the author in August 1984, and an article by Neil Swan, "Diversifying: Many Newspapers Own TV Stations,

but How About a Ranch or Truck Line?" *presstime*, June 1984, pp. 26–8.

Page 99
Until quite recently. Donald Graham, "New Times, Old Values," *Nieman Reports*, autumn 1984, p. 35.
In the annual survey. *Forbes*, special issues, fall 1982–1985.

Page 101
In a speech at Yale. Arthur Ochs Sulzberger, *Yale Daily News* annual banquet, November 9, 1984.
"We must do." Graham's speech at the University of Georgia, October 5, 1983.

Page 102
Burger gave his view. *First National Bank of Boston* v. *Bellotti*, Official United States Supreme Court Reports for the 1978–79 term, pp. 799–827.

Page 103
In her 1984 book. Mary Cunningham, *Powerplay* (New York: Simon and Schuster, 1984), p. 281.
Early in 1985. *Wall Street Journal*, January 10, 1985, p. 27.

Chapter 6

Page 108
In a short article. *Daily Nonpareil*, March 1, 1982.

Page 109
In an agitated. Letter dated February 11, 1983.
On the air. Transcript of newscast, March 4, 1982.
A second letter. Letter dated February 15, 1983.

Page 110
In a gracious. Letter dated February 28, 1983.
Joe Jordan. Interview with author, December 13, 1983.
Stu Nicholson. Interview with author, November 11, 1983.

Page 111
Don Hewitt. "60 Minutes Looks at Itself," aired September 22, 1981.
Hewitt often makes. "Playboy Interview: '60 Minutes,'" *Playboy*, March 1985, p. 160.

Page 112
"Entrapment applies only." Meeting of Investigative Reporters &
Editors, Miami, June 10, 1984.
"Ethics to me." IRE Miami meeting. June 9, 1984.

Page 113
Marion Goldin. IRE Miami meeting. June 9, 1984.
Geraldo Rivera. IRE Miami meeting. June 9, 1984.
At the convention. IRE Miami meeting. June 9, 1984.

Page 114
Two reporters "bit." *New York Times*, December 3, 1983, p. 9.
In 1976 he. *Playboy*, September, 1976, p. 63.
Scheer told the. Ken Auletta, "Would You Lie, Steal or Cheat to
Get a Story?" in *Hard Feelings: Reporting on the Pols, the Press, the
People and the City* (New York: Random House, 1980), p. 244.
They declare that. David Anderson and Peter Benjaminson, *Inves-
tigative Reporting* (Bloomington: Indiana University Press, 1976), pp.
6–7.

Page 115
The textbook. Virginius Dabney, "I'm distraught and unhappy
over what I see," *ASNE Bulletin*, November, 1982, p. 30.
"I'd say most." Note to author. September 1984.
In nearly two decades. Interview with author, July 24, 1984.
Much of what. Edward J. Epstein, *Between Fact and Fiction: The
Problem of Journalism* (New York: Vintage Books, 1975), pp. 6–7.

Page 116
Rivera's narration. *New York Times*, February 2, 1972, p. 78.
At a panel. "Eyeball to Eyeball: Dilemma in the Newsroom,"
Media and Society Seminars, a program of the Graduate School of
Journalism, Columbia University, initially broadcast on Public
Broadcasting System in January 1982.
In an influential. Alfred Hill, "Defamation and Privacy Under the
First Amendment," *Columbia Law Review*, December 1976, p. 1285.
"Trying to decide." Robert Sherrill, "Looking for Mr. Wunder-
bar," *Columbia Journalism Review*, September/October 1979, p. 65.

Page 117
The lawyers for. Sanford Ungar, *The Paper & The Papers* (New
York: E. P. Dutton & Co., 1972), p. 97.
However, Columbia. *New York Times*, May 2, 1972, p. 1
In an interview. Kissinger interview in *American Heritage* maga-
zine, August/September 1983, p. 53.

Page 118
In a column. Column excerpted in *News Photographer*, December
1981, p. 33.

Page 119
Arrington was shocked. *The News Media & the Law*, October/ November 1980, p. 32.
At the New York Court. Decided on April 7, 1982. Reported in *Media Law Reporter*, vol. 8, p. 1351.
He appealed to. *New York Times*, January 18, 1983, p. A20.
At one point. Brief of Cravath, Swaine & Moore submitted to New York Court of Appeals, May 7, 1982, p. 10.

Page 120
Eventually, the state. *presstime*, August 1983, p. 10.
The free-lancer who. Tim Malyon, "The Fateful Photograph," *Camera Arts*, October 1982, p. 26.
He was later. Dietemann immediately. *Life*, November 1, 1963, pp. 76–77; Floyd Abrams, "The Press, Privacy and the Constitution," *New York Times Magazine*, August 21, 1977, p. 13.

Page 121
Judge Hufstedler also. Vol. 449 of the *Federal Reporter*, second series, p. 245.
The Florida Supreme. *Shevin* v. *Sunbeam Television*. Decided on October 28, 1977, vol. 3 of *Media Law Reporter*, p. 1315.
The Federal Communications. Letter to author from Victor Kovner, a communications lawyer, December 14, 1983; Kent R. Middleton, "Journalists and Tape Recorders: Does Participant Monitoring Invade Privacy?" *Comm/Ent*, vol. 2, no. 2, p. 287.

Page 122
"It is more difficult." Frederick Taylor, "Reporters Taping Phone Calls: Why All the Shudders?" *ASNE Bulletin*, December 1982/January 1983, p. 19; interview with author, October 3, 1984.

Page 123
Then, a month. Memorandum distributed to employees of *The New York Times* on January 23, 1984.

Page 124
Crile said he. *New York Times*, June 16, 1983, p. C27.
That story prompted. *New York Times*, April 27, 1983, p. C24; *New York Times*, December 14, 1984, p. B11.
"The pity of." Burton Benjamin, at the University of California at Berkeley, November 1, 1985.
In connection. Don Kowet, *A Matter of Honor: General William C. Westmoreland Versus CBS* (New York: Macmillan, 1984).

Page 125
In this incriminating. *Los Angeles Times*, May 11, 1984, p. 9.
The tape ends. *Village Voice*, May 22, 1984, p. 25.

He said he. *New York Times*, May 15, 1984, p. C21.
"Our concern," said. Interview with author, July 21, 1984.
"Let me state." Letter from Mike Wallace to Hillel Black, April 11, 1984.
In response to this. *Washington Journalism Review*, June 1984, p. 5; *American Lawyer*, July/August 1984, p. 126.

Chapter 7

Page 128
Carla Cantor. Decision and finding of Judge Aldan Markson, Municipal Court of the Borough of Kenilworth, N.J., October 6, 1983.
The article that. *Morristown Daily Record*, August 3, 1983. p. 13.
At the trial. Judge Markson's decision of October 10, 1983.

Page 129
More than a quarter. Charles Burke, University of Florida, "Investigative Reporting in Local TV," Survey, 1983.

Page 130
Another survey. Richard G. Gray and G. Cleveland Wilhoit, Portrait of the U.S. Journalist, presented to the annual meeting of the American Society of Newspaper Editors, Denver, May 9, 1983.
Yet, with particular. Miami meeting of Investigative Reporters & Editors, June 10, 1984.

Page 131
By owning a tavern. Zay N. Smith and Pamela Zekman, *The Mirage* (New York: Random House, 1979), p. 4.
They interpreted. *The Mirage*, p. 13.
They distinguished. *The Mirage*, p. 13.
"The Chicago Police." *The Mirage*, p. 14.
Therefore, the authors. *The Mirage*, p. 13.

Page 132
Patterson said. Steve Robinson, "Pulitzers: Was the Mirage a Deception?" *Columbia Journalism Review*, July/August 1979, p. 16.
Several years later. Speech at the University of Florida, November 10, 1983.
At the time, Bradlee. Robinson, "Pulitzers: Was the Mirage a Deception?" p. 14; *New York Times*, April 18, 1979, p. II:4.
(Ten years later.) Miami meeting of Investigative Reporters & Editors, June 10, 1984.
Robert Christopher. Letter to author, October 25, 1983.

Page 133
In the tradition. Iris Noble, *Nellie Bly: First Woman Reporter* (New York: Messner, 1956).
In the late 1930s. Lee Israel, *Kilgallen* (New York: Delacorte Press, 1979), pp. 91–92.
In the early 1960s. Gloria Steinem, *Outrageous Acts and Everyday Rebellions* (New York: Holt, Rinehart and Winston, 1983), p. 29.

Page 134
In 1985 a television. It was shown on ABC-TV on February 25, 1985.
(In fact, she.) *New York Times*, December 11, 1984, p. C25.
Probably the most. Erving Goffman, *Asylums* (Garden City, N.Y.: Anchor Books, 1961), pp. 4–5.
In a 1974. *Pell* v. *Procunier*. Vol. 417 of official United States Supreme Court reports, p. 817.

Page 135
In 1982 an. "The Convicted: A Special Report on Arizona Corrections System," *Arizona Daily Star*, August 8, 1982, special supplement.
The exception was. Response to author's questionnaire, January 1984.
Richard Stewart. *Boston Globe*, December 27, 1983, p. 23.

Page 136
Stewart found prison. *Boston Globe*, December 29, 1983, p. 54.
Stewart notes. *Boston Globe*, December 31, 1983, p. 17.

Page 137
In a column in July. Carson City *Nevada Appeal*, July 16, 1984.
Probably the best. *The Official Report of the New York State Commission on Attica* (New York: Bantam Books, 1972).
An article in. William Hart, "LA's Giant Jail Is a Giant Headache," *Corrections Magazine*, December 1980, p. 32.
In December 1982. Bruce Porter, "California Prison Gangs: The Price of Control," *Corrections Magazine*, December 1982, p. 6.

Page 138
"I would limit." Response to author's questionnaire, March 1984.
In 1984. Response to author's questionnaire, January 1984.
Once it is determined. Sissela Bok, *Secrets: On the Ethics of Concealment and Revelation* (New York: Pantheon Books, 1982), p. 263.
"We stopped the practice." Response to author's questionnaire, January 1984.

Page 139
At NBC. "NBC News Policies & Guidelines," July 15, 1984, pp. 30–31.

At ABC. "ABC News Policy," March 10, 1982, p. II.11.

In its production standards, CBS. "CBS News Standards," updated periodically, p. 25.

For example, in 1979. *Rochester Democrat and Chronicle*, August 5, 1979, p. 1.

Page 140

In 1985 the. *Village Voice*, January 22, 1985, p. 44; interview conducted by Sean Tierney, July 25, 1984.

Page 141

Late in 1983. Leslie Linthicum, "When to Go Undercover? As Last Resort to Get Story," The National Ethics Committee, Society of Professional Journalists, Sigma Delta Chi, 1983, *Journalism Ethics Report*, p. 20.

At the *Denver*. Response to author's questionnaire, January 1984.

At the *Seattle*. Response to author's questionnaire, January 1984.

"I don't believe." Interview with author, October 19, 1984.

Page 142

In the summer of 1983. *New York Times*, August 31, 1983, p. B1.

In *Winners*. *Winners & Sinners*, November 24, 1983, p. 1.

"I used all." Speech, University of Florida, March 21, 1984.

Page 143

"As an investigative." Nicholas Gage, *Eleni* (New York: Ballantine Books, 1984 ed.), p. 613.

Eventually, Gage. Speech at University of Florida, March 21, 1984.

For example, in 1983. *Washington Post*, October 9–14, 1983.

In another series. *Washington Post*, March 4–7, 1984.

Page 144

In defending the. Letter to author, September 21, 1984.

In 1981 she wrote. *Buffalo Evening News*, July 10, 1981, p. 31.

Page 145

This was the case. *Miami Herald*, May 2, 1982, pp. 1, 20A.

In the early 1980s. Speech to meeting of Investigative Reporters & Editors, Miami, June 9, 1984.

Along with the Junior. *Miami Herald*, October 9, 1983, p. 9.

Page 146

Several months. Correspondence and telephone conversations, November 1983.

At the paper. Response to author's questionnaire, February, 1984.

He knew he. Unpublished term paper by Peter Muckley, University of Florida, December 5, 1983.

Page 147
In its guidelines. "ABC News Policy," March 10, 1982, p. II.12.
In 1982, Danny. *San Antonio Light*, May 23–24, 1982.

Page 148
"Our experience with." Letter to author, April 19, 1984.

Page 149
In the fall of 1984. *Washington Post*, November 2, 1984, p. 1.
Patricia Lynch. "Is Lyndon LaRouche Using *Your* Name?" *Columbia Journalism Review*, March/April 1985, p. 42.

Page 150
That subterfuge. *New York Times*, March 25, p. 1981, p. II. 5.
The department's Office. *presstime*, June 1984, p. 36.
A bill introduced. S. 804, The Undercover Operations Act of 1983; Letter to author from Bruce Sanford, a Washington lawyer, August 30, 1984.
In May 1984. Testimony before the Senate Judiciary Committee's Criminal Law subcommittee, May 16, 1984.

Page 151
In May 1984, nine. *Morristown Daily Record*, May 16, 1984, p. 8.
In view of that. *New York Times*, May 17, 1984, p. B2.

Chapter 8

Page 156
The dramatic photograph. *New York Daily News*, June 19, 1983, p. 19. The photograph appeared in the *New York Daily News* on June 12, 1983, p. 1.
After his disclosure. Sanford Ungar, *The Paper & The Papers* (New York: E. P. Dutton & Co., 1972), p. 137.

Page 157
A couple of weeks. "Why Zion Unmasked Ellsberg as Source," *Women's Wear Daily*, July 1, 1971.
"You had every." Sidney Zion, *Read All About It! The Collected Adventures of a Maverick Reporter* (New York: Summit Books, 1982), p. 71.
As David Rubin. Peter M. Sandman, David M. Rubin, David B. Sachsman, *Media: An Introductory Analysis of American Mass Communications*, 3rd ed. (Englewood Cliffs, N.J.: Prentice-Hall, 1982), p. 79.

Page 158

(In *Branzburg*.) *Branzburg* v. *Hayes*, Vol. 408 of official United States Supreme Court reports, p. 704.

"There was a." Letter to author, May 22, 1984.

In its written brief. Brief of Frederick A. O. Schwarz, Jr., Corporation Counsel of New York City, April 26, 1983, p. 25.

Page 159

At the oral argument. Held in Albany, N.Y., May 3, 1984.

Frye was insulted. Interview with author, May 3, 1984.

In its brief. New York City's brief of April 26, 1983, p. 24.

The concept of. David G. Trager, "Are Lawyers Professionals or Do They Only Profess to Be?" *New York Law Journal*, September 2, 1983, p. 1.

In ruling for. *Frye* v. *Commissioner of Finance of the City of New York*. Decision of Appellate Division, August 11, 1983, p. 4.

Page 160

In contrast to. Decision of the Court of Appeals, June 5, 1984, pp. 1–2.

Page 161

(It does not to.) Interview with David Rosen, director of the Harvard news office, December 5, 1984.

One recent study. *presstime*, September 1983, p. 133.

Warren Phillips. Letter to author, June 18, 1984.

Joe McGinniss. Letter to author, September 22, 1984.

David Broder. Letter to author, July 2, 1984.

Page 162

In 1938 Robert. Robert M. Hutchins, "Is There a Legitimate Place for Journalistic Instruction? No!" *Quill*, March 1938, p. 13.

Forty-five years later. *Our Country and Our Culture: A Conference of the Committee for the Free World* (New York: Orwell Press, 1983), p. 82.

"The general state." School of Journalism, University of Oregon, Planning for Curricular Change in Journalism Education, May 1984, p. 1.

The judge turned to. Memorandum by Sybil Hart Kooper of State Supreme Court in Kings County, New York, December 29, 1978, p. 6.

Page 164

In 1983 John. *Editor & Publisher*, October 8, 1983, p. 15.

Shortly after the Shah. *Columbia Journalism Review*, July/August 1979, p. 8.

To be eligible. Press Card Regulations of New York City Police

Department. Promulgated by Commissioner Robert J. McGuire, undated.

Page 165

The police also issue. Press Card Regulations.

Robert McKay. Memorandum to participants in seminar of Aspen Institute for Humanist Studies on "Cross-Profession Study of Ethical Standards," July 9, 1982.

Page 166

("Don't make misrepresentations.") International Business Machines, Business Conduct Guidelines, 1983, p. 15.

For example, door. Code of Ethics of the Direct Selling Association, as amended March 9, 1981, p. 1.

That code said. Nelson A. Crawford, *The Ethics of Journalism* (New York: Alfred A. Knopf, 1924), p. 183.

The *Seattle Times. The Ethics of Journalism*, p. 235.

In 1973 the Society. James C. Thompson, Jr., "Journalistic Ethics: Some Probings by a Media Keeper," Poynter Center, Indiana University at Bloomington, January 1978.

Page 167

"By not writing." *ASNE Bulletin*, October 1984, p. 43.

Without codes. Workshop on teaching ethics in journalism, The Hastings Center, June 6, 1984.

Geraldo Rivera. Miami meeting of Investigative Reporters & Editors, June 9, 1984.

(In the introduction.) "ABC News Policy," March 10, 1982, p. 1.

In September 1981. *Los Angeles Times*, September 23, 1981, p. 1.

Page 168

Just a little more. *Los Angeles Times*, Code of Ethics, November 16, 1982.

In a letter. Letter to author, June 21, 1984.

In the study. Charles W. Bailey, *Conflicts of Interest: A Matter of Journalistic Ethics* (New York: A Report to the National News Council, 1984), p. 35.

Page 169

(In 1983, a random.) Richard G. Gray and G. Cleveland Wilhoit, Portrait of the U.S. Journalist, presented to the annual convention of the American Society of Newspaper Editors, Denver, May 9, 1983.

Page 170

At the end. Pool report distributed by the Professional Football Writers of America, January 19, 1984.

One detail that. *Orlando Sentinel*, January 20, 1984, p. 1.

In 1985, a. *Oakland Tribune*, January 17, 1985, p. 1.

"We provide all." *Orlando Sentinel*, January 20, 1984, p. 1.
"It's like being." *Editor & Publisher*, February 11, 1984, p. 14;
Letter to author, September 24, 1984.

Page 171
The most lavish. *St. Petersburg Times*, January 22, 1984.
It was therefore. *Tampa Tribune*, January 21, 1984, p. B1.

Page 172
His picture was. *Gainesville Sun*, January 21, 1984, p. 2A; *Tampa Tribune*, January 1, 1984, p. 2B.
McEwen had recently. *Columbia Journalism Review*, September/October 1983, p. 26.
Afterward, a Budweiser. *St. Petersburg Times*, January 20, 1984.
In its exhaustive. *St. Petersburg Times*, January 19, 1984, p. D1.

Page 173
In one survey, conducted. National Ethics Committee, Society of Professional Journalists, Sigma Delta Chi, 1983 Journalism Ethics Report, p. 3.
In his study. Charles W. Bailey, *Conflicts of Interest: A Matter of Journalistic Ethics*, p. 18.
"I haven't gotten." Interview with author, October 12, 1984.
In response to a survey. The 1983–84 *ASNE Committee Reports*, p. 9.
"Collectively," said Charles. *ASNE Bulletin*, October 1983, p. 19.
"You'd never guess." *Editor & Publisher*, February 25, 1984, p. 12.

Page 174
"There are two." Interview with author, July 22, 1984.
Uriel Savir. Interview with author, March 16, 1984.
Writing about his junket. Michael Kinsley, "Cockburn the Barbarian," *Washington Monthly*, April 1984, p. 35.

Page 175
The advertisement of the Cigar. David Zinman, "Should Newsmen Accept PR Prizes?" *Columbia Journalism Review*, spring 1970, p. 37.

Page 176
For example, *The Philadelphia*. *ASNE Bulletin*, February 1984, p. 9.

Page 177
This was done. *New York Times*, November 22, 1984, p. D16.

In their book about. Zay N. Smith and Pamela Zekman, *The Mirage* (New York: Random House, 1979), pp. 230–31.

In 1984, in *The Wall. Wall Street Journal*, April 19, 1984, p. 31.

Page 178

In 1981, after. *Washington Post*, April 19, 1981, p. A15.

Three years later. Letter to author, August 17, 1984.

Benjamin Bradlee says. Interview with author, October 12, 1984.

Page 179

Nonetheless, the latest. Conference of State Court Administrators and National Center for State Courts, *State Court Organization 1980* (U.S. Department of Justice, National Court Statistics Project, Williamsburg, Virginia, May 1982), pp. 120–21.

In the fall of 1983. Interview with author, September 21, 1984.

That is what. Letter to author, December 2, 1983.

Page 180

The directive said. Directive of Governor Mario Cuomo, June 1, 1983.

Page 181

In theory, according to. Requirement of NYP registration and plates, issued by the New York State Department of Motor Vehicles, September 1980.

According to the New York State. The list of NYP plate holders was supplied by Duncan G. Macpherson, director of EDP services of the New York State Department of Motor Vehicles, on January 27, 1984.

Chapter 9

Page 184

In a survey of. Philip Meyer, *Editors, Publishers & Newspaper Ethics* (Washington: American Society of Newspaper Editors, 1983), p. 42.

In the early. John Brady, "Gay Talese: An Interview," *The Reporter as Artist: A Look at the New Journalism Controversy*, ed. Ronald Weber (New York: Hastings House, 1974), p. 92.

Page 185

On a Sunday. *New York Times*, January 22, 1984, p. 1.

"We wanted it." *Editor & Publisher*, February 4, 1984, p. 20; interview with Timothy Robinson, January 15, 1985.

Page 186

"I've felt for." *New York Times*, June 23, 1982, p. C21.

Page 187
Writing later in. *Washington Post*, April 8, 1984, p. 1.
He related the incident. *Washington Post*, February 13, 1984, p. 1.
For two weeks. *New York Times*, February 28, 1984, p. A20.

Page 188
"Government officials." William Greider, "Reporters and Their Sources: Mutual Assured Seduction," *Washington Monthly*, October 1982, p. 15.
"None of us really." William Greider, "The Education of David Stockman," *The Atlantic*, December 1981, p. 38.
In an interview with. Laurence Barrett, *Gambling With History: Ronald Reagan in the White House* (Garden City, N.Y.: Doubleday, 1983), p. 190.
In the accepted. William Greider, "Reporters and Their Sources: Mutual Assured Seduction," p. 15.

Page 189
In a poll. Ethics Committee Report, The 1983–84 ASNE Committee Reports, p. 15.
"Backgrounders and off." Speech to Southeast Regional Meeting of the Society of Professional Journalists, Sigma Delta Chi, Miami Beach, April 7, 1984.
"If you say." *Fort Myers News-Press*, August 20, 1983, p. 1.
Because of. *New York Times*, May 15, 1984, p. C21.
In its report. "Unauthorized Disclosures Regarding Abscam, Pendorf and Brilab, A Public Report of the U.S. Department of Justice," January 14, 1981, p. 14.

Page 190
In January 1984. *Columbia Journalism Review*, March/April 1984, p. 22.
Early in 1984. *New York Times*, February 6, 1984.
That article began. *Editor & Publisher*, February 11, 1984, p. 34.
To celebrate its. *USA Today*, September 15, 1983, p. 11A.

Page 192
The attitude of. A. M. Rosenthal, Speech to the Fordham Law Alumni Association, January 30, 1976.
In a speech. Floyd Abrams's speech at the University of Michigan, March 22, 1984.

Page 193
A summary of the Gannett. *New York Times*, July 8, 1979, p. E1.
Allen Neuharth. *New York Times*, July 8, 1979, p. E1.
Amid this hyperbole. *New York Times*, July 8, 1979, p. E3.

Page 194
  The Severo case. *Newsweek*, March 18, 1985, p. 80.
  (In a letter.) Letter to author, March 5, 1985.
  (Seven months earlier.) *New York Times*, October 22, 1982, p. A16.

Page 195
  The Apalachin case. Decided by the Second Circuit Court of Appeals, November 28, 1960. Vol. 285 of Federal Reporter, Second Series, p. 418.
  (In his letter.) Letter to author, March 5, 1985.
  When Kaufman was. *New York Times* July 29, 1983, p. A8.

Page 197
  In each of the six years. The following articles appeared in *The New York Times Magazine:* "Juvenile Justice: A Plea for Reform," October 14, 1979, p. 42; "A Legal Remedy for International Torture?" November 9, 1980, p. 44; "Congress v. The Court," September 20, 1981, p. 44; "The Insanity Plea on Trial," August 8, 1982, p. 16; "Reassessing The Fairness Doctrine," June 19, 1983, p. 17; "The Verdict on Juries," April 1, 1984, p. 42; and "Keeping Politics Out of the Court," December 9, 1984, p. 72.
  In the five-year. Op-Ed articles in *The New York Times* by Judge Kaufman appeared on the following days: January 24, 1981, p. 23; June 20, 1982, p. IV 21; November 4, 1982, p. 27; August 14, 1983, p. E19; December 7, 1983, p. 25; June 11, 1984, p. A19; March 26, 1985, p. 27; June 16, 1985, p. E21, and October 6, 1985, p. E21.
  On June 19. *New York Daily News*, June 19, 1983, p. 7.
  (A few years earlier.) *New York Times*, November 1, 1979, p. B9; November 4, 1979, p. 35; December 6, 1979, p. II 19; and April 10, 1980, p. II 15.

Page 198
  I once wrote. *New York Times*, June 27, 1978, p. 1.
  That story never. *New York Times*, March 18, 1977, p. II 4.
  She later talked. Rod Townley, "A Specter Is Haunting Irving Kaufman," *Juris Doctor*, November 1977, p. 20; Sol Stern, "Irving Kaufman's Haunted Career," *Village Voice*, March 6, 1984, p. 10; and interview with author, September 24, 1984.

Chapter 10

Page 201
  "D'Amato seldom left." Tom Goldstein, "D'Amato: At Home in the Senate," *New York Times Magazine*, February 13, 1983 p. 38.

Page 202
The rules of *The Christian.* Nelson A. Crawford, *The Ethics of Journalism* (New York: Alfred A. Knopf, 1924), p. 215.
The code of ethics of the Kansas. Crawford, *The Ethics of Journalism*, p. 203.
The code of the *Springfield.* Crawford, *The Ethics of Journalism*, p. 217.
One that does. ABC Code, March 10, 1982, p. II.3.

Page 203
The New York Times. Winners & Sinners, April 13, 1984, p. 1.
In the afterword. David McClintick, *Indecent Exposure: A True Story of Hollywood and Wall Street* (New York: William Morrow, 1982), p. 523.
In a note. Nicholas Gage, *Eleni* (New York: Ballantine Books, 1984 ed.) p. 624.

Page 204
In an effort to "rethink." Workshop sponsored by Hastings Center, Hastings, N.Y., on teaching ethics in journalism, June 6, 1984.
In *The Brass.* Upton Sinclair, *The Brass Check: A Study of American Journalism* (Pasadena, Cal.: Published by author, 1920), p. 404.
At a conference. Miami meeting of Investigative Reporters & Editors, June 8, 1984.
This approach was. Memorandum of January 28, 1981.

Page 205
Nearly a quarter. Alastair Reid, "Letter From Barcelona," *New Yorker*, December 2, 1961, p. 137.
In fact, the bar. *Time*, July 2, 1984, p. 66.
This rearranged scene. *Wall Street Journal*, June 18, 1984, p. 1.
It was followed. *New York Times*, June 19, 1984, p. 1.
"In reporting with." *New York Times*, June 19, 1984, p. 1.
The rationale. Interview with Martin Baron, January 25, 1985.
Subsequently, in a memorandum. *New York Times*, July 3, 1984, p. C9.

Page 206
Even though Reid's intent. *New York Times*, June 19, 1984, p. B20.
In an essay. John Hersey, "The Legend of the License," *Yale Review*, autumn 1980, p. 2.
All he needed. *Boston Globe*, June 20, 1984, p. 44.
For several years. James Boswell, *Boswell's Life of Johnson* (New York: Washington Square Press, 1965) p. 35.

Page 207
In *Scoop.* Evelyn Waugh, *Scoop* (Boston: Little Brown & Company, republished 1977), p. 56.

The editor reassures. Waugh, *Scoop*, p. 41.

A colleague tells. Waugh, *Scoop*, p. 92.

"With little disguised." Evelyn Waugh, *When the Going Was Good* (Boston: Little Brown & Company, republished 1984), p. 93.

Page 208

When the latest. *New York Times*, January 1, 1975, p. 8.

(He was also.) *New York Times*, June 30, 1951, p. 8.

Late in 1917. *New York Evening Mail*, December 28, 1917, p. 9.

Page 209

Readers, Mencken wrote. Robert McHugh, ed., *The Bathtub Hoax & Other Blasts & Bravos* (New York: Alfred A. Knopf, 1958), p. 11.

(Papers owned by.) Peter M. Sandman, David M. Rubin, David B. Sachsman, *Media: An Introductory Analysis of American Mass Communications*, 3rd ed. (Englewood Cliffs, N.J.: Prentice-Hall, 1982), p. 52.

It ran a "picture." Douglas Steinbauer, "Faking It With Pictures," *American Heritage*, October/November 1982, p. 52.

"The assumption was." Letter to author.

Page 210

Liebling wrote in. A. J. Liebling, *The Wayward Pressman* (Garden City, N.Y.: Doubleday, 1947), p. 51.

Liebling had used. Raymond Sokolov, *Wayward Reporter: The Life of A. J. Liebling* (New York: Harper & Row, 1980), pp. 61–62.

In a list of awards. Gay Talese, *The Kingdom and the Power* (New York: Bantam Books, 1970 ed.), pp. 449–56.

Page 211

In an advertisement. Ronald Weber, "Some Sort of Artistic Excitement," *The Reporter as Artist: A Look at the New Journalism Controversy*, ed. Ronald Weber (New York: Hastings House, 1974), p. 25.

In 1968, when. Joseph Eszterhas, "Legacy of the Silver Bridge," *Plain Dealer Sunday Magazine*, August 4, 1968.

Page 212

In 1974 the United. Vol. 419 of the official Supreme Court decision, p. 253.

John Hersey's. "The Legend on the License," pp. 2, 23.

Such is the. "Who Said That? A Report to the National News Council on the Use of Unidentified Sources," 1983, p. 2.

Page 213

An item on the *New*. *New York Daily News*, May 12, 1983, p. 9.

An example occurred. Henry Post, "Useful, Using, Used: Roy

Cohn and the New York Press," *Columbia Journalism Review*, May/June 1980, p. 55.

The erroneous assumption. *New York Post*, February 26, 1979, p. 6.

The *Village Voice*. Wayne Barrett, "The Birthday Boy," *Village Voice*, March 5, 1979, p. 24.

Then Liz Smith. *New York Daily News*, March 7, 1979, p. 6.

Page 214

The *Review*, in a subsequent. *Columbia Journalism Review*, July/August 1980, p. 70.

(The error was.) Interview with author, March 15, 1984.

"His nonconformist." *The World According to Breslin*, annotated by Michael J. O'Neill and William Brink (New York: Ticknor & Fields, 1984), p. xvi.

In the memorandum. *New York Times*, July 3, 1983, p. C9.

In the introduction. Calvin Trillin, *Uncivil Liberties* (New York: Ticknor & Fields, 1982), pp. 5–7.

Trillin's humor. *Uncivil Liberties*, p. 163.

Page 215

In 1975, Robert. Robert Darnton, "Writing News and Telling Stories," *Daedalus*, spring 1975, p. 190.

"Jimmy is 8." *Washington Post*, September 28, 1980, p. 1.

Page 216

In the middle of October. *Washington Post*, April 19, 1981, p. A13.

In April, after. *Newsweek*, April 27, 1981, p. 50.

Bob Woodward. *Time*, May 4, 1981, p. 50.

On April 13. *Washington Post*, April 19, 1981, p. A13.

Page 217

Bradlee had underlined. *Washington Post*, April 19, 1981, p. A12.

She was allowed. *Washington Post*, April 19, 1981, p. A14.

"She was a one." *Washington Post*, April 19, 1981, p. A15.

"Unfortunately and unfairly." Memorandum to staff, April 21, 1981.

Page 218

He made known. Presidential address, annual meeting of the American Society of Newspaper Editors, Chicago, May 5, 1982.

In a column. *New York Daily News*, May 6, 1981, p. 3.

"The question of." *New York Daily News*, May 9, 1981, p. 9.

Shortly after the resignations. *Editor & Publisher*, June 6, 1981, p. 78.

Without ever leaving. *New York Times*, December 20, 1981, p. 72.

"It was a gamble." *New York Times*, February 22, 1982, p. 1.

The *Times*'s checking. *New York Times*, February 22, 1982, p. 4.

Page 219

One survey showed. Richard G. Gray and G. Cleveland Wilhoit, Portrait of the U.S. Journalist, presentation to the annual meeting of the American Society of Newspaper Editors, Denver, May 9, 1983.

"If I did not." *New York Times*, January 29, 1982, p. 18.

In a survey done three. The 1983–84 ASNE Committee Reports, p. 15.

A memorandum of. Memorandum to staff from William F. Thomas, November 11, 1982.

Page 220

At *The New York Times*. Memorandum of September 27, 1984.

In an earlier. The 1983–84 ASNE Committee Reports, p. 16.

Page 221

Reid spoke at. *Time*, July 2, 1981, p. 66.

Page 222

Jones's elaborate. *Village Voice*, January 13, 1982, p. 10.

"I needed a." *New York Times*, February 2, 1982, p. 4.

It is a dirty. Roy Peter Clark, "The Unoriginal Sin," *Washington Journalism Review*, March 1983, p. 43.

Page 223

The following sentence. *New York Times*, August 19, 1984, p. F12.

But the reporter. *Washington Post*, May 11, 1984, p. C14.

In this case. *New York Times*, August 2, 1984, Index page.

James Greenfield. Response to author's questionnaire, February 7, 1984.

Charles Stabler. Response to author's questionnaire, February 1984.

In its *Deskbook*. Robert A. Webb, ed. *Washington Post Deskbook on Style* (New York: McGraw-Hill Book Company, 1978), p. 4.

At its seventy-fifth. *The Quill*, December 1984, p. 26.

Page 224

The most thorough. *National Observer Handbook*, undated, p. 9.

"It is, of course." Response to author's questionnaire, February, 1984.

"We consider it." Response to author's questionnaire, February, 1984.

In December 1982. *New York* magazine, March 22, 1982.

Page 225

Jordan began his. *Editor & Publisher*, December 24, 1983 p. 21.

That column began. *Editor & Publisher*, December 24, 1983 p. 21.
"I thought it." *Washington Journalism Review*, March 1984, p. 12.
(Hopcroft himself.) *National Law Journal*, May 28, 1984, p. 9;
Washington Journalism Review, December 1984, p. 17.
In explaining why. *Washington Journalism Review*, March 1984,
p. 12.
George Jordan's. *AIM Report*, February 1984, p. 4.

Page 226
On September 1. Roy Peter Clark, "The Unoriginal Sin," *Washington Journalism Review*, March 1983, p. 43.
In 1975. Jerry Bledsoe, *The World's Number One, Flat-Out, All-Time-Great Stock Car Racing Book* (New York: Doubleday, 1975), p. 87.
For Clark, who. "The Unoriginal Sin," p. 44.
Archdeacon explained that. *ASNE Bulletin*, November 1982, pp. 34–35.

Page 227
He apologized again. *ASNE Bulletin*, November 1982, p. 35.
He was chastised. *ASNE Bulletin*, November 1982, p. 34.

Chapter 11

Page 229
A week later. *Time*, October 26, 1981, p. 97.

Page 230
(Bradlee said later.) Interview with author, October 12, 1984.

Page 231
During the controversy. *Time*, November 2, 1981, p. 122.
In a study on. "Who Said That?" A Report to the National News Council on the Use of Unidentified Sources, 1983, p. 17.

Page 232
Jones, who had just. *Editor & Publisher*, November 12, 1983, p. 16.
In a 20,000. Calvin Trillin, "A Reporter at Large: American Royal," *New Yorker*, September 26, 1983, p. 57.
"Insignificant errors." The material concerning Donald Jones comes from an interview December 14, 1983, and correspondence during the following year.

Page 233
In a speech in the fall. *Editor & Publisher*, November 12, 1984, p. 16.

Page 234
"It's a cop-out." Interview with author, October 19, 1984.

Page 236
Several months earlier. *Kansas City Star*, August 21, 1983, p. 1.
"We'd sooner drown." Speech to the Media-Law Conference of the Florida Bar Association, Clearwater, February 25, 1984.

Page 237
This letter by a Polish. *New York Times*, August 28, 1983, p. 18E.

Page 238
"The tendency is." Interview with author, October 19, 1984.
This letter to *Newsweek*. May 2, 1983, p. 7.

Page 239
When the council was formed. Patrick Brogan, *Spiked* (New York: Priority Press Publications, 1985) p. 117.
James B. Squires. *Washington Post*, March 21, 1984, p. A2.
Creed Black. *New York Times*, March 21, 1984, p. A19.

Page 240
A rebuke. *New York Times*, April 22, 1983, index page.
A criticism. *New York Times*, July 12, 1983, index page.
The calling. *New York Times*, October 9, 1983, index page.
The singling. *New York Times*, December 24, 1983, index page.
In probably. *New York Times*, August 30, 1983, index page.

Page 241
The elegant formulation. Benjamin Bradlee, *Conversations With Kennedy*, p. 12.
In *Times Talk*. *Times Talk*, October/November 1983, p. 3.
Several months after. *New York Times*, May 29, 1983, p. IV7.

Page 242
It was reported. *New York Times*, September 29, 1983, p. 12 (national edition).
A few weeks later. "The Evans and Novak Show," Cable News Network, October 9, 1983.

Chapter 12

Page 244
On Tuesday, Lamm's. *Florida Times-Union and Journal*, February 14, 1984, p. D1.
"Whose side." Speech at Miami meeting of Investigative Reporters & Editors, June 9, 1984.

Page 245
For example. *New York* magazine, June 20, 1983, p. 14.
When it folded. *New York Times*, February 4, 1984, p. 37.
The ambivalence. Gerald Lanson and Mitchell Stephens, "The Man and his *Times*," *Washington Journalism Review*, July/August 1983, p. 23.

Page 246
Shortly after. Donald L. Barlett and James B. Steele, "The Full Story of Cianfrani and the Reporter," *Philadelphia Inquirer*, October 16, 1977, pp. F1–8.
After the *Inquirer*. Eleanor Randolph, "Conflict of Interest: A Growing Problem for Couples," *Esquire*, February 1978, p. 225.

Page 247
Similarly, in the fall. *Kansas City Times*, November 5, 1983, p. 1.
C. W. Gusewelle. *Kansas City Star*, November 9, 1983, p. 2A.
The columnist received. *Editor & Publisher*, December 10, 1983, p. 9.

Page 248
Early in 1984 *Fortune*. "Views from the Top—and Bottom," *Fortune*, January 9, 1984, p. 54.
The first hint. *Wall Street Journal*, March 2, 1984, p. 12.

Page 249
On April 2. *Wall Street Journal*, April 2, 1984, p. 1.
Two weeks later. *Wall Street Journal*, April 16, 1984, p. 33.

Page 250
Thomas Griffith. "Washing Dirty Linen in Public," *Time*, April 16, 1984, p. 83.
In the middle of May. *Wall Street Journal*, May 18, 1984, p. 2.

Page 251
By the time. *Wall Street Journal*, August 29, 1984, p. 2.
The editors defended. *Wall Street Journal*, April 16, 1984, p. 33.
The editors said. *Wall Street Journal*, April 16, 1984, p. 33.
In early May. Transcript of Norman Pearlstine's speech to ASNE, Washington, May 10, 1984.

Page 252
Jeff Greenfield. "60 Minutes Looks at Itself," September 22, 1981.
In 1981, he. Mike Wallace and Gary Paul Gates, *Close Encounters: Mike Wallace's Own Story* (New York: William Morrow and Company, 1984), p. 417.
A few months later. *Close Encounters*, p. 424.
In his book. *Close Encounters*, p. 412.

Page 253

Once he realized. *Close Encounters*, p. 425.

The jury and audience. *New York Times*, June 20, 1983, p. 33.

Several months after. Speech at Practising Law Institute Conference on Media Law, New York, November 17, 1983.

Page 254

Rather put his. *AIM Report*, October 1983.

Rather apologized. *Time*, October 3, 1983, p. 77.

In an interview. *Playboy*, January 1984, p. 274.

"Fair enough." *Playboy*, January 1984, p. 274.

Page 255

In the summer of 1983. *New York* magazine, August 15, 1983, p. 21.

The profile in US. Fred Ferretti, "Will Arledge Say Anchors Aweigh?" *US*, May 16, 1978, p. 41.

Page 256

Smith, for her part. *New York* magazine, September 26, 1983, p. 10.

A third paragraph. Letter to author, December 2, 1983.

After Smith's letter. Roone Arledge did not respond to the author's request to discuss the *New York* interview.

Amid all this. *Newsweek*, May 4, 1981, p. 55.

Page 257

More than fifty. Bruce Bliven, "Newpaper Morals," *New Republic*, May 30, 1923, p. 19.

"The jury found." *New York Times*, January 25, 1985, p. 26.

INDEX